AF738710

Propagations

Thirty Years of Influence from the Mental Research Institute

HAWORTH Marriage & the Family
Terry S. Trepper, PhD
Senior Editor

New, Recent, and Forthcoming Titles:

Christiantown, USA by Richard Stellway

Marriage and Family Therapy: A Sociocognitive Approach by Nathan Hurvitz and Roger A. Straus

Culture and Family: Problems and Therapy by Wen-Shing Tseng and Jing Hsu

Adolescents and Their Families: An Introduction to Assessment and Intervention by Mark Worden

Parents Whose Parents Were Divorced by R. Thomas Berner

The Effect of Children on Parents by Anne-Marie Ambert

Multigenerational Family Therapy by David S. Freeman

101 Interventions in Family Therapy edited by Thorana S. Nelson and Terry S. Trepper

Therapy with Treatment Resistant Families: A Consultation-Crisis Intervention Model by William George McCown, Judith Johnson, and Associates

The Death of Intimacy: Barriers to Meaningful Interpersonal Relationships by Philip M. Brown

Developing Healthy Stepfamilies: Twenty Families Tell Their Stories by Patricia Kelley

Propagations: Thirty Years of Influence from the Mental Research Institute edited by John H. Weakland and Wendel A. Ray

Structured Exercises for Promoting Family and Group Strengths: A Handbook for Group Leaders, Trainers, Educators, Counselors, and Therapists edited by Ron McManus and Glen Jennings

Propagations

Thirty Years of Influence from the Mental Research Institute

John H. Weakland, MFCC
Wendel A. Ray, PhD
Editors

Routledge
Taylor & Francis Group
LONDON AND NEW YORK

First published 1995 by The Haworth Press, Inc.

Published 2013 by Routledge
2 Park Square, Milton Park, Abingdon, Oxfordshire OX14 4RN
711 Third Avenue, New York, NY 10017, USA

First issued in paperback 2016

Routledge is an imprint of the Taylor & Francis Group, an informa business

Library of Congress Cataloging-in-Publication Data

Propagations : thirty years of influence from the Mental Research Institute / edited by John H. Weakland and Wendel A. Ray.
p. cm.
Includes bibliographical references and index.

ISBN 978-1-560-24936-8
ISBN 978-1-315-80090-5(eISBN)

1. Mental Research Institute–Influence. 2. Psychotherapy. 3. Brief therapy. 4. Mental Research Institute. I. Weakland, John H. II. Ray, Wendel A.
[DNLM: 1. Academies and Institutes. 2. Psychotherapy. 3. Psychoanalytic Theory. WM 24 P965 1995]
RC480.5.P713 1995
616.89'14–dc20
DNLM/DLC
for Library of Congress **94-32743**
CIP

ISBN 13: 978-1-138-98398-4 (pbk)
ISBN 13: 978-1-56024-936-8 (hbk)

To the Memory
of Joyce Emamjomeh,
Administrator of MRI
1985-1991

CONTENTS

ABOUT THE EDITORS

John H. Weakland, ChE, MFCC, a licensed marriage, family, and child counselor, is in private practice in Palo Alto, California. A Senior Research Associate of the Mental Research Institute, he is Co-Director of the Brief Therapy Center in the Institute, and Clinical Associate Professor Emeritus in the Department of Psychiatry and Behavioral Sciences, Stanford School of Medicine.

Originally trained as a chemist and chemical engineer at Cornell University, he received his degrees in 1939 and 1940, respectively. After six years of engineering practice in research and plant design, he returned to graduate school for work in anthropology and sociology at the New School for Social Research at Columbia University, from 1947-1952. His research centered primarily on culture and personality, the Chinese family and culture, and he worked under Gregory Bateson, Margaret Mead, and Ruth Benedict. In 1953, he moved to Palo Alto to work on Gregory Bateson's research projects on human communication, together with Jay Haley, Don D. Jackson, and William F. Fry, Jr. This research led to the "double-bind" theory of schizophrenia, the U.S. west coast beginnings of family therapy, and the founding of the Mental Research Institute by Jackson.

A fellow of the American Anthropological Association and of the Society for Applied Anthropology, and an advisory editor of *Family Process*, in 1981 he received an award for distinctive achievement in new directions in family therapy from the American Family Therapy Association. He is the author or coauthor of more than 60 professional papers and five other books: *Change: Principles of Problem Formation and Problem Resolution*, with Paul Watzlawick and Richard Fisch (NY: WW Norton, 1974); *The Tactics of Change: Doing Therapy Briefly*, with Richard Fisch and Lynn Segal (SF: Jossey-Bass, 1982); *The Interactional View: Studies at the Mental Research Institute, Palo Alto, 1965-1974*, edited with Paul Watzlawick (NY: WW Norton, 1977); *Counseling Elders and Their Families*, with John Herr (NY: Springer, 1979); and *Rigor and Imagina-*

tion: Essays from the Legacy of Gregory Bateson, edited with Carol Wilder-Mott (NY: Praeger, 1981).

Wendel A. Ray, PhD, MSW, a board certified clinical social worker and licensed professional counselor, is in private practice of individual, marriage, and family therapy in Monroe, Louisiana. He is a Research Associate and Director of the Don D. Jackson Archive, Mental Research Institute, Palo Alto, California, and an Associate Professor of Marriage and Family Therapy at Northeast Louisiana University, Monroe, LA. A clinical member and approved supervisor of the American Association for Marriage and Family Therapy, and past president of the Louisiana Association for Marriage and Family Therapy (1992-1994), he is author or coauthor of more than 20 professional papers and three other books: *Irreverence: A Strategy for Therapists' Survival*, with Gianfranco Cecchin and Gerry Lane (London, U.K.: Karnac Books, 1992, U.S. distribution: Brunner/Mazel); *Resource Focused Therapy*, with Bradford P. Keeney (London, U.K.: Karnac Books, 1993, U.S. distribution: Brunner/Mazel) and *The Cybernetics of Prejudices in the Practice of Psychotherapy*, with Gianfranco Cecchin and Gerry Lane (London, U.K.: Karnac Books, 1993, U.S. distribution: Brunner/Mazel).

Contributors

Prabha Appasamy, PhD, 36-H, North Parade Road, St. Thomas' Mount, Madras–600 016, India

Gregory Bateson, MA, (Deceased), Anthropologist who played a major role in the formulation of cybernetics and introduced communications theory into the work of social and natural scientists.

Janet Beavin Bavelas, PhD, Professor, Department of Psychology, University of Victoria, BC.

Insoo Kim Berg, MSSW, Director, Brief Family Therapy Center, 6815 W. Capitol Drive, Milwaukee, WI.

Michael Bloom, PhD, Family Practice Center, Inc., 2300 S. Dakota Ave., Sioux Falls, SD.

Hendon Chubb, PhD, Director, Brief Therapy Institute, 65 Johnson Road, West Cornwall, CT.

William Cohen, MD, Assistant Professor of Pediatrics, University of Pittsburgh School of Medicine and Director, Child Development Unit, Children's Hospital of Pittsburgh.

Steve de Shazer, MSSW, Founder, Brief Family Therapy Center, 6815 W. Capitol Drive, Milwaukee, WI.

Celia Elzufan, LIC, Director, Centro de Terapias Breves (Brief Therapy Center), Buenos Aires, Argentina.

J. Scott Fraser, PhD, Associate Professor and Director of Training, School of Professional Psychology, Wright State University, Dayton, OH.

Douglas J. Green, DMin, First Congregational Church, Ithaca, NY.

Helen Haughton, BA(Sc), DIP(Psch), Rockspring, Hillcrest Road, Dublin, Ireland.

Hugo Hirsch, MD, Director Centro Privado de Psicoterapia, Buenos Aires, Argentina and Co-Director, Centro de Terapias Breves.

Giorgio Nardone, PhD, Director, Cenro di Terapia Stra Strategica, Corso Italia 236, 52100 Arezzo, Italy.

Eddie Oshins, MA, MS, Visiting Scholar, Department of Physics, Stanford University, Stanford, CA.

Mara Selvini Palazzoli, MD, Founder and Director, Center for Family Studies, Milan, Italy.

Klaus Pothoff, MD, Storgatan 17, 352 31 Vaxjo, Sweden.

Stefan Priebe, MD, Rothenbaum Chaussee 237, Hamburg, Germany.

Jules Riskin, MD, Senior Research Fellow, MRI, Palo Alto, CA.

Fabia Schoss, PhD, Via Tiraboschi, 8, 20135 Milano, Italy.

Carlos E. Sluzki, MD, Department of Psychiatry and Behavioral Sciences, Berkshire Medical Center, Pittsfield, MA.

Terry Soo-Hoo, PhD, Co-Director, Difficult Kid Center, MRI, Adjunct Faculty, University of San Francisco, CA.

Yosef Soroka, MSW, Private Practice, 43 Freud Street, Hiafa, Israel.

Ray Storts, ACSW, LCSW, LMFT, Family Services, 11740 E. 21st Street, Suite E, Tulsa, OK.

Paul Watzlawick, PhD, Senior Research Fellow, MRI, 555 Middlefield Road, Palo Alto, CA.

Diana Weyland, LIC, Director, Family Therapy Program, Mental Health Hospital San Isidro, Buenos Aires, Argentina.

Senior Editor's Comments

When Wendel Ray approached me last year suggesting a book honoring the Mental Research Institute (MRI) through the writings of its alumni and disciples, I frankly had mixed feelings. On one hand, I was quite intrigued with the concept. After all, MRI has been one of the most influential groups in the psychotherapy field since Freud's "inner circle" of the early part of this century. A book discussing MRI's origins, vicissitudes, and influences would be an exciting work, particularly for historians of psychotherapy.

On the other hand, I feared that such a book might end up to feel "self-serving" rather than instructive or insightful. I have read other books which were tributes to a person, place, or idea, and in their attempt to commemorate they lost their critical edge. "Tribute" books are usually, frankly, boring to read unless you are personally involved with what is being celebrated.

I realized early in the evolution of this book, however, that this would be no "awards banquet" for MRI, with one author after another citing the importance of the Institute. Instead, what developed into *Propagations: Thirty Years of Influence from the Mental Research Institute* was a work of profound clinical scope from some of the foremost leaders in psychotherapy. Through chapters ranging from the theoretical to the case study, the theme of how this amazing Institute has profoundly impacted our therapeutic thought is woven dramatically, but subtly.

This book could certainly be read as a compliment to the MRI influence, but it could also be read to discover and savor the important contributions of those influenced *by* MRI. It is like watching a festival of films by filmmakers influenced by a master director: The tribute to the master is clear, but the films by the disciples stand on their own. In *Propagations*, certainly the tribute to the MRI influence is clear, but the chapters by the alumni stand on their own as well.

I think the reader will be as amazed as I at the depth and power of the MRI influence, which extends to theory, all aspects of psychotherapy practice, other professions, and other lands. Even if one is not an MRI devotee, this book offers outstanding conceptualizations, writing, and clinical ideas that will be immediately useful to clinicians, academic researchers, students, and others interested in how people change.

Terry S. Trepper, PhD
Senior Editor
Haworth Marriage and the Family

Preface

John H. Weakland

One cannot–or more accurately should not–say that anything is more unique or less unique; there is no comparative for singleness. But it should be permissible to say this book is nearly unique, or unique so far as I know.

The work might perhaps be characterized as an "institutional festschrift." That is, it resembles the usual academic festschrift in being a collection of papers by different authors to commemorate an occasion. But instead of being produced in honor of a particular individual–usually a distinguished scholar or scientist–at or near his retirement, the chapters here relate to a particular institution, the Mental Research Institute, now renamed simply MRI. And we sincerely hope that MRI is not at, nor near, retirement; rather, we hope and trust it will continue productive work for a long time yet.

The year 1989, however, marked the thirtieth anniversary of our Institute's founding by Don D. Jackson, MD, and in thinking about an appropriate way to take note of this, the staff of MRI came up with an idea: to invite "alumni" of the Institute–mainly professionals who had participated in our training or monthly residency programs, but including some former staff members who had left to work in other pastures, and a few people who had never worked here but whose work we had influenced at a distance by our writings or personal contact–to write about how their contact with MRI had influenced their subsequent work. This book is the result of the responses we received to that invitation, and the Institute is indebted to all those who took the trouble to reply, although not all of the contributions we received could be included here.

Some characteristics of the work that follow directly from the genesis sketched above should be pointed out. Most important is the range and diversity of its contents. The terms of our invitation were purposely broad, with no restrictions other than some suggestions about maximum length. The chapters included here certainly reflect this; they vary greatly in approach, style, subject, and what might be termed "finish"–from preliminary musings to rather formal reports. Certainly, to use a favorite term of Gregory Bateson, a major forefather of our Institute, they constitute a "mixed bag."

It is quite possible that some potential readers will see this as a weakness or defect in this collection. After all, we do live professionally in an age of great specialization and positive statement. To our eyes, however, the view is different. Beyond, or rather beneath, our concerns to improve the practice of psychotherapy, MRI has always had an exploratory bent–an interest in large, unresolved, even murky questions–and a corresponding concern with basic concepts about human problems and the nature of change. From such a vantage point, the course of scientific and professional development does not appear as a unitary, clearly organized and logically structured progression (though this is probably the most prevalent image), but something that moves ahead, often tentatively and fitfully, out of a combination of curiosity, observation, reflection, and experimental behaviors, by a number of different people. Certainly the authors here came to MRI from different backgrounds, with different purposes, and had different sorts of contact with us.

For all these reasons, then, it seems that a "mixed bag" is an appropriate result of our invitation. We might even hope that, in addition to the value of the specific content of each chapter, this "mixed bag" arising from one source might offer a useful example of how, in actuality, new ideas and related practices develop and diversify from a broad common core.

In any case, we owe thanks to all those who have helped make this volume a reality–first of course everyone who sent a paper in response to our invitation, but also all of the members of MRI's professional and office staff who took part in the conception and carrying forth of this project.

Introduction: MRI–A Little Background Music

John H. Weakland
Paul Watzlawick
Jules Riskin

The charter of the Mental Research Institute (MRI) states that its purpose is "to conduct and encourage scientific investigation, research and discovery in relation to human behavior for the benefit of the community at large." One of our letterheads makes matters a bit clearer by characterizing MRI as "A research and training institute for the interactional study of the individual, the family and the community." We might add some further specifications to this. The Institute's work started from an initial concentration on the study of family interaction and teaching of family therapy. However, from early days its activities have included a broad range of concerns, generally involving the role of human communication and interaction in shaping and ordering behavior, especially in the genesis, maintenance, and resolution of problems in the family and in other sorts and sizes of social organizations–that is, how people continually and systematically, though often unwittingly, influence each other for worse or for better. Our work has always involved an interdisciplinary staff with diversified backgrounds including psychiatry, psychology, social work, anthropology, and human communication. This has led to over 50 completed research projects, more than 40 books, with many foreign editions, over 400 other publications, and a number of international conferences.

Yet, such a formal description may not convey much about the fundamental question here: What sort of a place has been the seedbed from which the variety of papers in this volume have sprouted?

A related concern arose within MRI some years ago when it appeared that many newer members of the staff seemed unfamiliar with what might be called the origins, traditions, and ethos of the Institute. This was met by holding a staff meeting which presented a "trialog" between three "old hands"–Jules Riskin, Paul Watzlawick, and John Weakland. So now, in the hope of conveying some of the "feel" of MRI to a wider audience, we re-present this "trialog" in a somewhat condensed form.

JW: I think it is appropriate that I start because, while we are discussing the history of MRI, I am an anthropologist and I really want to start with the prehistory of MRI.
JR: Which is why I suggested that you start.
JW: In a sense, I think it is very true that MRI began before it came into existence. It began not really from, but in a way, out of Gregory Bateson's projects on communication. You might also say that it began by the conjunction of those projects, and the people involved with Don Jackson. Bateson's projects started in the late fall of 1952 when he got a grant from the Rockefeller Foundation to study communication somewhat broadly but, in particular, to study paradoxes in communication related to differences in levels of abstraction, levels of communication, levels of classification. Bateson got this initial grant from the Rockefeller Foundation because he knew the president of the Foundation, who specifically OK'd it personally and directly.

Gregory, who was my first anthropology teacher, asked me to join him, and I came out here in the beginning of 1953. Jay Haley had met Gregory at Stanford where Jay was studying in the Communications Department, and had been invited to join also. So we started to work over at the Menlo Park VA Hospital. Later we were joined by Bill Fry who was just finishing his psychiatric residency.

Q: And why at the VA?
JW: Gregory had a job there as the Ethnologist of the VA Hospital. In a way, this was sort of fortuitous. It probably had a lot to do with the directions that things took, because I don't know if we would have ever gotten into studying schizophrenia (which led to family work), and certainly not as soon, had we not been there. We started studying communication in about as many ways as one might

imagine. I'll boil a lot of it down. Some of it I couldn't have imagined–observing things from otters and monkeys playing in the zoo, to the training of guidedogs for the blind, to a ventriloquist communicating with his dummy–a little of everything; it was all very exploratory. But there was a central theme going through all this, which was that we were interested in different levels of communication, channels of communication, and how one message modified another or had to be taken into account in understanding the significance of another. And, I would say at that time we were thinking of significance mainly in terms of meaning, but yet, in a way, that was already beginning to move over toward significance in terms of *influence*, which I think is one of the main things that came out of this work and one of the main things that persisted as very important, even now. I'll give you one example. Bateson was very interested in what he described and wrote about as the message "This is play" in animals. He had noticed otters playing and they did things that looked like they were fighting but they weren't fighting and they didn't respond to each other as if they were fighting. So, he put this into words in terms of: they must also be exchanging a message, "This is play." This playful nip was not the bite of fighting. Well, that is partly a description in terms of meaning, but it is also a statement in terms of behavioral influence. When animal *A* nips animal *B*, what happens is not that it is a fight, but that there is a return nip and then they run all over the place and tangle and roll –they play.

From there, we began to think more broadly and generally about the fact that there is always more than one message going on, and that these messages modify each other. There is no simple message. There are messages about messages which qualify their meaning. We began shortly to look at human communication and, since we were sitting in the VA Hospital and there was a lot of strange communication going on there, we began–I believe at Jay's initial suggestion–to look at schizophrenics. And to think of this in terms of, "Is there a way to understand their messages in the terms we were thinking about? Is there some way of interpreting them? Is there some sort of framing by which they could be understood, even though they seem nonsensical in ordinary terms? Is there some sort of framing these messages lack that makes them look so crazy?"

This led us to the idea, among other things, that a lot of what schizophrenics say is rather readily understandable if you see it as a metaphor, where there is no label saying "This is a metaphor," but where it looks like a straight factual statement–only the facts don't make any sense. When a patient says, "I've got concrete in my stomach. My stomach is full of concrete," he says it like a literal statement and it makes no sense. If you tell him, "That doesn't make any sense," he will insist on it, and in much the same way as when you argue with anybody, he gets more stubborn about what he just said. But, if you begin to discuss the food in the hospital, then you may get a very different response because that may be what he is metaphorically talking about.

From there, we began to think about the style, the patterns generally of schizophrenic communication. We began to think about how they came to talk this way; how did they learn it? These days, I think we might think more in terms of: "How is it that this type of talk is reinforced and perpetuated?" But in those days, we were still thinking more about origins, and we began to wonder, "How did they learn it?" Since we couldn't find out what actually happened in childhood, we thought we would do the next best thing, and we began to get their families in and audiotape schizophrenic families, to see how things might fit together between the way the family communicated and the way the patient communicated. By this time, which was only two and a half years after the beginning of the project, we had invited in Dr. Jackson–first, as a sort of consultant on schizophrenia and dealing with schizophrenics, since he was a teacher in the residency program at the VA. He rapidly became a full working member of the project, where he had some theoretical ideas and a whole lot of data. He already had some experience with schizophrenics, and with their families as well, a lot of interest in treatment, and some ideas about homeostasis even at that early date, which fitted in with some ideas we had about feedback and cybernetic systems. So, having got the patients, the families, and ourselves into a room, the next thing that happened was attempts at family therapy. My usual statement about that is: We did this partly to repay the families for their cooperation, partly for curiosity to see what we could do, but in my own case, at least, it was also a means of self-defense because the impact of the schizophrenics and their families pulling at you while you interviewed them was too damned big to stand if you didn't try to do something to change the system. Fairly late in the 1950s, we got one more grant. This one was from NIMH (National Institute for Mental Health) to do a study on family therapy with schizophrenics and their families. This was, by Gregory's insistence, carried out through the Palo Alto Medical Research Foundation (PAMRF), although at that time Don was just starting MRI, originally as a division within the PAMRF. So that is, I would say, the prehistory. I might have a comment or two later about what I see all this is about, but that is how it developed.

Q: By this time, the year is?
JW: It is 1958 or 1959 by now.
JR: From just hearing John talk, I realize that my notes here have less to do with ideas and more to do with some rather blurred, fragmented memories of people more than of the ideas. So it might take a somewhat different dimension now.

I first heard about the schizophrenia project at an American Psychiatric Association meeting in 1956 in Chicago, in which an evening workshop was presented by Haley and Bateson. I don't know if any of you were there. It was jammed. It was a room for 100 people and there were people hanging from chandeliers. Were you there?
JW: No. The only Chicago workshop I went to was when Jay and I went to a sort of get-together there at a big hospital to speak to the staff–but never to a big meeting.
JR: Well, as I say, it is very blurred except that there was a very big, interested, and eager crowd. I do remember that there was a picture show of two or three families being interviewed for a few minutes. And the cameras didn't work, and all that.

I was in training in Cincinnati and I was interested in working with schizophrenics. The professor who was particularly interested in schizophrenia and language was Louis Gottschalk, who has since for 20 years now, worked in content analysis. He is now at UC (University of California), San Diego. He gave me a paper that he thought I might be interested in, in a volume I had never heard of, called *Behavioral Science*, Volume 1. One of the first papers in the first issue. And I couldn't understand a word of it; he agreed and we both thought it was very exciting.

JW: This is *the* paper, to which he is referring (Bateson, Jackson, Haley, and Weakland, 1956).

JR: The double-bind paper.

Q: John told us how he got involved, Gregory Bateson, Don Jackson–but how did Jay Haley get involved? Nobody has said.

JW: I told you how Jay Haley got involved. Jay met Gregory at Stanford when Gregory was a Visiting Professor in the Anthropology Department. He was the longest-term Visiting Professor in the history of the University. I think he was a Visiting Professor for ten years consecutively.

JR: I.e., he was never accepted by the in-group.

JW: And Jay, who was studying for a Masters in the Communications Department, took a course or two from Gregory.

JR: Then during Christmas of 1957, I made my semiannual trip out to my home in Oakland, and arranged through prior correspondence to visit the Bateson group. I guess I wrote to Jackson actually. A couple of things I remember about that meeting. First of all, it was like I was reading a book by Stephen Potter (1971). This may not be the way you would characterize the meetings, but, goodness, it was just a magnificent display of one-upmanship back and forth. It was consistent with what came out which was very active and intensive. I also remember at the end of the meeting, a fellow named Haley–somehow I mentioned the name of Nathan Ackerman; I had just read a book by him on the family, and Haley said, "What did you think of it?" We were already at the beginning of "Who got the answers first?"

Following that, which was late 1957, I wrote a letter to Don Jackson, saying I was planning to move back out there; was there any place for me in the research project? He passed the letter to Gregory and I got this letter back from Mr. Bateson which I cannot find. I still remember fragments of it. It had to do with research being like the priesthood; you must be wholly dedicated to it; it is like following a difficult path; there is no room (I am paraphrasing now a bit) for the luxury of having a clinical practice, having a comfortable living, and so on. And I didn't know what had hit me, but I knew I had been hit. I moved out here in August of 1958, and had a meeting with Jackson, showed him this letter and in his very characteristic way, (he could smooth over, in the most remarkable way, any difficulties), he said, "Don't bother about it. There was a little incident between Bateson and me. You just happen to be the one who is the recipient. That is all." I think partly what it represents was an ongoing struggle that even continues as late as Gregory's latest book written a couple of years ago, about who was in charge, who got credit for what, and this sort of thing. I am referring to the fact that the Mental Research Institute is not at all mentioned in *Steps to an Ecology of Mind* (Bateson, 1972), and I am not sure if Jackson is mentioned, but certainly not the Mental Research Institute. That was a kind of running conflict that went on for a long time. Anyway, I arrived here in August of 1958 and started in September. Don had meetings at his house in the evening. A woman, who was tall and wore very funny hats, attended–Virginia (Satir) whom I met then. She had just come from Chicago and partly came out because she had heard of Don Jackson. I am not sure that was the only reason. Also, I am not sure if he had heard of her, but she had heard of him and the Bateson project. She had been doing some work at the Psychiatric Institute in Chicago, doing family therapy. So she came, along with a psychologist from Stanford by the name of something like Winters, he went to Michigan since, and Jerry Oremland who was working with Don and subsequently has become a fairly traditional-minded psychoanalyst in San Francisco.

JW: I might mention that there was a whole group of interested young residents most of whom had come through the VA about that time.

JR: Yes, there was a very strong following for Don.

JW: They were very much involved with Don and with the project that I mentioned on schizophrenia and family therapy. They have gone a variety of ways since.

JR: We met three or four times over a few months. The idea was to set up a longitudinal study to study schizophrenia. Then I began hearing more about a research institute to be called the Mental Research Institute. In late 1958, Don already was trying to secure backing from wealthy people. He had a remarkable ability to get these people interested in the kind of work he was doing; he was charming and charismatic, as you've all heard many times. The actual starting was dependent on getting some hard money. I heard at one time how the word "mental" got in; I don't remember what the reason was, but I think it was some kind of compromise. The organization officially got started on March 1, 1959–after the hard money was in hand. It was $50,000 from the Wheeler Foundation plus a few other tens of thousands. At that time, these private contributions were available and Don had just an amazing ability to be the one who knew how to be the recipient of these contributions. I don't know exactly what went into it, but it was quite remarkable. The original site was the Palo Alto Medical Research Foundation. Marc Krupp was the director then and still is, and he was very supportive.

Q: You said that you wrote to Don Jackson and I assume joined the staff . . .

JR: Yes, so he starts the MRI and there are four of us who begin the MRI–Don, Virginia Satir, Ella Zvigne who was secretary, and I, in the old house that is now part of the main building of the Palo Alto Medical Clinic. Here with a professional staff of three, Don invited me to be the Associate Director and I didn't have the courage at that time to ask him what as Associate Director I was supposed to do. I think, in hindsight, that it was very important to him to have an MD working with him, for political reasons.

Q: You were in private practice?

JR: No. I had just come out and I started half-time at the San Mateo Adult Clinic, and half-time with Don.

Q: And where was the Bateson Group?

JR: Still at the VA.

Q: The only tenuous connection . . .

JR: Yes, I'll mention a little about that because it is a sort of coming together, pulling apart, coming together, quite tenuously and really quite difficult to pinpoint precisely where the connections were. I imagine that there are at least a couple of immediate goals he had in mind when he set it up. One was that he wanted to have an umbrella to do a longitudinal study–that would be a most immediate, obvious goal. I think it is clear he had in mind a long-term goal of setting up a research institute which would be somewhat parallel to the Research Foundation – that would do its own thing in the behavioral sciences. At the time we got started, there were a couple of other projects also going on at the PAMRF that Don was directly or indirectly related to. One was the family therapy and schizophrenia project that John already mentioned, and the other was the LSD Project. MRI started, housed at the PAMRF and as a subsidiary group within the PAMRF. However, it was not parallel to the other PAMRF divisions because it had its own Board of Directors, and its own name, so it was part in and part separate. And that was the beginning of a lot of later complications and troubles.

JW: To add to the complexity, the family therapy and schizophrenia project was a project in PAMRF but not in the Mental Research Institute for one–(I was going to say simple reason but that word doesn't exactly fit)–for one *overriding reason* and that was that Gregory was officially the Director of the project and I was the Co-Director, and Gregory by that time was unwilling to work as Don's employee.

JR: Yes, he was *not* going to work for Don.

JW: He was willing to work with Don on the project under Krupp, but he wasn't going to work *for* Don.

JR: Again, that is part of what I referred to, in the letter I got earlier. This was going on continuously. OK. There was the Bateson Project and the LSD project, which was to determine if LSD could help loosen up patients who didn't move after three or four or five years in therapy. It went on for a while and then kind of petered out.

I mentioned the professional staff–Virginia, Don, and myself–the first thing we worked on was a longitudinal study for schizophrenia. I would be very embarrassed to go back and look at that proposal, but you have to learn someplace and that was our learning point.

By January of 1960, we moved to 777 Bryant Street. By this time, Don was getting much more involved–or continuing but more so–in writing, going across the country, and lecturing. Let me come back to that. We had conferences, and sometimes some of the Bateson group participated, and sometimes it was people in the LSD project. I remember that they were exciting though I don't remember much more about their specific nature. Don had a very remarkable ability to pick up ideas from people in the most diverse disciplines and try to pull something out of them and develop them. That was a particularly exciting part. I am not sure, but I think Jay

and John joined the MRI formally around 1961. Virginia, from the very, very beginning, began interviewing families. She used the LSD Room, and she used the Charles Addams House. Was that what we called the old house that was on Channing Avenue where Gregory's project did its interviewing?
JW: Yes.
JR: And where some of the films were made, and Virginia did some of her interviewing there. This was mostly evening work and very quickly she got the interest of a lot of local professionals–psychiatrists, psychologists, and social workers. Jerry Rose was involved very early, and Don Ehrman, Manny Silver, are some old-timers around here. She would interview and they would go out and have pizza and beer later on and discuss the interviews until late at night. I may be romanticizing the past, but it was kind of exciting. I did some cotherapy with her, which was where I started to learn family therapy, and that was kind of a bizarre experience. I felt like I was on the outside of a jet airplane. Sometimes she would show up and sometimes she wouldn't, and we worked those problems out.
JW: She had one thing in common with Don.
JR: I'll jump ahead here; I have the note "twins." As I got to work with both of them, and I'll come back in a minute to what the specific work was, I kept on seeing them as twins. They were very creative, very gifted, totally unreliable in terms of keeping appointments, but maybe appointments aren't the most important thing in the world. As creative and as gifted and as full of new ideas as they were, coming up with new ideas every second (I think by hereditary constitution), they were absolutely incapable of following a syllogism through to its logical conclusion–both of them. They just didn't work that way; they were artists. It was a family, the three of us. It was a complex and stormy marriage. They were the parents and I was the kid. I think I mentioned the "twins" bit once to them, and that didn't go over too well.
JW: Let me mention something. I think both in relation to working for Gregory and for them, the position is much more that of parental-child.
JR: Okay, right. It was reversed sometimes because if we had a deadline to meet, I would become the parent.
JW: Yes.

JR: Like getting this first project out and getting it organized.

In 1960, Virginia got funded from the Hill Foundation in Minneapolis, and that carried her through for the first two years of the family therapy training project. She got a very large grant from NIMH from 1962 to 1966, I think, for five years. So she got much more involved with that. The thing that Virginia, Don, and I worked with for many months was listening to one tape for about five minutes–five minutes of one tape. Don had clearly demonstrated to many people his remarkable ability to take a section of an interview, listen to it, turn it off, and predict precisely what the next interchange would be. Virginia could do the same thing but, at least for me, they were not able to clarify what they based these predictive abilities on.

JW: I'd like to make a comment along that line. One of the main things that took place from very early on, beginning with the Bateson project and then going on through, was that this was damned near the beginning of anyone really taking down material–the whole record–in the psychiatric and behavioral fields and going over and over it. Up until then, it was someone giving you an account of how he ran a therapy session, and he doesn't have a record himself, so he gives you an account from memory. So, first it was taping, and then it was observation, and then it was filming, and finally videotaping. This was just something totally new–to really have data and look at it.

JR: Yes, and one of the reasons it was new was that there was a tradition in the psychoanalytic model that the nature of the relationship between the therapist and the analysand would be interfered with seriously if there were a tape recorder present. This was just a very serious "no-no."

There were a couple of other groups who were doing somewhat parallel things. For example, Theodore Lidz (Yale), Nathan Ackerman (New York), and NIMH where Lyman Wynne was. We got a hold of a tape that Lyman Wynne had of a family interview he conducted. We listened to this damned tape for many, many months; we spent several hours every week. This was where there was a reversal, where the two artists were performing and I was trying to get them to tell me what they were basing these things on. Out of this came the paper of the five-minute analysis of the tape.

Also around this time, we got a letter from someone in Philadelphia about a psychologist from Philadelphia who was interested in communication, was interested in coming out here, and wondering if there was a place open for him? This was around 1960. I remember we looked at this fellow's C.V. and we were struck by how many different places he had been in the last 15 years, and we wondered if he would stay here a year. Paul, take over.

PW: To explain how this happened, you may have already gotten the feeling that Don had a sort of tendency to pick up stray dogs. I had been working down in San Salvador at the National University where I had the Chair of Psychotherapy. After three years, I began to feel that somehow things had exhausted themselves and there was nothing much more to expect, except more of the same. So I decided that it was time to move on again. At that time, the only place in the States I really wanted to see was Philadelphia–John Rosen's place, the Institute for Direct Analysis, which was also called the Institute for the Study of Psychotherapy. I wrote to John Rosen and he immediately wrote back and said yes, it was fine and I could come, and I could undergo training there in direct analysis. So I sold my office furniture and my air conditioner and I canceled my office contract, and then, just to be on the safe side, on the 18th of December of 1959, I wrote to John Rosen and said, "I am coming," just in case he had forgotten. On the 24th of December, as a Christmas present, I got a letter from John Rosen, saying any prior promises or commitments on his part were canceled. I went to Philadelphia anyway and John Rosen looked at me and said, after finding out who I was, "But, I told you not to come." I said, "Yes, but you told me on the 24th of December after our correspondence had been going on for months." And, as so often in my life, this seeming disaster turned out to be an advantage because the rest of the Institute, including Al Scheflen and Spurgeon English, who at that time, was Chairman of the Department of Psychiatry at Temple, felt so badly about this business that they bent over backwards to help me. By the time I arrived, however, the great days of the Institute were over, Rosen's methods had come increasingly under doubt while, at the same time, I think it is hard to imagine how great the impact of–as it was then known–the Palo Alto Group, was on areas outside of Palo Alto. Their articles, and not only the double-bind articles, were really making an enormous splash. I mentioned to Scheflen that I was interested in their work and he said that was fine because Jackson was coming out in October. So, I met Jackson; I had written him before and he had said, "Come out; I can't promise you money, but if you want to come out here, that is fine." So, at the end of November, 1960, I arrived here.

Many of the things I could say you have heard and I need not repeat, but not enough has been mentioned about Don's rather flamboyant personality, and his rather special ways of dealing with people. Jules has mentioned his ability to raise funds that has never been matched by anybody. He was fantastic in this. Admittedly, it was much easier then, but still he had a way of insuring ample supplies to the Institute. It was quite remarkable.

Also, I was very struck by his capability; I have never seen a therapist of his caliber anywhere. It was incredible to watch him sit through a family session–at times, in a rather characteristic pose, looking down on the floor and then suddenly coming to life and doing something that had long-range implications; he just picked up what was going on here and now. Jules mentioned his remarkable ability to somehow pick up information that was contained in the verbal interchanges. Janet Beavin and I–Janet having graduated from a secretary to a Research Associate in those days–met with Don for many, many weeks for several hours per week, and we played him blind segments of structured interviews–that is, the couple's response to "How, out of the millions of people in the world, did you two get together?" We had 60 such examples which ranged from two to five minutes approximately. Don did not know the people. He had never seen them; we did not give him any information, not even the ages. Don would come up with the most incredibly concrete kind of diagnoses at the end of listening to these very, very brief interchanges, of which, of course, he only had the verbal and paralinguistic parts; he did not see the facial expression and the body language or anything. He just listened to the tape. He would then say something as concrete as, "All right, if they have a son, he is probably a delinquent." If they have a girl, she probably has some psychosomatic problem." He was right every bloody time. And we would say, "For God's sake, Don, how do you do it? What made you say this?" He would say, as if it was the most obvious thing in the world, "Well, because of the way they laugh here." We still did not know what was the thing that made him say it, but he was always right. I remember one funny incident in particular. We tried to get a control group of so-called normals, and we rounded up three normal couples. I remember one was a father and a mother, whose marriage seemed to be very much all right after something like 17 years. They had a 15-year-old daughter and she was doing well at school and there were no problems. So they qualified for our idea of normal. We played this particular part of "how did you meet" for Don, and for the first time Don said, "I don't know; to me they sound normal."

The main methodological and ideological difference between Don and Virginia was that Virginia was heavily history-oriented and all her training in those days, of which she did a lot, was based on this. People were supposed to take painstaking histories, and Don was just the opposite. I did not have the feeling that they were two parents. In fact, I would only think of Virginia as Mrs. Rosen after having been exposed to John Rosen in Philadelphia. By this I mean, extremely intuitive, very effective but quite unable to explain why she was doing what she was doing, just like Rosen.

JW: Don was willing to explain, but unable to explain.

PW: He was willing to explain, and he thought he had explained it. In those days, many of the projects we ran were all based on the belief that clinical diagnosis must reflect itself clearly in the interaction between family members. We were looking for delinquent interactions (Jerry Rose's project), patterns of asthmatics (John Weblin, a New Zealander who was here for a while and studied these families), a couple of normals, psychosomatics, ulcerative colitis families with Irv Yalom, schizophrenics, of course, and underachievers. As I say, all of these studies were based on the assumption–a wrong assumption–that clinical diagnosis must be relatable in a clearly definable and limited way in the patterns of interaction of these families. It never worked out.

In those days, Gregory–to mention another nice sort of historical fact–had a thing called the "Tuesday Evenings"–an open house at his home. I think every single one of them was really an experience–intellectually, a very gratifying experience. He usually had some guests from either related fields or from some totally different fields like astronomy or economics or so on. There was a lot of interchange and cutting across boundary lines taking place there. As I say, these were the early days.

Those were, indeed, the early days, when an institute populated by very diverse people arose when a very general and largely theoretical interest in communication and interaction merged with a specific and largely practical interest in the family and psychotherapy. Much has changed since then. Many of the founders are no longer with us. There is probably less intuition and less excitement, but also less of the confusion and uncertainty that naturally accompanied our early explorations into very new territories. Yet some fundamental things remain much the same. A variety of new people have come; our work is still stimulated by the diversity of our interests and backgrounds. And though we believe that many of the questions of our early days have been answered, new questions have arisen from these very accomplishments, so we are still seeking to extend our interactional view of human behavior and problems further, and to pass on some of our answers and questions to others. We hope this book will provide an interesting sample of what has resulted.

SECTION I: INFLUENCING FIELDS OF INTEREST AND VIEWPOINTS

In less than 40 years of history the field of family therapy has grown very rapidly. This has, quite expectably for a field involving immediate application, led to an increasing emphasis on practice. But it is important to remember that MRI's work arose from a context–the Bateson research projects–that involved a strong conceptual/theoretical emphasis, and that such an emphasis still underlies all of our practice. Our essential focus has always been on taking an interactional view of communication and behavior, as outlined most broadly in *Pragmatics of Human Communication* (Watzlawick, Beavin, and Jackson, 1967). In addition, probably because our work, especially in its early stages, involved radical rethinking and restructuring of established psychiatric theory and practice, there has also been a basic interest in how such change (which presents significant parallels to the kind of change sought in psychotherapeutic practice) comes about.

One result of this is that our work has had relevance beyond the specific field of psychotherapy and it seems appropriate to begin this volume with several papers concerned with this more general level of MRI influence.

Chapter 1

A Research Worker Is Permanently in Debt

Mara Selvini Palazzoli

The MRI's letter reminding me of the Foundation's thirtieth anniversary prompted me to recall what, for me, was an emblematic occasion. In 1979, I accepted an invitation to be present in San Francisco for the commemoration of the MRI's twentieth anniversary. We had all been asked to contribute to a conference bearing the felicitous title of *The Present Imperfect*, set up after the manner of an ancient "certamen." The speakers were called upon to expand on one and the same theme, which had been broken up into four questions, the first of which was, "Why did you decide to become a family therapist?" My answer involved owing up to being what I am and always have been, namely an obstinate, inquisitive creature who will stop at nothing in her quest for further knowledge–not even at making 180 degree U-turns in her chosen path.

I had started on a career in internal medicine at the University Clinic in Milan. It was there, in 1950, that I came across my first anorectic patients. I was absolutely fascinated by this mysterious clinical puzzle. Quite sure that my medical competence offered no clues for solving it and having decided that I had to, I threw my budding career in internal medicine to the winds and got into psychiatry and psychoanalytic training.

This fact of becoming a psychoanalyst had been in my life, which is characterized by many changes of route, an important one. I treated many patients (including a considerable number of anorectic patients) and for a time I was happy because I had the impression that I was understanding everything! But, with time, I began to feel a sort of disenchantment. The reason for that disenchantment was not only in the enormous personal effort (aside from the vast expenditure of time demanded by the psychotherapeutic treatment) when viewed against the paucity of results, at least in numerical terms. I realized that many questions remained unanswered. For example, why, among hundreds of thousands of girls, who in conforming to occidental fashion begin to diet, only a few are not able to stop and thus become anorectic? I felt it was necessary to look for new conceptual models which could offer a wider range of answers and more efficient tools for treatment.

It then became clear to me that the occasion for another change in direction for my career was arising: from psychoanalyst to family therapist. This change was characterized by a groping and proved itself to be more laborious than the previous one.

It is amusing to observe how faithfully my courses in the university reflected my exploratory activity. The classic works of Wynne and Singer (1963), concerning thought disorders in the families of schizophrenics, had been decisive in my making the switch from the monadic to the relational viewpoint. So I began the incredible difficulty of translating that paper into Italian (including the bizarre expressions used by members of schizophrenic families). My new course, concerning *Communication in Psychiatry*, replaced my previous one on *Psychoanalytic Theory*, and was especially dedicated to the study of the papers by Wynne and Singer.

During the translating of the paper, a suspicion came to my mind when the parent of a schizophrenic patient who, after looking at the four Rorschach's tables, gave the following answer–"a sort of species for a special occasion." He was probably able to see something more precise, but, for some reason connected with his learning experience, had chosen to give an answer which was an attempt not to answer. To speak clearly, in his experience, could have been a very risky affair! How happy was my surprise when later, in my wandering through papers and books (as self-taught people do), I found my suspicion confirmed. Don Jackson's papers on family's rules and homeostasis (1957a) and the fundamental work of Jay Haley (1959) pointed out the basic rule in the schizophrenic family: precisely the taboo of defining the relationship. Everybody can easily understand that, "If I won't define my relationship with you, I must be as confusing as I can."

Coming back to my autobiography, in 1965, I stopped my profession as a psychoanalyst. For two years I was especially dedicated to studying and reading the articles and books of the pioneers in family therapy. In 1967, I organized a week long residential course dedicated to family therapy; inviting Nathan Ackerman and R.D. Laing as teachers. It was the time of student revolution and on that occasion my initiative was heavily attacked by a group of ideologists, accusing me of being a bourgeois, striving to support an institution–the family–which had to be destroyed.

Notwithstanding that objection, in the same year, in two dark and damp rooms in a cellar (which reminded one very much of catacombs, but equipped with tape and one-way mirror), I started the Center for Family Study, which, in its progress has reached its current arrangement. I did not apply for grants and thought at the time, that nobody would be inclined to give money for such an enterprise. I also stayed free from ties with institutions, for fear of interferences, whether out of ideological or administrative reasons. This certainly limited the range of our experiences. At the same time, staying free of institutional control offered many advantages.

I began to work without any form of family therapy training. I made only a brief trip to Philadelphia in 1967 where I could observe a few family sessions given by Barcai, Nagy, and Framo. I was also present for the meeting for family therapists organized by the Eastern Pennsylvania Psychiatric Institute where I met, for the first time, Paul Watzlawick who later became our friend and mentor.

Back in Milan, I invited to work with me, at first, a Jungian psychologist who was expert in group therapy, and later, some other colleagues with a psychoanalytic background. We worked along, groping in the dark in a state of mental confusion, using the interpretative model to which we were accustomed: pointing out to the family what was going on, etcetera, with disappointing results.

This last turn in my career, in 1971, was the hardest and most painful because it brought war in the team. During the last year, I again changed my course in the university, using as a textbook, *Pragmatics of Human Communication*, by Paul Watzlawick, Janet Beavin, and Don Jackson (1967). Concerning the work with families, I had decided to become what, at that time, was called a "system purist," and I tried to impose Haley's and Jackson's papers and books on my team. However, three members of that team, (at that time composed of seven people) who had recently completed psychoanalytic training at great personal sacrifice and expense, not only refused to apply what was taught in these books, but even to read them. Separation was the only possible solution to that situation.

Consequently, at the end of 1971, the first "system purist" team was formed: Luigi Boscolo, Gianfranco Cecchin, Guiliana Prata, and myself, all psychiatrists with psychoanalytic backgrounds. Our common decision was to adopt the systemic circular model, with a particular emphasis on avoiding any contamination with linear causal models. When we began to work with families, at last without any conflict in the team, we made an amazing discovery. It was as though we had gotten, all at once, new eyes to see . . . we were becoming clever! In this way, we could learn through our own experience. At some point a competitive struggle can make people blind . . . one cannot see anything else other than his own struggle to prevail. Notwithstanding the progress we experienced after the end of the fighting within the team, another fight took place inside each of us: the fight against our own linguistic condition, i.e., the linear-causal model of thinking.

Nevertheless, we remained stubborn and decided to be taught by the understanding of our mistakes, rather than by teachers. Much later we realized that in this way we remained very different from most other family therapy centers which invite well-known therapists to visit, adopt different models and, therefore, create a certain confusion. In short, we wanted to go our own way in research. We were, above all, exploratory researchers–a little group of four, isolated but very compact. We passed from moments of discomfort to moments of joy and astonishment in the face of certain effects our interventions suddenly provoked in families, and which were totally unimaginable before.

To me, this was especially surprising with families presenting anorectic patients. During my previous career as an individual psychotherapist, especially skilled in treatment of anorexia nervosa cases, very often I needed hundreds of sessions before obtaining a positive result. Working with families, one well-centered intervention could be enough to provoke radical change.

In the years 1972 and 1973, we profited from trips to Europe by Paul Watzlawick, to whom we submitted our work for his evaluation. We are indebted to him for his confirmation and encouragement. He followed us in our work, exchanging letters and translating one of our first papers for *Family Process*, himself.

Although we knew Gregory Bateson through his many writings, in the fall of 1972 we had an enthusiastic encounter with his book *Steps to an Ecology of Mind* (1972). I cannot say how many times we have read and reread its chapters, every time finding in it something new–an indication of our progress in the new epistemology. But our problem was–How could we apply these fundamentals in our work? How could we derive from them new ways for therapy? The decision to work with schizophrenic families was precisely a result of these problems and efforts. We hope to have contributed something in this direction by establishing *positive connotation* and in devising family rituals and systemic paradoxical prescriptions (Palazzoli, Boscolo, Cecchin, and Prata, 1978).

The year 1972 was very important for me for another reason. Along with research on the family "in schizophrenic transaction," I encountered the possibility of conducting research on bigger systems. This opportunity was offered to me by my ex-pupils at the Catholic University. At the end of their course, they invited me to be the leader of a research group. The goal was that of investigating whether the systemic model, which had showed itself so valid for the family, could be applied to the study and solution of problems met by the psychologist in his work in the school.

The work of this group, which lasted two and a half years, ended with a publication of the book *Il Mago Imagato* (*The Magician Without Magic*) (Selvini Palazzoli, 1976). With this epithet we synthesized the absurd dilemma of the psychologist in Italian schools where all the members of the scholastic community (director, teachers, pupils, parents), while refusing to become defined as "a client," expect the psychologist to produce a magic solution. Consequently the effort of the research group was directed towards finding a method which would permit him to structure his own professional context.

In 1976, I began to work with a second group, this time composed of psychologists professionally employed by heterogeneous organizations: industries, businesses, hospitals, boarding school, and planning and consulting services. General System Theory and Cybernetics were applied to the examination of relational patterns observable within the various institutions as well as in the interaction between the psychologist and the various subsystems of the organizations. I cannot speak at length on this research, which was also published in the USA with a foreword written by Paul Watzlawick (Selvini Palazzoli et al., 1986). I may only say that our work was especially dedicated to recording *similarities* and *differences* of the phenomena observed in the various organizations. Concerning the similarities, we have found and described in very different organizations redundancies which are isomorphic and have the same pragmatic effect: the maintenance of control in the hands of people at the summit. As to the differences we have observed in big organizations, in comparison with the family, one of the most interesting is the following: the presence of "double binds" in big organizations has unquestionable effects of discomfort and unhappiness on some of their members, but very seldom do they have the psychotic effect, often observed in families. The explanation of this phenomenon lies in the fact that in organizations we do not find relationships so vital and intense as in families. For organizations, turnover and firing is easy, therefore, it is also easy to leave the field. The difficulty of being unable to leave the field appears to be a crucial point in family dysfunction.

The research on the larger systems is very interesting because it allows comparison with the family system. Similarities and differences enlighten both fields of research. "In principle, extra depth in some metaphoric sense–Bateson said–is to be expected whenever the information from the two descriptions is differently collected and differently coded" (Bateson, 1979).

My original team split up in 1979 and once again, I set off on a radically different tack: the idea of shedding new light on the mystery of so-called grievous mental disorders that appear during infancy and adolescence. After working for four years with Guiliana Prata, in 1982 I began working with the team I work with at present. By then we had abandoned paradoxical methods and invented a new one that has proved useful both in therapy and research. Although the methods may have changed, the final purpose of all my efforts has remained the same, namely, to seek for the relational roots of what is commonly spoken of as mental illness.

The work we have been doing during these last ten years, described in our book (Selvini Palazzoli et al., 1989), has been a radical conceptual departure from our previous line of research. However, what we are doing now undoubtedly owes very much to what was done before. No research worker can honestly renege on his debts, no matter how boldly he may strike out in an entirely new direction. Those 17 years of psychoanalytical work, and ten years after that during which I followed the teachings of Gregory Bateson and the MRI, are an invaluable part of my experience that I could not have done without. So, every research worker is indebted to all those who provided him with the ideas that fired his imagination and enthusiasm and helped set him off on some fascinating new adventure–one I always look upon as an unmerited existential privilege.

Chapter 2

A Note on Metacommunication

Janet Beavin Bavelas

This short article, originally written in 1966 and previously unpublished in English, is a report on a series of meetings held at the MRI in 1966 to discuss *metacommunication*. Its historical significance arises initially from the participants in the seminar: a combination of the "first generation" MRI theorists (Don D. Jackson, Jay Haley, John H. Weakland, Paul Watzlawick), visitors (Veron, Lennard), and a younger MRI generation (Carlos Sluzki, Janet Beavin, Art Bodin). Although much of the work of the MRI was stimulated by meetings of this kind, few explicit records exist. The present note illustrates the high level of collaborative discussion in which important tenets of a general theory of communication (not limited to pathology or the family) were examined, clarified, and advanced.

In our view, there is not only historical but contemporary theoretical value to the ideas discussed and the distinctions proposed–distinctions that have often been treated subsequently with considerably less subtlety than is evidenced here. For example: The relation of verbal to nonverbal aspects of a message is *not* isomorphic to communication and metacommunication (or to content and relationship, or to fact and emotion, or any other simple dichotomy). It is suggested that digital and analogic encodings be put on a continuum and examined for similarities rather than always being contrasted. The generality and utility of the Theory of Logical Types for nonverbal information is questioned. Three concrete definitions of "context" are offered, and some useful connections to information theory and general linguistics are implied.

This paper was submitted in 1966 to *Family Process*. Jay Haley (as Editor) sent it to Gregory Bateson, who recommended publication along with a comment of his. Somehow, we dropped the ball (probably because Sluzki returned to Buenos Aires and Beavin began graduate school), and this note was published only in Spanish, in a slightly abridged version.[1] The original, below, has had only trivial corrections, as has the Bateson comment (which has some prophetic comments about "twenty years hence").

In the words of the old radio program, "Return with us now to the days of yesteryear . . . "

A NOTE ON METACOMMUNICATION

Carlos E. Sluzki and Janet Beavin

The term *metacommunication* was introduced by Gregory Bateson (1951) and defined as "communication about communication," that is, all exchanged cues and propositions about either codification or the relationship between the communicators, or both. This concept has been subsequently found useful and adopted by different researchers in psychiatry and human communication: For example, Watzlawick (1964) described metacommunication as the *relationship* (as distinguished from the content) aspect of communication. Scheflen, Birdwhistell, and their colleagues (e.g., Scheflen, 1965a, 1965b) have used the term in their context analysis. Morris and Wynne (1965) report finding the metacommunicational level especially relevant in the study of schizophrenics' parents' communication. And, as is well known, the Double-Bind Theory (Bateson et al., 1956) based a description of certain pathological communication patterns within families on a distinction between communication and metacommunication, and further work following this line has, implicitly or explicitly, assumed metacommunicational phenomena. But adoption also meant adaptation. The term has been framed quite differently by different researchers and, in many cases, not framed at all, the result of which was lack of clarity as to the meaning or meanings of the term and its framework.

With the aim of discussing and perhaps clarifying the field of metacommunication, a seminar was held at the Mental Research Institute, Palo Alto, for seven meetings during the second half of

January and the first half of February 1966, with the full-time participation of Janet Beavin, Jay Haley, Carlos E. Sluzki, Eliseo Veron, Paul Watzlawick, and John H. Weakland, and the part-time participation of Arthur Bodin, Don D. Jackson, and Henry Lennar.[2] The following is a report on this seminar, which the senior author organized and directed.[3]

Several points which underlie the concept of metacommunication were reviewed: (1) We immediately encounter the general difficulty of having only natural language with which to discuss and understand communication and metacommunication (rather than, for instance, some additional symbolic language); there are formal problems regarding the consistency of a model for which the language and framework are the same as the object of observation, and in human communication, this problem of self-reflexivity is a profound one. (2) At a more specific level, it was agreed that there is not necessarily ever any "primary" message[4] (e.g., the verbal component) to which the other aspects (e.g., the nonverbal elements) are "meta-messages." That is, no assumptions were made of an isomorph between logical levels and communication channels.

(3) Regarding verbal and nonverbal channels of communication, it was recalled that they have been to some extent distinguished as digital and analogic, respectively (Bateson, 1951; Bateson and Jackson, 1964), but this distinction should be seen as a continuum, not a dichotomy. That is, although problems of "translation" from one mode to the other can be noted, it is as important and valuable to examine their similarities and interrelations as their differences. It is inadvisable to assign primacy to either, in any sense of "reality" or "the basic message." We can, of course, have a metacommunicational relation between analogic and digital messages, with all the usual possibilities for ambiguity *or* clarification, but the situation is basically similar to the cases where both messages are analogic or both digital.

(4) The Russellian Theory of Logical Types, the most frequently used analogy for the notion of *levels* (especially level and metalevel) in communication (Bateson, 1951; 1954) usefully illustrates the importance of distinguishing levels, although its specific concepts of class and member were felt to be more strictly appropriate

for metalinguistic (purely verbal) relations than for natural (including nonverbal) communication.

(5) Two principles of the linguist Jakobson (1956) were introduced in order to explore their usefulness for comprehension of metacommunicational relations, especially in other than linguistic channels: (a) Through a reconstruction of the code, the observer can establish the relations of a given message to the other signs of the code (the complete, implicit set composed of the chosen message and all the alternative messages that *could have been used* instead of the one chosen), that is, the *selection* made by the sender. The message, hence, conveys not only the information of its own content, but also information about the decision made by the sender to use *that* message, out of all the possible others. (b) Through an analysis of the context in which any message is sent, the observer can also study the contiguity relation between that sign and the rest of the signs in the message package, as well as those in the temporal vicinity of the sequence, that is, the *combination* of elements made by the sender.

Partly on the basis of the above, a series of progressive distinctions, or identifications of areas in the field of communication, were made:

First, there is the problem of the meaning of the term *about* in the definition of metacommunication (communication about communication). Specifically, *to whom* is a message *about* another message–to the sender, the receiver, or the observer? For if one wants to avoid subjective conceptualizations such as *intentions*, it does not seem possible to establish the existence of message and meta-message according to the properties of the message itself. What the observer does is to reconstruct the operations of the sender on the one side and, in order to establish the validity of thes model, may predict responses of the receiver to whatever communicational stimuli he or she decides to study. From the observer's point of view, the assessing of the *about* is not a logical problem, but essentially an instrumental one, that is, entirely conventional.

Second, there are *explicit* and *implicit* meta-messages. Only the metalinguistic messages–those whose test refers to the meaning of other messages, for instance, definitions–would seem to be truly explicit (with their content thus generally clear, although ultimately the observer is still responsible for the analytic labeling and description of even this material, as was mentioned above). All others must be reconstructed by operations of the observer; both their existence (as they are not explicitly contained in the communicational material) and their content are solely products of analysis.

Third, it seems that the study of implicit meta-messages corresponds to the study of *messages in their context* and thus more or less coincides with what has generally been called, after Morris (1938), the "pragmatics" of communication. Three ways to specify the nature of the context were identified:

(i) The *code* as the context in which a message is sent. This is related to the selection operation, that is, the message has a relation of substitution with other elements of the code, this relation implying a meta-message. The code is any set of possibilities; as Ashby has illustrated this:

> The information carried by a particular message depends on the set it comes from. *The information conveyed is not an intrinsic property of the individual message.* That this is so can be seen by considering the following example. Two soldiers are taken prisoner by two enemy countries, A and B, one by each; and their two wives later each receive the brief message "I am well." It is known, however, that country A allows the prisoner a choice from
>
> *I am well,*
> *I am slightly ill,*
> *I am seriously ill,*
>
> while country B allows only the message
>
> *I am well*
>
> meaning "I am alive." (Also in the set is the possibility of "no message.") The two wives will certainly be aware that though each has received the same phrase, the information that they have received is by no means identical. (Ashby, 1956, p. 124)

(ii) *Other emitted messages*, more or less continuous to a given message, as its context; this type corresponds to the combination principle. Bateson described this principle independently and offered the example of an extemporizing dancer:[5]

For any given movement within a sequence of movements, it is evident that . . . the dancer's choice is influenced (largely) by the ongoing characteristics of his sequence of action, and even, perhaps, by the ongoing dancing of a partner (Bateson, 1951, p. 184). See also the "quasi-courtship" cues described by Scheflen (1965a). The juxtaposition of messages over time or across channels results in a metacommunicative combination.

(iii) The *interactional situation* in which the message is emitted as the context which specifies its content, which may thus vary with the character of the interactional situation, each situation presenting a code of social (interpersonal) restrictions that limits and, up to a certain point, determines the repertoire of possible metacommunicative meanings.

These three ways of specifying context (and metacommunication) imply very different research strategies.

Fourth, comparing successive conceptual models in the literature, as well as within the discussion during the seminar, there seems to be a movement from the description of single items (whether this item be a message or a person) to the *relational* level, taking as minimal unit of observation *at least two things in relation to each other*–two levels, persons, messages, item and class, etc. The lack of many precedents for this approach, and the lack of a suitable model for the conceptualization of this focus, made it necessary to restate it very carefully once and again, especially since the usual focus in the science of human behavior and, thus, the habitual thinking of its researchers, are more centered on the single element than on relationships.

COMMENT
Gregory Bateson

If something remains 20 years hence of what we were trying to say in the VA project, I would hope that the ideas will then look quite different and be dressed up in a quite different language. I doubt if *meta-communication* will be a fashionable term, and I am sure that *analogic* and *digital* will be dropped from these contexts. C. F. Hockett's term *iconic* is already better than *analogic*. Of course, there will surely be some sort of classification of the ways in which one bunch of physical events or objects can give "information" about another, i.e., a classification of ways of coding–perhaps several such classifications.

Sometimes I wonder whether we ever treated seriously enough the most basic premise of communication theory: that there are no "things" or reifiable entities within the explanatory system–*only* coded message material. There therefore can be no "explicit" message. The "name," however iconic or representational, can never be the thing named. The percept is never the thing perceived. And so on. The reference to the thing can only be *implicit* in the name, never explicit. The nearest thing to an explicit message is the case where an event or object seems to propose the fact of its own existence. But, of course, this is still nonsense. What enters through our sense organs is still only a transform or coded version of the referent.

If I tell you "this piece of paper is square" and you want to check the truth of my message, you will not compare my message with the paper. You will, either by perception or use of instruments, prepare another *description* of the paper. You will then compare my description with that other. In other words, my description is not "about" the paper. It is about other descriptions of the paper. What I assert by saying "this piece of paper is square" is simply that there will be overlap of information, i.e., redundancy, between my message and other descriptions of the paper. In this sense, messages are always and only about other message material.

So it all boils down to *redundancy*. If it is raining and I say "it is raining" and you look out the window, you will get less information from the perceived raindrops than you would have gotten, had I not spoken. A message is *always* about other message material (e.g., about percepts, which we erroneously call "things"). It is convenient to refer to one part of the double system as a *referent*. But a message is simply that which creates redundancy in the system made up of message-plus-referent; and redundancy is always a *mutual* overlapping.

The reference or subject matter of meta-communication is always this redundancy-creating *relationship* between some lower order message and its referent. It was surely a mistake to speak of a meta-message as being about another message. I should have said that a meta-message is about the *relationship* between some other message and its referent. It was *almost* all right to say that if message A is about the coding of message B, then A is meta to B. After all "coding" is not a characteristic of a message, but of a relationship between a message and its referent.

The questions is: into what universe or domain does what we used to call a *meta-message* bring redundancy? It is a *meta-message* if it brings redundancy into the universe,

[M = (m + r)], where M is the meta-message
m, the lower order message
r, the referent of the lower order message.

The great advantage of stating all this in terms of "redundancy" is that this latter term is always reciprocal, referring to an *overlapping* of informational content.

This being so, the + signs in the above expression are not simply additive. What is intended is that units bracketed constitute a domain which contains redundancy; and the redundancy referred to is such that information is repeated across the + sign. (m + r) means that m contains some information which is also contained in r.

It is interesting to note that *reinforcement* is the prototype of meta-communication. The diagram is: [Reinforcement + (Stimulus + Response)] The attached diagram may help–perhaps.

And that is, I guess, why the typical sequences of experimental learning contain these *three* components. There must be three items if one of them is to be about the *relationship* between the other two.

Note that this diagram is itself an M, such that [M + (m + r)]. Also *any* message about the relationships in this diagram is an M. For example, the message "in (m + r), m is in verbal English," would partly tell the receiver where to look for the attributes of m which will be redundant (i.e., correlate with) attributes of r.

DIAGRAM OF (m + r)

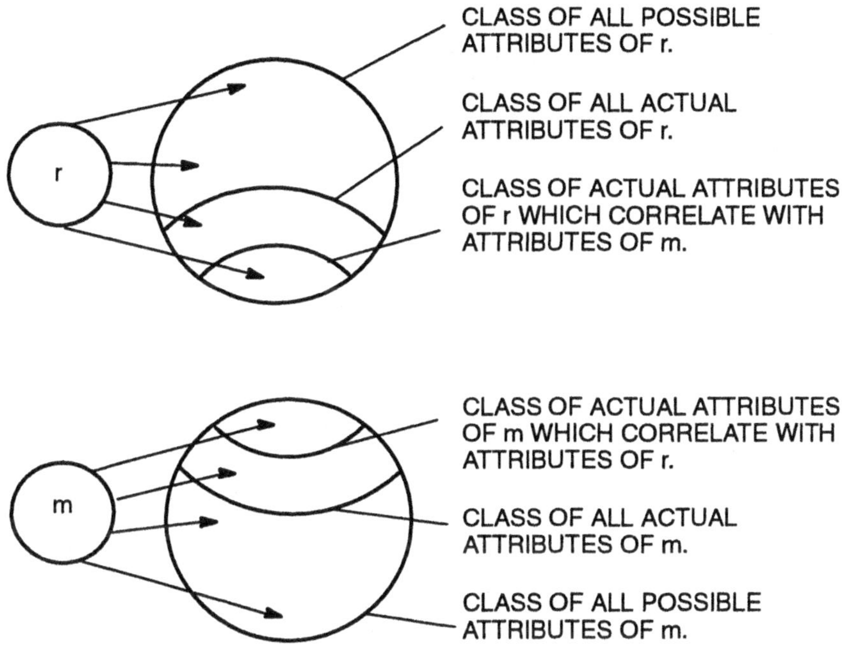

NOTES

1. Dluxki, V. R. (1966). Seminario sobre metacommunicacion. *Acta psiquiatricia y psicologica de America latina, 12*, 2-4.

2. Beavin, Bodin, Haley, Lennard, Sluzki, Watzlawick, and Weakland are Research Associates of the Mental Research Institute, of which Dr. Jackson is Director. Veron is Associate Professor, University of Buenos Aires, Department of Sociology. Lennard is Associate Professor of Psychiatry at the University of California School of Medicine. Sluzki is also Chief of the Research Department at the Psychopathology Service, G. Araoz Alfaro Hospital, Lanus (Prov. of Buenos Aires), Argentina.

3. The ideas herein are thus a product of collective work for which the authors must give credit to the group, while retaining responsibility for their present formulation.

4. The term "message" is used in this note to refer to any of the analytic elements of the communication package. At this early stage of the study of human

communication, these components have yet to be exhaustively identified. They certainly include, at the least, the content, syntactic, and semantic structure of the text of the verbal utterances, the tone, pitch, and rhythm of the voice; gestures, positions, and movements of the body; and structural or temporal relations between these (the latter, we will suggest, being one form of metacommunication).

5. He called this "progressive integration," having described something very like selection as "selective integration."

Chapter 3

The Interactional Theory and Therapy of Don D. Jackson

Wendel A. Ray

It has been more than 25 years since Don Jackson died unexpectedly at the age of 48. He continues to be revered as having been a gifted clinician, theoretician, and one of the most influential forces ever in the field of family therapy. Brilliant and perennially idealistic, Jackson was convinced that the shift within the behavioral sciences from viewing the individual in isolation to envisioning the individual in context announced the beginning of a new age of understanding about the interconnected nature of human behavior.

Jackson is best remembered for his leading part in the development of such concepts as family homeostasis, family rules, relational quid pro quo, and, with Bateson, Weakland, and Haley, the theory of the Double Bind. And yet, with the exception of a few scattered tributes highlighting important aspects of his work (Ackerman, 1970; Greenberg, 1977; Weakland and Greenberg, 1977; Zuk, 1981) Jackson's contribution to family theory, phenomenal for its breadth and scope, has never been adequately documented.

He was the first clinician to uncompromisingly maintain a higher order cybernetic and constructivist position in the practice of therapy. The essence of his model is seeing the client as a "family-surrounded individual with real problems in the present day" (Jackson, 1967c). Brief in orientation, the primary focus, questions asked, assignments and tasks given are *always* on the *relationship*

Originally printed in *Zeit Schrift Fur Systemiche Therapie,* 14 pp. 5-30, 1991. Reprinted with permission.

between members of the family. The basic characteristics of Jackson's *theory and therapy* will be delineated, followed by an analysis of a family interview he conducted.

FUNDAMENTAL PREMISES OF INTERACTIONAL THEORY

While there is a possibility of historical, genetic, or so-called hereditary factors, such ingredients are not independently observable except in cases of severe mental or physical deficiency. Therefore, "symptoms, defenses, character structure and personality can be seen as terms describing the individual's typical interactions which occur in response to a particular interpersonal context" (Jackson, 1965a, p. 2). The focus of therapy is on observable behavior taking place in the present between the members of the client's primary relational context (Jackson, 1964; 1965a). All behavior (including symptoms) . . . is viewed as communication and, therefore, inseparable from its context (Jackson, 1964). Among the first to adopt a constructivist position, Jackson believed that *any* belief shared by members of a group constitute the reality they experience (Jackson, 1965a; 1965b; 1967a; 1967b; 1967c). The therapist, as participant observer, is seen as an active participant in creating descriptions of behavior imposed on the family (Jackson, 1965b).

Participants in relationships are seen as continually attempting to define the nature of that relationship. In every communication participants offer to each other definitions of their relationship in an effort to determine the nature of the relationship. "Each, in turn, responds with his definition of the relationship–which may affirm, deny, or modify that of the vis-à-vis" (Jackson, 1965a, p. 8). As time passes in this process, certain behaviors are maintained as acceptable while others are excluded such that observable, redundant patterns of interaction emerge. These redundancies can be metaphorically understood as the rules governing relationships within a given family system (Jackson, 1965b). These patterns connecting family members are the focus of therapy.

The more rigid and restrictive the rules of the relationship the less adaptive the family is to change (i.e., the less requisite variety available to the members) and the more probable one or more members will be identified as "symptomatic" either by themselves, other members of the family, or by outside members of the greater community (Jackson, 1967a). So-called symptomatic behavior emerges in families when the rules of the relationship are so restrictive that family members are unable to adapt to the natural changes experienced as the family evolves over time, and/or when participants are unable to arrive at consensual validation about the changing nature of their relationship (Jackson, 1965b; 1967a).

The desire to be able to predict reality, the illusion that one can control the behavior of others, fear of change and the desire to maintain some sense of stability are at the center of most attempts to define the nature of relationship (Jackson, 1959; 1961; 1965a; 1965b; 1967d; 1967e). When attempts are made to arrive at a point of consensual validation (Jackson, 1965a; 1965b) about the nature of a relationship, one might observe such typical "pathologies" as a marital relationship in which each partner uses various means of coercion to force the other to accept their definition of the relationship (Jackson and Yalom, 1964), triangulation by one spouse of a member of the previous or next generation in a family in coalition against the other spouse (Jackson, 1959, 1965b; Jackson cited in Haley, Hoffman, and Jackson, 1967), and other variations in behavior around the theme of overt and covert maneuvers on the part of one spouse in response to the efforts of the other spouse to define the relationship in their own way (Lederer and Jackson, 1968). These so-called symptoms or pathologies are examples of how individuals, caught in the illusion that they can control the other, attempt to define the nature of the relationship.

Assessment

The therapist, as participant observer (Jackson, 1949), develops hypotheses about the family as a homeostatic system inextricably involving, influencing, and being influenced by the behavior of the symptomatic member (Jackson and Yalom, 1964). The symptom bearer's behavior is conceptualized as serving a vital, present function in balancing the relationships of all family members. His difficulty protects the viability of the family. It is *as though* it is the function of the symptomatic member to have difficulties (Jackson and Weakland, 1959). The identified patient's difficulties, in turn, provide an opportunity for other family members *not* to exhibit overt difficulties. Viewed in this way, the relevant assessment question becomes: "how can one elucidate and verify the context so that crazy behavior becomes meaningful to the observer" (Jackson, 1964).

Attempts to change the behavior of the symptomatic member, without taking into consideration the advantages and disadvantages of such change for all members of the family, are frequently "foolhardy and futile" as a consequence of the tendency of the family system to attempt to maintain stability and "resist" adaptation and change (Jackson, 1954a, b; Jackson and Yalom, 1964; Weakland and Jackson, 1961).

Intervention

When a family member attempts to introduce new behavior that is not part of the preexisting repertoire of acceptable behaviors within the family (i.e., transgress the rules), problems can, and often do, emerge as the system organizes itself to maintain the status quo (Jackson, 1967a). "Tampering" (Jackson and Yalom, 1964, p. 83) with redundant patterns of interaction around the symptom is an important method of triggering change.

Working with double levels of messages, context, and behavior *as* a message are hallmarks of Jackson's style of therapy (Jackson, 1959; 1961). Another theme of Jackson's work is the assumption that people make the best choices available to them at any moment considering the context (Jackson, 1952), and his reliance on the human ability to adapt and simulate behavior (Jackson, 1961). Other techniques characteristic of Jackson's clinical work include: attending to the illusion of alternatives, the game without end (Watzlawick, Beavin, and Jackson, 1967), changing verbalizations into action, and making the overt covert (Jackson, 1960; 1961). Jackson pioneered the shift of thinking from one level of abstraction to another for the purpose of assessing how symptomatic behavior makes sense and for the purpose of intervention. Recognizing that what appears illogical at one level of abstraction is logical at a different order of abstraction is the essence of therapeutic work commonly described as paradoxical. Examples of this include accepting the behavior and premises of the client and extending these to the point of absurdity (Jackson, 1959; 1961; 1963); the use of well-timed "spontaneous" laughter or a facial expression of astonishment to indicate preverbal understanding of the untenability of a family member's position (Jackson and Yalom, 1964); and utilization of so-called therapeutic double binds and prescribing the symptomatic behavior (Jackson 1959, 1961, Watzlawick, Beavin, and Jackson, 1967).

The following interview (Birdwhistell, 1964) illustrates Jackson's surgeon-like precision in applying interactional theory in therapy. Commentary interspersed throughout the transcript, consistent with Jackson's interactional theory, provides a conceptual understanding of the strategies and techniques utilized.

THE FAMILY INTERVIEW

Dr. Jackson waits until all family members have entered the room and seated themselves before taking a seat for himself.

Comments: In a discussion with the family's primary therapist after the interview, Jackson reveals that he typically chooses *not* to sit until all family members have an opportunity to seat themselves in order to begin assessment of the relationships between family members based upon how the members elect to arrange themselves in relation to one another. Jackson goes on to comment that, in this instance, he immediately observed that Bruce (the identified patient) sat away from the rest of the family group. This suggests, before any verbal exchange takes place, the possibility that Bruce is the focus of a triangle involving his father and mother. Waiting until all family members sit has become a common first move for assessment purposes used by therapists in many schools of family therapy. The children are Bruce, 12; Sonya, 9; Lisa, 6; and Brian, 18 months.

Jackson: How do you do? I'm Dr. Jackson.

Norman: I better introduce us. I keep forgetting it.

Jackson: Sure.

Norman: My name, I'm Norman. This is Bruce, this is Lisa, this is Sonya, this is Carol, and this is Brian.

Jackson: Hmm. Now I don't know anybody's name.

Norman: Well, I thought maybe you might. [Pause]. Do you want me to go over it again?
Jackson: No. No, the main thing isn't so much the names as it is the problem. I don't . . . see I've been deliberately not told what, you know, problems you have so that I wouldn't get somebody else's ideas canned.
Comment: Jackson's choice not to want the family member's names repeated brings up questions pertaining to the issue of joining in therapy. Many therapists place great emphasis on going slowly initially, carefully attending to building rapport with family members before moving into a discussion of the difficulties which bring them to therapy. This particular interview was one of four made with this family in one day, as part of a research project. In one sense, immediately moving to a discussion of the problems facing the family can be explained as having been necessitated by the immediate reality that Jackson had one 30-minute opportunity to conduct an assessment interview, while demonstrating his theory and therapy. Jackson's interactional approach is, however, both problem-focused and brief in orientation. The information Jackson attends to pertains to what transpires between members of the family. By moving immediately into a discussion of what the family members see as problematic, Jackson continues the assessment process by setting up a situation in which differences emerge between members around how to define the problem.
Norman: Yeah. Well, we were having trouble with Bruce on understanding and listening to anything.
Jackson: Um hmm.
Norman: And it's caused quite a bit of aggravation I think with Carol here and . . . Uh, one thing you better know, this is a second marriage. These two children, Bruce and Sonya are from . . .
Jackson: Your first?
Norman: . . . my first marriage.
Jackson: Uh huh.
Norman: And Lisa is from Carol's and Brian's from ours. And it's quite a situation here but . . .
Jackson: What the French call ménage, ah, a household.
[Sonya and Lisa are sitting beside one another looking at some pamphlets when Bruce joins in with his sisters.]

Norman: Now we are going to have a little more understanding. Give me the pamphlets please, OK?
[Jackson observes this interaction while the baby, Brian, is crawling across the floor.]
Jackson: This gets a little bit on my nerves.
Norman: Oh, I understand.
Carol: Yeah, they don't know how, they can't sit still very long.
Norman: They can't sit still very long.
Carol: You understand it's for their benefit as much as ours.
Norman: If we let them go we wouldn't get nothing done. You wouldn't even be able to understand the problem.
Jackson: Ah, what do you two differ on about how Bruce should be handled?
Comment: Consistent with his interactional theory, Jackson does *not* immediately agree with the parents' statement that Bruce is the problem, or allow the parents to expand their description of how Bruce's behavior is the problem. He avoids the unverbalized implication that there is something *wrong* with Bruce which is causing him to act this way. Instead, by posing this question, Jackson remains consistent with his interactional theory, beginning to test out the homeostatic hypothesis that "symptomatic" behavior on the part of a child frequently serves to balance the relationship between other members of the family, and possibly indicates a struggle between the parents over how to define the nature of their relationship. By asking a question about *how* they differ, Jackson implies not only that difference exists, but that this lack of a united opinion about how to handle Bruce is part of the difficulty. In turn, this immediately begins to expand the definition of the problem to include not only Bruce, but mom and dad also. Using what today is called *triadic* or *circular* questioning, the very questions Jackson asks begin to suggest an interactional explanation for Bruce's behavior. Many present-day therapists have adopted Jackson's circular method of questioning.
Norman: Well, I tell her not to scream and holler so much, to act.
Jackson: Um hmm.
Norman: And when he does something, ah . . .
Carol: Instead of letting them work me up and build up inside. In

other words just have some authority. And I try and it just doesn't work [giggles].

Comments: Carol's finishing her husband's response by providing a statement which implies, through voice inflection and other non-verbal mannerisms, that she would handle the situation more competently if she could, but she is helplessly unable to do so and needs her husband's help. A tentative picture begins to emerge of the *quid pro quo* between wife and husband. Carol appears to be attempting to control the definition of the nature of their relationship through one-down maneuvers of helplessness. This portrays Norman as big, strong and able to handle situations that are beyond the abilities of a mate who is helpless to handle the situation without him, thus *allowing* him to feel in charge. Norman's actions, in turn, are equally a part of this relationship definition dance.

Jackson: Um hmm.

Carol: Brian [calls the baby to her].

Jackson: Did you know you were such a problem before you got called on?

Bruce: What do you mean?

Jackson: Well, I mean had you decided that you were supposed to be the problem in the family? Or did it just happen?

Bruce: Happened.

Comments: In posing this provocative question Jackson immediately builds upon the confirmation received from the parents about how they differ in terms of how to handle Bruce and Carol's inferences of helplessness. He suggests that the family context is such that the son's behavior is not only appropriate but has somehow been evoked as a way to balance relationships between other members of the family. In one sense, the behavior of Bruce may appear to be inappropriate, but in another sense his behavior may serve a protective function for the parents. As long as Bruce is seen as misbehaving, the parents can focus on him rather than work out differences that may exist between them in their own relationship.

Asking this question in the presence of the parents, suggests that the situation is more complicated than the son misbehaving for no apparent reason. Based upon the homeostatic hypothesis, and through his method of questioning, Jackson is beginning to construct a therapeutic reality based upon the information provided by the family members' responses while continuing an assessment process based purely on interactional theory, the responses of family members to his queries, and observable behavior of family members in the present context.

Jackson: Um hmm. Do you find your new mother harder to obey than your old mother?

Bruce: Yeah.

Comment: Continuing to view Bruce's behavior as adaptive and contextually appropriate, this question cuts to the heart of one of the binds children frequently find themselves in when parents divorce and remarry. Loving both mother and father, children sometimes feel torn by the love and loyalty they feel for both parents. In the midst of this, the child and both sets of parents must work out new rules for their relationships and make major adjustments in their lifestyles to accommodate to these changes. Additionally, by posing this question to Bruce in the parents' presence, Jackson begins to normalize what the family is experiencing while continuing to expand the definition of the difficulties being experienced to the whole family, rather than remaining focused on Bruce as *the* problem.

Jackson: Um hmm. Well that's kind of natural isn't it?

Bruce: What?

Jackson: That's kind of natural. [Turning to the mother]. And besides, you expect to be not obeyed as well, don't you?

Comments: Focusing on the relationship between Bruce and his new mother, Jackson recasts the difficulties being experienced in interactional terms. Maintaining a focus on normal developmental difficulties commonly experienced in the working out of relationships between newlywed spouses, the way the family members talk about their difficulties begins to shift. Carol describes her experience of being thrust into a position of having to define the nature of her new parental relationship with the children of her new husband.

Carol: Yeah . . . well, see, ah, like I was saying before I was out working and I had this one baby. And I guess all of a sudden I had four children. It's an adjustment for me too.

Jackson: It's a big one.

Comments: While normalizing the situation, Jackson continues to join with the family through a process of asking questions in ways which convey respect for all members of the family and demonstrate appreciation of the complexity of their situation. The responses of the mother begin to move away from a focus on Bruce's behavior as the problem to describing the difficulty she is experiencing adapting to her new life situation.

Carol: And ah, they are all good children, and I'm not, more or less, used to all the children, you know? I mean ah, in the beginning I just had them on weekends and all. And, oh, everything was great and I figured it would be real easy. But it just didn't turn out as easy as I thought. And like Norman says I'm high-strung.

Jackson: Um hmm, yeah. How does Sonya strike you in comparison with blonde [Lisa]?

Comments: By *not* following up on the mother's leading statement that "I'm high-strung," Jackson maintains a theory-consistent stance, continuing to focus on triadic processes which serve to balance relationships within the family. Gatekeeping what clues the family provides, Jackson continues to develop an interactional hypothesis essential to the creation of a workable therapeutic reality. By not focusing on the mother's comment about being high-strung, Jackson continues to imply that there are possible advantages to having a problematic child in terms of balancing the relationship between the parents. Jackson then attempts to shift attention off of Bruce to the behavior of the other children in the family. Doing this suggests that the behavior of the other siblings may be just as much of a problem, and simultaneously suggests that focusing on the behavior of the children provides a method for parents to distract themselves from reaching consensual validation about how they will define the nature of their relationship. This technique has been adopted by clinicians across a number of systemically oriented schools of family therapy.

Norman: Oh, you mean Sonya and Lisa?

Carol: Yeah, Sonya is ah . . .

Jackson: I . . . Sonya and Lisa as far as temperament?

Norman: Oh, as far as temperament, she [Sonya] has a temper.

Jackson: Um hmm.

Norman: And she'll flair up and let hers go, but not very much. She's usually quiet and much more timid. Where Sonya, I mean ah, I don't think Sonya has as much of a temper.

Carol: Yeah, she does.

Norman: Well, I never see it very much.

Carol: He's not around them as much as I am.

Norman: But one thing I do know she'll talk your leg off, and ah, other than that I don't see where Sonya is too much of a problem. It's just the idea our problem is, he [Bruce] will not obey anything. And ah, I think now that we, this is coming to a standstill and we might be picking too much. I mean noticing everything, in our aggravation, to try and bring him down a little bit off his [inaudible, sounds like obstinate?].

Jackson: Well what strikes me as odd is, you know, you obviously are a pretty strong fellow and you obviously are a good bit bigger than this [Bruce] over here. So, if it was simply a matter of his obeying you would pulverize him.

Comments: As soon as Carol shifts from talking about Bruce as the only problem to talking about other difficulties she is experiencing, Norman takes up the task of reiterating the system stabilizing the *myth* that things would be fine if only Bruce would behave. This cues the mother to join the father in continuing to obscure the relationship-balancing function served by maintaining the focus on Bruce as the problem. Rather than dispute this at the same order of logic and risk creating resistance, Jackson accepts the premise that the parents are helpless and unable to control Bruce. Jackson acquiesces to the parents' position and begins to push it to the point of absurdity.

Carol: Oh, he does.

Norman: Oh, I do every once in a while.

Carol: But it doesn't do any good.

Norman: But, umm . . .

Carol: I've seen him try and talk to him. And I'd like to have a nickel for every time he says "Now, Bruce I'm not going to yell at ya. I'm not going to hit ya. We'll sit down, I'm trying to understand you. Let's have a talk."

Jackson: Um hmm.

Carol: I'd like to have a nickel for every one of them. I'd like to have another nickel for every time he waffles him. But he just doesn't seem to get anywhere.

Jackson: Well, you've seen pictures of people that are in concentration camps. Maybe you've even known some. You know what they look like. If you really wanted to fix him so that he would obey, it could be done.

Comments: Jackson continues to push to the point of absurdity the parents' premise that they have no ability to influence the behavior of Bruce. In doing so the possibility begins to emerge that there may be disadvantages to the stability of the relationships between other family members should they successfully handle Bruce. Mother and father could successfully gain control of Bruce's behavior, but at what cost? If they no longer have something to distract them it could result in their having to work out some level of consensual agreement about how they will define the nature of their own relationship. This may be frightening for them, given that each has a past history of difficulty working out a marital relationship. It would appear less threatening to have a problem–in this case Bruce's behavior–to focus on. Bruce, in turn, seems willing to accommodate.

Norman: Oh I know it could be done . . .

Jackson: So what strikes me is that the first problem that I see in the family is that you don't quite want this [Bruce] to obey, because you could do it if you wanted to.

Comments: By continuing to push the premise Jackson evokes a shift in the parents' response from helplessness to one in which they begin to talk about ways they have gained control over Bruce's behavior and past successes they have had in doing so.

Carol: We could?

Jackson: Um hmm, yeah.

Carol: Well, one thing we have, I think we've conquered, we had a big problem with him stealing.

Jackson: Um hmm.

Carol: I mean he stole, and think that got on the wrong side of me because he . . . well in the beginning when I first got him he stole $20 out of my pocketbook. And then we went to my sister's house one time and he stole a silver dollar out of my little nephew's bank.

Jackson: Um hmm.

Carol: And all these things sort of stuck with me, you know? And he was stealing right and left from us and I think just in the last, I'd say, it

was only recently that we caught him stealing again, a couple weeks ago. But I think it's starting to, ah, that's one problem I think we . . .
Jackson: Well, what would you think of, of something like this. This is just a theory I'm testing out on you. What would you think if Bruce were very obedient and did everything exactly the way that both of you wanted.
Comments: The parents acknowledge that when they take a firm stance, they are successful in setting limits which Bruce does not go beyond. Yet, as the parents continue to focus on Bruce, Jackson continues to tamper with the myth that things would be perfect if only Bruce would behave. By suggesting that even if Bruce was perfect there would be problems, Jackson challenges the family myth by pushing the parental premises to the extreme.
Norman: Oh, I don't think that any child can do that.
Jackson: Well just imagine, suppose he could. I agree it would be rare but suppose he did that. Wouldn't it suddenly put a strain on the marriage?
Comments: By asking the parents to imagine what life might be like if Bruce were perfectly obedient, Jackson begins to lay out the difficulties that change might precipitate in the marital relationship. This statement implies that there might be advantages derived from the parents' unsuccessful attempt to take charge of Bruce. Jackson continues to build a therapeutic reality in which the family members, particularly the mother and father, must consider the interactional implications of their statements of helplessness. It could be concluded that Jackson is attempting, through these comments, to provide the family with insight into the interactional nature of their situation, and through this insight they might change. This *is not* the case. For Jackson, the goal in therapy is not to evoke insight, but to trigger a change in the present patterns of transaction around the "problem" behavior in an attempt to alter the existing patterns of interaction. By suggesting that the marriage might be strained if Bruce's behavior improved, Jackson is utilizing what Penn (1985) calls "feed-forward" questioning to challenge the myth that things would be fine if only Bruce would behave, while simultaneously suggesting that the balance of the parental relationship is somehow involved in Bruce's behavior being viewed as problematic.

Carol: [In a quiet, tentative voice.] I don't see how it would put a strain on the marriage, no.
Jackson: It's funny but I think it would, you know.
Carol: I don't think I'll ever be faced with the situation so I don't have to worry, [laughs nervously] but ah . . .
Comments: Often when a client rejects the therapist's observation, the therapist gets inducted into the family's mythology and backs away, thinking they may have missed the boat. But consistent with interactional theory and with nerves of steel, Jackson continues to push the premise by offering one possible disadvantage of Bruce becoming obedient. Every comment used by Jackson is meaningful in that the interactional nature of the situation is highlighted.
Jackson: But just in a funny kind of way you could get an approximation of that if he got much more obedient. For example there is something very funny that would come up and that is that you would suddenly discover that there are more problems about whose kids were being better behaved than whose.
Carol: Yeah, we're going to have those problems till . . . let's face it . . . till they're grown up and on their own.
Jackson: But you don't have them now because yours are [Norman's] the worst behaved.
Comments: Carol reacts to Jackson hitting too close to the central issue (i.e., both Norman and Carol being unsure of themselves and both being unwilling at this point in their marriage to directly focus on working out a mutually agreed upon definition of the nature of their relationship). She attempts to obscure the interactional process by minimizing any disadvantages which may arise if Bruce's behavior improves. By refusing to abandon the triadic process he has observed in the family, Jackson continues to keep the pressure on by pushing the premise and not letting Carol talk him out of it.
Carol: But he's the oldest too.
Norman: [Interrupting Carol.] No, ah, a lot of the time I say this, I say this to her . . . Different times she'll say this to me and I'll say "that's children."
Comments: Carol cues Norman to respond, and then obscures the topic of conversation by trying to shift the focus away from the issue at hand, i.e., that Norman's children's misbehavior draws attention away from the strains existing in the marriage. These

strains would be more apparent if Bruce's behavior improved and was no longer a problem. Jackson's comment implies that Bruce's behavior may be appropriate considering his age and position as the oldest child. Now that Jackson has opened up the possibility that there might be some advantages being derived from focusing on Bruce as a problem (i.e., helping the couple avoid working out differences that may exist over the nature of their relationship), Carol attempts to shift focus (and blame) from Bruce and the other children and onto the biological mother. In doing so the triangle being used to balance the marital relationship also shifts.

Carol: [Interrupting Norman.] Well, I realize . . .

Norman: She'll say something to me and I'll listen to her . . .

Carol: [Talking while Norman speaks] . . . mine are going to get bigger. And I told him as soon as she's older [Lisa] and she pulls the same thing I'm going to do the same thing to her because . . . I tried to tell him, like I love Brian, he's ours, I love him as much as I love Lisa. But if she ever does, you know, it is going to be the same difference.

Norman: Yes but ah . . . I . . .

Carol: [Interrupting Norman.] And even now I'm starting to discipline her. The trouble is the children were never disciplined by their mother. Like if Norman would say something, I've heard this from Dr. Peachy [the therapist the family has been seeing]. If he would discipline them there would be a big fight . . .

Jackson: Um hmm.

Carol: And the children knew this. And they thought they were going to get the same thing with me. Like if I would go against it all the time.

Norman: But she never goes against me. Ah, about that ah, I think they're, ah, I don't know how to express it. They're children. I mean she says they are going to get the same thing, I mean she's liable to do the same thing . . . Lisa.

Comments: Norman agrees with Carol and compliments her by implying that by never opposing his stance with the children, she agrees with his premise (i.e., that the children's behavior is developmentally appropriate). Jackson's silence supports this show of agreement between the spouses about how to handle the children. Jackson does not immediately follow-up on Carol's blaming Nor-

man's first wife for problems they are having with his two children, instead waiting to see if the statement is repeated. If the biological wife is blamed a second time, then it may indicate a redundancy, another triangle Norman and Carol use to balance their relationship.
Jackson: Um hmm.
Norman: She's liable to correct her and what's going to happen–that's what I was trying to bring out–what's going to happen when this result doesn't bring anything? How are you so definitely sure that this result of correction can, continued correction with Lisa, might bring the result you want?
Carol: I'm not. There's no guarantee.
Norman: Look at the results. My father would knock me in the corner with his fist. And the results, what happened? I just walked right away from him. I mean that's not . . .
Carol: Yeah, but he thinks I should just . . . discipline her like I discipline Sonya and there is almost five years difference. Now I can't expect the same. Why should I punish her now?
Norman: No, I wasn't even mentioning . . .
Carol: No, we get in arguments over that.
Jackson: You see, it seems to me that one thing that happens is that, that you're trying to do your best. And this is difficult to begin with because anyone that is trying is worse off than somebody that's just being spontaneous, you know? But you can't help but try, that's all you can do. But in your trying, what you seem to be running across is you don't realize how much these two are alike.
Comments: Building upon the demonstration of mutual agreement between the spouses that emerged earlier, Jackson makes a comment on the normal kinds of relationship accommodations facing this blended family and the paradox inherent in *trying* to do one's best. He then again tries to shift focus off of Bruce onto his sister.
Carol: Which two?
Jackson: That [Bruce] and Sonya.
Norman: They are. They are very much alike. I admit that. She [Carol] says she can see an awful lot . . . that she is improved and she's much better, but I ah, I think they're kids.
Carol: I'm saying since I've gotten her she's improved a lot.
Jackson: Um hmm.
Norman: I think they are kids in most ways . . .

Carol: Cause I had quite a few problems with her . . .
Norman: But like this stealing, that I don't think is kids, something like that, because I stole. I think all boys steal some time or other.
Jackson: Most of them I know did, yeah.
Comments: Jackson aligns with Norman when he characterizes Bruce's behavior as being *both* inappropriate, in that stealing is not acceptable behavior, *and* normal, in that it is developmentally appropriate when children push limits by exhibiting such experimental behavior as stealing. While aligning with Norman, Jackson utilizes the technique of unbalancing the marital relationship to bring out into the open any overt disagreement between the spouses over this issue. Frequently, it is through disagreement over how to handle child-focused issues that disagreement are played out between the spouses about how to define their own relationship.
Carol: But not continuously.
Norman: Not continuously after you're forewarned, maybe, a couple of times.
Jackson: Um . . .
Norman: I mean this is what I'm getting at that I can't control. 'Cause I've talked with him, I've hit him, I've deprived him of quite a few things and ah, never done any good. But then I noticed lately that he has not taken anything and he's been fairly well that way.
Carol: The other problem we had and I tried to tell him, he would lie continuously.
Jackson: Um hmm.
Carol: He got to the point where he was supposed to be at a football game, and he gave me a blow-by-blow description, and he was not even at the game. You know he is supposed to be there and he, and he's really giving me a vivid description you know and he . . .
Jackson: Are you able to openly criticize your husband when you feel like it? Just, just right off the top of your head or do you have to prepare for it and sort of build up to it?
Comments: Rather than tracking the content of Carol's statement, Jackson continues to tease out the possible interactional advantages being derived from keeping the focus on Bruce. Questions address the process (i.e., the triadic implications) implicit in Carol's comment by exploring how Carol and Norman are working out the nature of their relationship.

Carol: I don't know what you mean.
Jackson: Well, you've got some gripes. We all have gripes about something.
Carol: Oh no, I come right out with my gripes.
Jackson: Right out? Same day, you don't even have to think about it?
Carol: No, maybe that's my fault.
Norman: We don't have much argument. She and I together don't have any arguments.
Jackson: Do you think you argue enough?
Comments: Continuing to push the premise, Jackson hints that it is normal to have differences, particularly when newlywed spouses are working out the nature of their relationship.
Norman: Oh we argue enough, enough I mean.
Carol: Enough to make up [laughs].
Norman: But it's not like, ah, I think, like I said to the other doctor before, these [points at the kids], I mean it was continuous argument which was never anything developed out of it but more argument.
Jackson: Umm.
Norman: And no, ah, that way we got further away. And where some families when they argue they may get closer together in some ways but in continuous argument. I mean in everything you do, everything you say. Well, then I realize this today through other therapy and the help Dr. Peachy gave me and my second or first marriage. [Norman turnes toward Sonya and says] Sonya would you sit over there like your father said?
Carol: [To Sonya] You might want to listen to what the doctor says and if you're paddy-caking you might not be able to hear what the doctor says.
Jackson: Well, the difference in my approach to some other people is, and you have already had three people see you, is that I think when kids are this age the parents have an awful lot to say about what happens to them. So do a few other things like school, if they get physically sick, the doctors. So I can't get very excited about kids this age misbehaving because I don't think they are lost yet.
Comments: Having drawn some tentative opinions about the developmental appropriateness of the family process he has experienced thus far in this newly formed, blended family, Jackson normalizes the situation. Making a slight semantical shift, Jackson

begins to describe Bruce as *misbehaving* in ways which are age appropriate, given the family context of which he is part.
Carol: Oh, well, Norman says he [Bruce] is.
Jackson: Yeah?
Carol: Norman feels like Bruce, we can't do nothing more because . . .
Norman: I just [inaudible].
Jackson: Um hmm.
Norman: Where I think that, ah . . . all the troubles . . .
Carol: He feels with all the trouble that's been, it's not going to change.
Jackson: Hmm.
Norman: He'll have to change himself. That's how I feel; he'll have to change himself. And sooner or later when he gets out in the world or when he gets a little older and he gets the bumps and the knocks and things it is going to come out of him one way or the other.
Jackson: You make him about ten years older than he is.
Comments: Suggesting the father's expectations and behavior are as much a part of the puzzle as Bruce's behavior, Jackson persistently frames the situation in terms of on-going relationships between members of the family.
Norman: No.
Jackson: Um hmm.
Carol: Some ways he does and some ways thinks he's too young.
Norman: That's what I was telling her–she thinks that these are older children and they're not. They're[an] 11-year-old boy and ah, they don't understand what I'm saying that's what I'm getting around to. She says to me do that, why did you do this, why did you do that, they're children.
Carol: Well if you had a ten-year-old son that carries around matches constantly, always had matches in his pockets and you knew he was smoking, what would you do?
Norman: Well how many times have I done, . . .
Jackson: I have a ten-year-old son that doesn't smoke so you see so I'm stuck. I can't tell you.
Carol: Ah . . .
Norman: Yes but what would you do?

Carol: Yeah, but he just says, "I can't do nothing about it."
Norman: Because I'm always cracking him. And that don't do no good. I can put him in his room that don't . . .
Carol: He's only–I mean matches, he's going to put himself on fire.
Norman: He goes right behind my back and does it.
Jackson: Well, there's one thing that maybe . . . have you ever asked Bruce what to do?
Norman: Oh yes.
Jackson: What do you say Bruce? What am I going to do with you, you tell me?
Comments: Attempted solutions the parents have tried in dealing with Bruce all fall within one class which could be called *control by cajoling, coercion, and punishment*. The parents are genuinely frustrated by their *apparent* inability to gain control of Bruce's behavior. As children grow up they strive to become more independent and this developmental reality dictates that the nature of the relationship between the parents and children must change in order to accommodate. Jackson's question to Bruce acknowledges this. Simultaneously, at yet another level of abstraction, the parents lack of success in dealing with Bruce serves to maintain the homeostatic balance of the entire family system. The parents' inability to control Bruce helps manufacture a "magnificent enemy" (Jackson, 1967e), i.e., a problem on which they can focus and join together. This, in turn, helps balance their relationship by allowing them to avoid working out (or even acknowledging) differences which exist between them. Repeated use of this class of solution may be isomorphic to how Norman and Carol related with one another. Jackson questions tinker with this balance.
Bruce: [Brief silence.]
Norman: That's the same answer I get.
Bruce: I don't know.
Norman: Continuously. Now I know he's young, but I [mumble, indistinguishable].
Carol: We'd like him to open up but he won't open up. This is the third doctor and all he'll say is "I don't know."
Jackson: He said a lot more than that.
Carol: What did he say?

Jackson: He looks as wise as a Supreme Court Justice. Look at that [gesturing toward Bruce].

Comments: Calling attention to the analogic aspect of Bruce's "silence" and "I don't know" response, Jackson cuts through the stability maintaining myth that Bruce is somehow being defiant toward his parents. Put in terms of communication theory, the *command* aspect of Bruce's behavior may just as well be conveying a message which says "just give me a clear, unambiguous message that tells me what to do and I'll do it."

Bruce: [Giggles.]

Carol: Oh, looks, yeah.

Jackson: Oh, but looks say a lot, you know?

Carol: Yea I found that out. 'Cause he's [Norman] always telling me my looks give me, my eyes give me away.

Norman: Wonder what my eyes do. [Laughs.]

Jackson: Well what would you think about having an agreement, maybe you already have, that no discipline for Bruce came from you at all?

Comments: Jackson believed the most effective way to trigger change was not through evoking insight, but by tampering with the redundant patterns of behavior around the "problem" behavior. Here, he begins to construct a between-session task which, if carried out, will alter the family's patterns of interaction. In turn, this may provide an opportunity for family members to expand their requisite variety of behavioral alternatives.

Carol: From me?

Jackson: Yeah, all . . .

Carol: But I don't think I could, um, I have a temper.

Jackson: Oh I'm not saying you can't lose your temper. But you, it's just agreed that what you say doesn't count as far as having an effect on Bruce's actions.

Norman: No, what he's saying is what you say doesn't seem to affect Bruce. He doesn't seem to get anything out of it.

Jackson: But suppose you had a rule? That even if you get mad Bruce is supposed to ignore it? He doesn't necessarily do anything you say, that all his discipline has to come from his father?

Comments: The task utilizes existing covert patterns of behavior by making them part of an overt rule. The parents have complained about Bruce not doing what Carol tells him to do. In turn, a helpless Carol complains to Norman who then steps in to handle Bruce. Utilizing what he termed a *therapeutic double bind*, family members are asked to continue what they have been doing, but now they have been asked to do it. If they follow through with the task, patterns of behavior will change and the probability exists that Bruce's "problem" behavior too will change. If they do not carry out, or modify the assignment, the probability is still that the patterns of behavior will change. Regardless, the family members will find it difficult to continue to relate to one another in the same way in relation to Bruce's "problem" behavior.

Carol: Yes, but his father works such horrible hours.

Jackson: Um hmm. I think Bruce kind of likes the idea, I'm guessing, that maybe he could be disciplined by his dad. Now, of course, if he were burning the house down then you would interfere with the house being burned down.

Carol: Now that's another fault of mine . . .

Jackson: Do you feel like burning the house down, Bruce?

Comments: Pushing to the point of absurdity the parental premise that Bruce is a "bad boy," Jackson tightly wraps a semantic frame around a between session task by incorporating Carol's comment about Bruce's playing with matches in the construction of the assignment.

Bruce: No. Where would I sleep?

Jackson: Yeah. The kid's smart.

Comments: Through his use of language Jackson begins to connote the meaning of Bruce's behavior in positive ways, providing the parents with the possibility of constructing a different view of him as something other than a problem.

Norman: Oh he's very smart, I never said, there's nothing dumb about him.

Jackson: Um hmm.

Norman: I think he's a very bright boy in most things, except when it comes to discipline.

Jackson: And then we come to the actress over there. What do you think the problem in the family is?

Comments: Jackson again attempts to shift focus to the other children. If the parents are able to shift focus to the other children, this might take some of the pressure off Bruce.

Sonya: I don't know.

Carol: Oh no!

Jackson: Oh you picked that up from your brother.

Carol: She usually talks to beat the band, I mean she's been telling the whole story all day long.

Jackson: Maybe she's tired of telling the story.

Norman: Move over, Sonya, somebody move over.

Jackson: How do you get along with Bruce?

Sonya: Terrible.

Jackson: Terrible, huh? Well do you get along with blonde [Lisa] there?

Sonya: Umm, I don't know. Sometimes . . .

Bruce: All the time.

Sonya: Sometimes.

Bruce: Except when she doesn't turn the [inaudible] [giggles].

Jackson: Do you find Lisa easier to control?

Carol: Oh, I don't know whether she's easier to control because she's mine. That's part of . . . he thinks it's because she's my own. But actually anybody that's ever watched her, she's quiet. She can color and she can amuse herself. Because when I had to go to work I'd take her to my aunt's and there wasn't any children there. And she's learned to use her imagination and play by herself. And she doesn't bother me too much.

Norman: Yeah, but do you think she would now? She won't even let you get out of her sight.

Carol: She's still afraid. I used to go, but I mean, yeah, Norman. I can go do my cleaning and she'll go in the room and play ah . . .

Norman: Oh yes, I agree with you.

Carol: She plays very well by herself.

Norman: Yeah, I agree with you. No she's much smarter than my children, but there's an age difference too.

Jackson: Yeah, yeah, I'm aware of that.

Norman: And I never correct her because I don't think she needs the correction. I leave it up to her. I mean with her ways, I've watched, ah, . . . every once in a while I might grumble or something at her. Other than that she doesn't seem to cause a lot of ruckus or anything. If I say, "Go to bed," she goes to bed. I can tell them 20 times go to bed sometimes until I really make up my mind this time this is it and start after them, then they really . . .

Jackson: Well, what you've recognized is that if you started after them the first time. In other words if you really mean it, then he would do it the first time.

Comments: Jackson remarks on the *command* aspect of communication between these two newlyweds and the dis-ease which exists between them about how to work out a satisfactory relationship. (I.e., the behavior of the children in relation to Carol, is as much a comment on the nature of the relationship between Norman and Carol, as they are a comment on the personalities and ages of the children.)

Norman: That's what I've been doing lately. I say that's it, jump.

Carol: I guess I don't. I give them too many chances, and then by the time I, like I'll tell them one, two, three, and by the fourth time I'm blowing my top and then . . .

Comments: The couple has worked out a *quid pro quo* which seems to involve Carol being "helpless" in handling Bruce, providing Norman an opportunity to demonstrate competence in this area of their relationship. Through such exchanges, the marital relationship is balanced in that Norman can feel competent and needed to handle certain aspects of their life together that Carol is "unable" to. By acting, and at the level of conscious awareness probably feeling, helpless, Carol can maintain a sense of control over the nature of the marital relationship.

Norman: I don't want to tell them more than twice. Once.

Jackson: What do you and Bruce do together?

Comments: Again Jackson leaves the content of the conversation to explore the process of relationships in the family, focusing on other areas of the relationship between Bruce and his father. Looking at what is done, rather than what should be done, Jackson begins to expand the conversation beyond the presenting problem.

Norman: Not much, that much I can say, not much. Ah, I wanted to take him fishing this summer . . .

Carol: He took him crabbing.

Norman: I ended up taking him crabbing.

Jackson: Um hmm, you're apologizing.

Norman: [Uncomfortable laugh.]
Carol: Yeah, well, we're not married that long. And like I said the hours he works.
Norman: I'm never, I'm not at home that much.
Carol: And I like to have him around. I follow him around like a puppy dog when he's home.
Jackson: Um hmm.
Carol: He can't do anything that I'm not right behind him, 'cause I want companionship. I'm with four kids all day and I don't have an adult to talk to. I mean a neighbor or something like that. And, ah, Bruce, during the summer, we get up 8:00 in the morning. Go fishing all day long, pack his lunch, till 5:00 at night, eat his supper, and go to football. He has more freedom than any child, any of them. He had more fun as far as I'm . . . I mean he loves to fish. He goes fishing every day.
Norman: He goes fishing every day.
Carol: And I felt like I, and I wasn't out, one time I got with the doctors and dentist. But he has a free day off and he's going to go fishing . . .
Jackson: You changed the topic on me, you know that?
Carol: No.
Jackson: Yes.
Carol: How did I change the topic?
Jackson: I was talking about how do Bruce and his dad get together and you end up telling me that life is difficult. And I'm not arguing with you 'cause I think life is . . .
Carol: No, I'm trying to tell you how I felt when he said about fishing.
Jackson: Well, I think we have put our finger on something that may be, you know, one of the sore spots and that is that somebody is going to get shortchanged. On different days it will be some different person maybe, it will get shifted around.
Comments: Jackson shifts the focus of the conversation from centering on the "problem" of Bruce's behavior to the normal, real-life difficulties involved in the blending of two families with four children. As Jackson persistently focused on the interaction of the family, the nature of the problem definition changes from Bruce's

behavior to the nature of the relationships between all members of this newly formed family.

Carol: Well, I don't know what he did in his first marriage but . . .

Norman: But there is one thing you say about being together. [To kids.] Now let's knock it off. Ah, I'll take these. Any place I go I take the family.

Jackson: Umm.

Norman: And he gets out that way. I mean if I go swimming we all go swimming. If I go here, we all go here. And my hours, I went to work 8:00 in the morning yesterday and came home 11:00 at night. Six days a week. What, when would I see my wife? I mean, so I see them all together. That's the only means available. So I understand. I mean I've often thought of this. Like I'd like to take him fishing.

Norman: [To Sonya.] Sit down. [To Carol.] Where did he go?

Jackson: Ah, I was not worried about Bruce going because you know, it seems to me that Bruce is pretty hip. And probably hearing what he has in these interviews he's developed even more.

Comments: Jackson wraps what is happening back around to the on-going efforts being made by Carol and Norman to define the nature of their relationship. Maintaining his focus on the triadic processes in the family, all comments made by either Carol or Norman are framed in relational terms. In so, doing adjustments being made between the spouses as they work out the rules of their new relationship, are normalized while Bruce's behavior is framed as appropriate, given the present family context.

Norman: Um hmm.

Jackson: And that is he sort of says, "Look you guys, work it out yourselves and then let me know what it's about."

Norman: That's correct. Yes, I think it's that attitude.

Jackson: Yeah, but this is, this is about, this is right for 11 years of age as far as I'm concerned.

Comments: By framing Bruce's behavior as normal for an 11 year old, Jackson shifts focus from Bruce to the nature of the relationship between Carol and Norman, offering Carol and Norman an opportunity to begin to view the situation in a different way.

Norman: That's exactly what I have been saying.

Carol: What's that?

Norman: That, his attitude. He doesn't, he's not an adult. He does not have the, ah, I mean the correction of it, but he does not have an adult attitude.

Jackson: No.

Norman: And you think . . . I'm liable to say something to him a couple of times but when he moves and I get after him he moves. He knows it then. But it's liable to take a . . .

Carol: But I don't find it that way with me. That's what I said to the other doctor, he's only going to do something when his father's home.

Jackson: Yeah, I think that's right and I think that is understandable. But it puts too much burden on you if you think that you should control Bruce at this point.

Comments: Jackson normalizes the difficulty Carol and Bruce are experiencing as they attempt to work out their relationship.

Carol: Yeah but, see, that's another one of my problems. Dr. Peachy, I said on one of these um, what do you call one of these things, that I have to be right all the time?

Jackson: Obsessional?

Carol: Like my dishes. They have to be clean . . .

Jackson: Compulsive?

Carol: I wish I could stop it but I can't. And I get to the point when I'm banging my fist on the table 'cause I get so angry.

Jackson: And you feel like you're 11 years old.

Comments: Jackson comments on how easy it is for a parent to be seduced into relating with their children in an equal, or peer-like manner, rather than maintaining a parental position with a child. The homeostatic function of Carol, at times, not being in charge of the children is highlighted. If she is competent, she no longer needs Norman to come to the rescue and help her control Bruce. How can Carol competently parent Bruce if one way her relationship with Norman is kept in balance is by being helpless to handle Bruce?

Norman: [Laughs.]

Carol: I don't know. I guess I act like I'm 11 years old, I don't know. I can see there are a lot of things the children were never taught. It's not their fault.

Norman: She was raised something like me, with an iron hand and I don't agree with it.

Carol: I was raised by my father. If you talk back to your father, if I talked back to my father, I got slapped down. He talks, many a time, to his father like he is a kid and I don't like it. And I don't like him talking to me like that. And he always has an answer. No matter what I say to him he has to come back with another answer. He has to answer back all the time. And I guess that it's the way I was brought up.

Jackson: That may be the way you were brought up but, but Norman doesn't entirely object to it you know. He sort of likes having somebody have an answer.

Comments: Jackson gatekeeps the direction of the conversation by *not* following up on the clue Carol provides about her history. Instead, he brings the focus of conversation back to the here and now by focusing on the protective function Bruce's behavior serves in balancing the present relationship between Norman and Carol.

Norman: Well in a way, I mean . . .

Carol: Well, he don't mind, no. But I don't like it.

Jackson: No, I, but that's why I say I think you've got to make your own mind first and then tell Bruce what's up.

Comments: Reiterating the need for Carol and Norman to be united on how they handle the children, Jackson maintains a stance consistent with the interactional hypothesis that behavior problems evidenced by a child often indicate disagreement between the parents (or parental figures) over how to handle the situation.

Norman: Many things have I told him. He's ah, I think I've told him too much maybe. He's 11 and he knows quite a bit. And I told the other doctor, he's going to have to face it. When he gets older and I'm not here to take care of him or she's not here to tell him and he's got to depend on himself and I think a lot of times a lot of children like that. They learn their selves through this, from this stage. And he either goes wrong or he goes good.

Jackson: Does Bruce get to see anything of his mother?

Comments: Having maintained a relational focus, in the discussion of the family's difficulties, Jackson now begins to expand his investigation to explore the relationship between Bruce and his biological mother. Lack of consensual validation between Bruce and his mother with regard to the nature of their relationship would be likely in light of the difficulties being experienced.

Carol: No. He hasn't for a year and a half. He could, they could. She doesn't make a move to see them. We've written letters and all and she could go to court. She could even have them if she wanted to. We'd be willing to, but she just doesn't ah, but I think he [Bruce] wants to stay with his mother. That's another way, one of my strong . . .

Jackson: I don't know how Bruce could know that he'd rather be with his mother since he doesn't really know her. He hasn't seen her in a year and a half did you say?

Carol: Yes, but they say that for four years that was . . . [Carol gets up to keep the baby from leaving the room.]

Norman: For four years what?

Carol: You told me and a lot of people told me she blocked herself off from him for four years.

Norman: Nor Sonya she never wanted. She'd tell her constantly she never wanted her. But, I know the way he feels because . . . Well that should tell you, the woman was a child. She was just like a child with one of her playthings.

Jackson: Have you written to your mother, Bruce?

Bruce: [Nods, saying nothing.]

Jackson: You have not written her yourself? You have? And she answers?

Bruce: No.

Jackson: Well? You kind of get the picture or do you?

Comments: Continuing to probe the nature of the relationship between Bruce and his mother, Jackson explores one of the relational binds Bruce might be experiencing. If Bruce is not clear about where he stands with his mother, working out the definition of relationship with his father and new mother will be that much more difficult. Viewing Bruce's behavior as adaptive and contextually appropriate, Jackson returns to a line of questions around the binds children are often caught in when they feel they are torn by the love and loyalty they feel for both parents.

Bruce: What do you mean?

Jackson: What do you think I mean?

Bruce: I don't know what you mean.

Jackson: I don't know what you don't know about what I mean. You write her and she doesn't answer.

Comments: By not accepting Bruce's "I don't know" stance and pushing him to respond, Jackson jumps levels of abstraction and replies with a statement which implies "I know that you know that

I know that you know what I'm talking about, so stop fooling around and answer my question." Refusing to be entranced by Bruce's use of a confusion technique, Jackson continues to explore the nature of Bruce's relationship with his biological mother.

Bruce: She answers sometimes.

Jackson: When was the last time you wrote?

Bruce: About May.

Jackson: Um, did she answer that one?

Bruce: Uh huh, she answered Sonya.

Jackson: You see you're up against one of the toughest obstacles there is and that's a ghost.

Bruce: What?

Carol: Yeah?

Jackson: A ghost, your mother's partly a ghost. Because how can you prove something that isn't there?

Comments: Jackson pushes the point that Bruce needs to have some sense of closure with regard to his relationship with his biological mother. As long as ambiguity exists with regard to where he stands with his mother, it will be more difficult to work out the nature of the relationship with his father and/or new mother.

Carol: And I went through the exact same thing as him. My mother walked out on me when I was seven. And I didn't see her again until I was 13; my father brought me up. My father had me for six years and babied me to tears.

Jackson: Well, they can't get as wrapped up in their father as you could because you're pretty wrapped up in their father, and that makes for competition.

Comments: The focus of conversation is again wrapped back around to the ongoing effort to define the nature of the relationship emerging between Carol and Norman. Discussion has completely moved away from how "bad" and uncontrollable Bruce is. All of the children's behavior begins to appear more and more coherent within a family context in which closeness and distance issues between Norman and Carol are played out through the children.

Carol: Oh, they could before. I was talking about. . . . I was wrapped up in my father . . . I was talking about before he remarried. After I just got, you know. But Norman, he's not affectionate. I told him, I said if I can't be that way, why don't you try to be a little affectionate towards them because they need it. Now I can kiss Sonya.

Norman: I'm not affectionate. Don't ask me why, I'm just not. It's the person I am. I mean I love my children and I guess I can't expect them to understand the way I love them, right now completely.

Jackson: Yeah, but love isn't demonstrated necessarily by hugging and kissing.

Carol: No, but they still need . . .

Norman: That's the way I feel.

Carol: I know but they still need a certain amount of it, especially Sonya. When I got her she would want to just sit on my lap and hug me all day. And I used to say to her that I'd never get any work done if all I did was sit here and hug you all day. Finally I broke it, but she was kissing me constantly.

Jackson: Yeah, but who was getting the most out of it? You or Sonya?

Comments: Refusing to accept the characterization of the children's behavior as a product of innate individual character traits, Jackson focuses attention on the manner by which the behavior of the children has been prescribed and proscribed by the behavior and expectations of the parents. Continuous exchange of messages between various members, particularly Norman and Carol, over how to define the nature of their own relationship, form the context in which personal characteristics and behavioral repertories are reinforced or limited.

Carol: What the kissing? I was not getting my work done.

Jackson: Oh, but you knew what Sonya felt like because you were a little girl. But you don't know what Bruce feels like.

Carol: But I know Bruce, I don't think Bruce could ever love me. I know she cares for me.

Jackson: But she's a girl and Bruce is a boy.

Carol: That true, I said I can't hug and kiss him. I mean you know, he doesn't want that.

Jackson: You think he's an old man already.

Comments: Jackson continues to tamper with the belief system underlying Carol's statement. His comments suggest that Carol's stereotyped assumption about Bruce said as much about her own uncomfortableness in demonstrating affection toward the boy as it did about what Bruce may have wanted and/or desired.

Norman: Well, I don't think he wants it. He never did want hugging and kissing.

Carol: He's like his father, he's not affectionate. Now a little girl, it's different.

Jackson: This is where we came in; he's like his father.

Norman: [Laughs.] I understand and try to understand you too, I guess.

Jackson: I guess. Considering that you have to work so hard and she has to take care of four kids, I really can't get very excited about the fact that you have this many problems. Because, you know, it is pretty understandable. There are so many things stacked against you.

Comments: The family's difficulties are again framed as normal and developmentally appropriate. By commenting on how well the family is doing, considering the complexity of their situation, Jackson's compliment not only suggests competency on the part of all members of the family, but conveyed respect for how well the parents were doing in creating this newly blended family.

Norman: That's the same way, because I mean . . .

–End of Interview–

This analysis reflects the observer imposed biases of the author. Others may view it differently depending on their choice of punctuation (Bateson and Jackson, 1964) and theoretical orientation.

CONCLUSION

A number of Jackson's former colleagues (Bodin, 1988; Haley, 1989; Weakland, 1988) suggest the preceding interview is not the best example of Jackson's clinical work. An assessment interview only a half hour in length, conducted under quite artificial circumstances in which the family was seen by four different psychiatrists in one day, and that Dr. Jackson had only one brief opportunity to demonstrate his theory and therapy, combine to make this seem to be an unrepresentative, inelegant example of his work.

The difficulties and constraints inherent in the context where the interview takes place can, however, be viewed as advantages and strengths. Being filmed and having only 30 minutes in which to work created a situation in which Jackson had to be in top form, using as many of his own resources as possible to successfully demonstrate his model. Rather than a poor example, the viewer gets a precise, highly condensed illustration of Jackson working at his best under very difficult circumstances. He executed his therapy with a level of intensity and concentration rarely seen in the work of others. His performance was lean with no time spent on frills or unnecessary moves.

In 1964, when this interview was conducted, the family therapy movement was in its infancy. The Brief Therapy Model later developed at the Mental Research Institute, Haley's Strategic, Minuchin's Structural, the Milan Systemic models, de Shazer and Berg's Solution Focused model and other so-called second-order cybernetic models had not yet been articulated. The theoretical assumptions and premises enunciated and clinical techniques pioneered by Jackson and his colleagues during the 1950s and 1960s, remain the bedrock upon which much of the field of family therapy now stands. Every therapeutic move used by Jackson in this interview, conducted 30 years ago, is presently utilized across schools of family therapy.

When viewed through the lens of his own Interactional Theory, Jackson's clinical work exhibited the characteristics of a great performing artist. His conduct flowed in pure and meticulous form out of his Interactional Theory. Jackson did not become distracted by comments and actions of family members which could have drawn him into peripheral issues. Rather, he adhered to an interactional view of family process. Questions asked laid bare the relationships between various members of the family. Jackson's comments acted to push the underlying premises of the family to the point of absurdity. Each move provided the family members an opportunity to begin to frame their situation differently, along normal developmental lines. Suggested assignments pointed a way out of the dilemma. When conducting therapy, Jackson was the embodiment of his Interactional Theory.

SECTION II: INFLUENCES ON CLINICAL WORK

The first part of Section II presents accounts by three clinicians reflecting how their own work has been influenced by their contact with MRI theory and practice. Since the authors are from Israel and Italy, this group of chapters might also have been grouped with those in the first part of Section III on MRI influence in foreign parts–but perhaps it is best to see this as one indication of the underlying interrelationship among the apparently very different and diverse chapters in this volume.

The second part of this section presents chapters primarily concerned with influence not on individual clinicians and their therapies, but with influence on other professional groups. The most important theme among these chapters is, perhaps, that to effectively incorporate a new and quite different orientation into the work of an existing professional group is difficult, and it is not just a matter of intellectual comprehension. Rather, this involves a process of promoting change in the group members' thinking and behavior that is rather analogous to what is required for successful therapy.

Chapter 4

Unfaithfulness in the Marital System: Paradoxical Therapy Using the Idea of Revenge

Yosef Soroka

When couples commit themselves to mutual fidelity, they believe that on the basis of their marital union they will achieve emotional, physical, and social security (Masters and Johnson, 1975). Masters and Johnson note that commitment is the key word in comprehending the concept of fidelity. Commitment is the consent to do something. They say to each other "I promise" and the promise is kept and realized. Without the commitment, without people relying on one another, the interpersonal relations will suffer lack of confidence. The mutual obligation of the pair is accompanied by mutual care, spontaneous concern, and availability.

Fromm (1973) mentions concern and responsibility as basic elements in the concept of love. To that he adds the concept of respect as an additional essential element in any form of love. When these conditions are achieved, the couple will permit itself physical and emotional exposure. Should one partner break this cycle of commitment he or she will disrupt the balance that maintains the marital system. A break of the commitment accompanied by an extramarital intimate relationship is an act of unfaithfulness which will be dealt with in this chapter.

Two specific cases will serve as a basis for the analysis of the theory. We will also discuss the special dynamics that develop between the pair, and bring one of them to break out of the marital system. We will further deal with the necessary ways of intervention in order to bring a new balance to the disrupted system, as a basis for new adjustments in the couple's life. Emphasis during the discussion will be on a paradoxical approach as a basis for the search for a solution.

A DESCRIPTION OF TWO COUPLES WHO UNDERWENT A PROCESS OF CHANGE AFTER AN EVENT OF UNFAITHFULNESS

Case I

The husband initiated the request for advice. It appears that his wife had exposed a year-long affair that he had had with another woman. He was not interested in breaking up the family unit, and therefore turned for advice for him and for his wife.

The couple was in their early thirties, married for ten years and parents to three children. Both proclaimed the intent to maintain their ties, but the wife, being betrayed and hurt, displayed jealousy making it difficult for the couple to return to a balanced way of life.

The woman told that during the years of their marriage she had been in the husband's shadow. While he worked and studied, she saw to all the household needs. When she used to ask him to spend more time with her and the children, he always had good reasons to decline. It left her frustrated. The husband's story completed the picture his wife had portrayed: during the years of their life together, the wife had supervised all his acts. In order to keep up with her demands, he had to reduce working and studying hours. This hampered his progress towards achieving the objectives he had undertaken in order to promote himself at work and to better his family's condition. When it had become clear to his wife that he could decrease his activities out of the home, she intensified her demands. This led to his feeling that she was no longer supporting him. At this stage he met a woman with whom he kept a relationship for a year. When the crisis between him and his wife broke out, he asked for professional advice.

Case II

This is the case of a couple, married for 15 years, with three children. The wife had an extramarital intimate relationship, and when she was about to decide to leave her husband, she decided to tell him about her unfaithfulness. Due to the resulting crisis, they turned for advice, which evidently the wife had initiated. Both wanted to keep their marriage intact, but the wife insisted on it being done with the help of a therapist.

Their story is that of a happy family through all their years together, a fact neither disputed. The man was the focal point of the family's life: he worked, saw to the family's needs, and spent many hours with his wife and children. Most of their activities were done together. When the children grew, he encouraged his wife to acquire a profession and fulfill her personal needs out of the home. The woman developed quickly; she acquired a managerial profession, found employment, and quickly reached a high position. At this stage, she met a man with whom she kept a relationship for a short while. Interested in keeping her relationship with her husband, she told him what had happened. She had felt she was being engulfed by the marital system and was being put on a level with the children, while out of the home her relative strength was differently appreciated. She wished to change her status in the family.

The above cases focus on the partners' attempts to change their status in the marital system. These are forceful processes which aim to upset an existing balance in favor of a new balance, by breaking away from the marital obligation. Masters and Johnson (1975) note that beyond all rationalization, extramarital affairs reflect two things:

1. Both partners are unable to provide their mutual physical and emotional needs.
2. They regard each other as not unique, exchangeable, as sources of pleasure and gratification.

But there is also another possibility in which one partner wishes to warn, by being unfaithful, that he or she is desirable and that it is better not to be disregarded and to be treated with respect and esteem, as perceived by him or her.

This possibility, as well as analysis of the interpersonal processes which lead to the search for external forces and the different ways to manage the crisis in order to obtain renewed trust, will be the subjects dealt with in the following sections.

The Interpersonal Model

Communication determines the existence of relationships between people (Watzlawick, 1979). This means that relations between people influence their self-concept in relation to others. Their status–whose stable character influences its surroundings–is not a result of an inner truth and is not to be shaken. Relationships resulting from communicative ties are described by Bateson (1958) and classified into two types: the first type of relationship is defined as complementary, and the second as symmetrical. In the first kind, the communicating people try to polarize each other. In the second type, the partners try to keep changing ties in order to avoid competition. The relationship changes according to changing circumstances of life.

More complex are the meta-complementary and meta-symmetrical relationships (Watzlawick, Beavin, and Jackson, 1967). In the meta-complementary relationship, one person imposes on or allows the other to show responsibility for him. In the meta-symmetrical relationship, one person imposes on or allows the other to be equal to him. Understanding these relationships explains the special nature of the relations of a couple where one partner has decided to be unfaithful. This situation illustrates nonacceptance of relations, done on a one-sided basis. It is a show of strength, a step usually taken when all other options are barred. Not every system about to change necessarily undergoes a major crisis. A crisis occurs when one partner feels that his status as an adult is hurt.

In the first case, the man felt his wife was not treating him properly according to his self-concept at that stage of his life. In the second case, the woman felt her husband was restricting her opportunities of self-expression, after undergoing a major change in her life. The restlessness expressed made them search for a solution which would cause a systemic change in their marital relationship.

The Benefit of Unfaithfulness

During a life cycle, a person experiences different stages to which he or she must flexibly adapt. Changes according to varying circumstances lessen the intensity of the crisis. Lederer and Jackson (1968) describe a flexible relationship which changes according to circumstances. They stress that such a relationship is essential for continuous adaptation to changing conditions. When there is a new reality which demands a change in the couple's relationship, and the change does not occur, a confusion arises concerning the nature of the relations which kept the system going till then. For example, a woman who had stayed home for years wishes to complete her education, expects her husband to encourage and help her. If the woman is unable, to the best of her understanding and feeling, to realize her hopes and aspirations, and if she is convinced the change is prevented by her husband, the crisis is almost inevitable. Often sex is used to solve such a crisis; sometimes sex is denied to the spouse, at others, there is a break from the marital system, and a search for an extramarital relationship. Both actions indicate the possibility of independent ways of self-fulfillment. Kopp (1972) notes that there are two reasons for the tactical use of sex: the first, that by their very nature, sexual relations are based on personal relations. The second, that denial of sex does not cause severe physical harm nor does it bring disastrous results. The serious harm is on the level of personal relationships and personal feelings. It seems this is the course considered by the participants as the surest and most painful way of attaining for themselves the desired advantage in order to reach their goal.

Reactions to Unfaithfulness

Jealousy is the strongest emotion expressed in cases of exposed unfaithfulness. Reactions of jealousy are accompanied by extreme anger, hostility, and aggression. These feelings are the result of a sense of humiliation due to injured self-esteem and injured physical self-image. Kaplan (1973) stresses that these feelings are almost uncontrollable, and being destructive, they delay the possibility of achieving the desired goal, unless it is a destructive one.

Jealousy also has another aspect, that of a desire to hold on to something which is of value to the individual. When an act of unfaithfulness is exposed, the person is caught between hostility and jealousy, with both feelings being similar. If there is an expressed wish to overcome the crisis, then the aim is to remove hostility, which is essentially destructive, and to channel jealousy into renewed cooperation between the couple.

This chapter deals with those cases in which there is a conflict between the destructive hostile feelings and that part of jealousy which aims at retaining the existing relations. This conflict creates a confusion which is the basis of any change, therefore it is not surprising that the couples, despite feelings of deep pain, are prepared for a penetrating explanation of their relationship. In other instances there is a conviction in the actions of the individual and they hasten to separate. The specific reaction to jealousy differs according to factors such as past experience, self-confidence, a feeling of self-esteem and basic confidence (Im, Wilner, and Breit, 1983). These facts have to be taken into account when planning interventions.

From Crisis to Renewed Confidence

Clinical experience shows that when balance is disturbed due to exposed unfaithfulness, the unfaithful partner generally initiates the request for treatment. It is the unfaithful partner who is prepared to cooperate with the therapist, in order to restore the balance to his relations with his deceived partner. Framo (1982) reports similar experience. He notes that women who had extramarital relationships had turned to him requesting help to return to their husbands. This observation is important for two reasons: (1) establishing who initiated the treatment enables determining the person most interested in bringing about the change (Watzlawick, Weakland, and Fisch, 1974). (2) The unfaithful partner has no direct interest in the destruction of the natural marital system. This enables us to deduce that the break from the marital frame was functional in a specific, focused area: the deceived partner, as opposed to the other, does his or her best to polarize the relations even more. The methods used include limitation of free movement outside the house, threats of harm to the partner or to the third party, threats of suicide and others. As mentioned, these attempts succeed in polarizing the relations that were the cause of the break. This way, the system gets more and more complicated, making it more difficult to influence the interpersonal processes. Teismann (1979) describes this complexity and notes three models of coping with states of jealousy:

1. Personal/cognitive. According to this model, change is achieved when the jealous individual changes his assumptions, expectations, and concepts on the act of adultery. This way he or she is available to the partner without the jealousy which formerly characterized the behavior (Ellis, 1972; Protinsky, 1977).
2. Interpersonal/capabilities model. In this case, change is achieved when partners develop the ability to recognize jealousy-provoking situations, thus restraining their reactions.
3. Problem solution model. According to this model (Weakland, Fisch, and Watzlawick, 1976) what is said or done is of importance in influencing the direction of the relations.

Understanding the interpersonal or intrapersonal dynamics or supplying explanations, can preserve the already problematic relations. Any rationalization can be worse than the act itself.

The solution on which we will concentrate is based on the last approach. Such a solution is also suggested by Im, Wilner, and Breit (1983), and is named "Sin and Punishment" by them. This technique proposes use of punishment by the deceived partner, when the breach of mutual commitment by the spouse's act of unfaithfulness is discovered.

The technique we use is identical. The punishment we propose sounds very extreme, because we indicate revenge. We expressly intend, though, that by refusing to do what we suggest, the individual will do what we really want him to: give up revenge, forgive and renew the tie with the spouse on the basis of relations functional to them in their next stage in life.

Orwell (1967) dealt with this subject of revenge, and his story inspired the choice of treatment. He describes an experience he had during the Second World War. At the time, he was a military correspondent, and as such, visited a German POW camp. During the tour, he was accompanied by a young Jew who had formerly been detained in this camp. During the visit, he saw the young man kick a German officer. He describes what he saw and felt: "What I saw on this occasion and on others made me realize that the idea of punishment and revenge is a childish daydream; more precisely, there is no such thing as revenge. Revenge is something you wish to do when you are powerless and because you are powerless. When you remove the image of helplessness, you also remove the desire for revenge" (p. 3-6).

In this description lies the direction for the solution of the hostility/jealousy problem: Give the hurt partner power to forgive the other from a position that holds no humiliation. Only in this way can the couple derive any benefit from the crisis they experienced, and can carry on their life together.

Description of the Interventions–Case I

From the start, it was clear that the relations between the couple had created a state of jealousy which worsened as the relations became more polarized. The relationship between the couple had been complementary: the husband worked and at the same time acquired an academic degree, whereas the wife looked after the household needs. The more the husband studied, the more he had to make up for his absence from work. The result was that his direct contribution to the family life lessened. His wife continued to cultivate the house and raise the children, at the same time nurturing the thoughts that one day he will not want her any more because she will no longer keep up with his new expectations, likely to be raised due to his graduation and his promotion at work. She began to demand from him more and more consideration for her and for the family needs. This included a demand for less working hours and a reduction of his studies. For the man, these were signs of lack of consideration and faith in his personal responsibility and care for the family. He had undertaken a lot in order to shorten the duration of his studies, so as not to harm the family too much. When unable to get the appreciation for his efforts from his wife, it was very easy to receive it from another woman. Naturally, this appreciation was based on completely different matters.

When his wife found out about his extramarital ties, it confirmed her earlier fears. She demanded immediate divorce. Apparently, this was an undesirable possibility for the husband. He wished to keep the family ties, promising not to break the marital system again.

Now the relations changed; the wife supervised her husband's behavior whereas he felt more and more compelled to act contrary to his wishes. It was a heavy penalty to "pay" for his sin, having to bear it for an unspecified time and in an unknown manner. Fearing the marriage would disintegrate he asked for professional intervention.

According to the strategy that hostility must be removed by giving power and control to the deceived side, it was decided to have a personal talk with his wife. She was told that, estimating their relationship, it appeared that she held the key to their continued ties. Should she wish, they would continue, should she not want, they would fall apart. In order to strengthen this estimation, she was also told that her husband appreciated her support and that he was convinced that without it, he would not have achieved so much. At the same time, she was explicitly told the therapy session was held in order to convince her not to forgive easily, otherwise, he might think she was not very hurt. In order to impress on him how hurt she was, she must take revenge with a single, focalized, and painful act of revenge.

Apparently, the words fell on receptive ears; the woman said that for quite a while she had been contemplating just such revenge, the means being adultery, that "he may feel what she had felt." Her feelings and intentions were accepted, with a request to limit it to a single act, so as not to turn it into a new way of life instead of revenge. It turned out that the woman had gone so far as to encourage someone to flirt with her. The general idea appealed to her, but she wished to think it over, because her original idea had been to develop a prolonged affair, such as her husband had had.

A week later, she called to say she was no longer interested in the therapy, because the aims of the therapy negated too soon the process of revenge she herself had planned. Some time later, in a follow-up phone call, it turned out that she had given up her original plans. Her husband had agreed to an old wish of hers to move to another apartment, which for her was a clear sign of the stability of their ties, her husband sincerely trying to compensate her for the pain he had inflicted. For her, the process was over. It is important to point out that from the couple's viewpoint, things ended spontaneously.

Case II

In this case, the couple's ties were based on mutual love. Their relationship was complementary. The man worked and saw to the family's income, and the wife saw to the household needs. When the children grew up, the man encouraged his wife to find an occupation outside the home. With his encouragement, she acquired a profession and in a short while, reached a managerial position. At the same time, her self-esteem changed, and with it, her concept of her status in their marriage. Though on the surface, her status was the same as her husband's, she felt she needed his confirmation for too many things. His concern, guidance, and directions made her feel as though he put her on a level with the children. When she tried to do things by herself, he was offended. Her explanations only made him more concerned for her, because he felt "something was happening to her." The woman interpreted his behavior as insecurity and as a reaction to the possibility she might exceed him. She didn't notice she was undergoing a change, and that her husband needed time to get accustomed to it.

At that point, she met a man who saw her at her new stage in life. She won his esteem due to the fact that she was "one level above him"; this served him and was a compliment to her. In this situation, she expressed herself differently than in the opportunities available to her at home. She was prepared to leave her home and her family for the new connection. As she was about to carry out her decision, she retreated and told her husband what had happened to her during that period of time. The pain and the crisis were unavoidable. The relations became unbearable, until the woman suggested therapy.

At first, the treatment focused on their interpersonal relations, definition of points of tension, and the prevention of jealousy. This process exacerbated the tension between the couple even more. The attempt to explain the woman's behavior strengthened the husband's feeling that she was unreliable when given freedom. She left a good protective home and showed weakness of moral values which would not have happened had he controlled her more closely. The only possible conclusion was that she must be guided strictly; lacking inner guidance, he would supply the needed control. This was a return to the old, known, and unwanted pattern of their relations.

In order to try to change this pattern, it was decided to change the tactics. The man was invited to a personal talk in which he told of the distress and pain his wife had inflicted on him. It was proposed to him, that he "settle accounts" with her, so that she should feel the pain he had felt. The idea was that he avenge himself by committing adultery. He replied he had seriously contemplated such a possibility, but rejected it because such behavior was not like him.

His choice not to take revenge was reenforced, pointing out his being above petty accounts. Having shown remarkable capabilities of forgiving but not forgetting, there was no problem to induce him to give his wife, who had shown momentary weakness, a second chance. His wife was told to ask him to be available for her anytime she felt in distress because of the rapid changes she had lately experienced. From a position of power, he agreed to give her right of self-determination in the marital system, which she had wanted, after having attained a position of influence at work.

The complementary relations changed into alternating relations which better suited the couple's reality. The man had shown preparedness to adjust himself to the new situation only after he had the opportunity of allowing her to carry on in the new direction to which he had encouraged her in the first place.

Summary and Discussion

Solving the problem of jealousy necessitates moderation of the hostility it generates, and giving the opportunity to find a constructive channel for it. The therapist has to figure out how to compensate the offended partner and at the same time, enable the unfaithful partner to return home strengthened.

This process takes into account the complexity, and yet offers an opportunity for the offended partner to spontaneously accept his or her mate. Any other way will cause the offended partner to act under compulsion, and will make the process of conciliation difficult.

The paradoxical use of the idea of revenge is a suitable answer when confronting the complexities of the problem. In the cases dealt with, the partner is in a position to forgive or take revenge. This is a choice between two possibilities, each of which releases the person from the desire to show hostility. If the person chooses to forgive, then all that remains is to accept the partner and rebuild their relations. If the person chooses to avenge the wrongs, and then carries out that revenge, he or she forgoes the moral superiority to demand from his or her partner a higher moral behavior. It seems people are aware of the trap, and they usually choose the first possibility. In any case, this is one of the two desirable possibilities for the therapist, in order to achieve a complete solution.

Extreme caution must be used, of course, when using this method. There is always a possibility that people will accept the idea literally. In that case, they may carry out the idea not quite according to the therapist's intentions. There is also danger that the therapist will be accused of trying to use disqualified methods.

For the proper implementation of the process, note these steps:

1. Identification of the offended partner. On the face of things, it is usually the deceived person. But one must be alert to a situation in which the deceived person takes on responsibility and stresses that he or she was the one who drove the partner to adultery. In this case, the unfaithful partner is the offended one!
2. The willingness of the offended person to cooperate should be examined and estimated in order to achieve a change of relations. Sometimes the cooperation is only tactical, and serves as a base for later justification of a demand for divorce: "I have tried everything but there is no other choice but to separate."
3. The offended person is invited to a separate talk, with the consent and cooperation of the other. During this meeting, the person is "recruited" as an active partner in the treatment, being told that he or she has the power to achieve the change.

Chapter 5

The Case of Anna C.

Fabia Schoss

THE PROBLEM

Anna, aged 42, was married at about 20, and has two daughters, one adolescent and the other a child of five with Down's syndrome. She works as a secretary part time in order to be able to look after her handicapped daughter as much as possible. About six months ago, her husband went to live with another woman, and he comes to see the children less and less, about once every ten days. During the first session, while recounting her life to me, often crying and in a confused state, she calmly said that each morning, going to work in her car, she hoped that another car would crash into hers, causing her to fall into the canal running alongside the street.

I sympathized with her as much as was possible. I said that I myself would think of ending it all in her situation, but that if she was willing to try, perhaps I could help her to face one of the problems that tormented her so much. She looked at me in a rather surprised fashion, and politely pointed out to me that I must have a mistaken idea of the type of person that she is. Deep down she is optimistic and positive; she has struggled all her life in difficult conditions, and if she asked me for help, it was because she wanted to find a way of feeling better.

Her greatest problem is her inability to accept that her husband left her. She feels that she has failed and is alone. Her chief aim in life has always been to have a united and happy family. Her father left home when she was a child and she still remembers how much she suffered and that she had decided that her life would be different and happy. She is living through the collapse of all her most deeply felt hopes. She feels guilty toward her daughters: the smaller one has a great need of stable points of reference, affection, and attention to be able to achieve some degree of autonomy. The older one is rebellious and "takes advantage of her father's absence," to do what she wants. Anna is tired of "fighting," and would like to have an open dialogue with her daughter.

She feels guilty toward her mother who is so good and kind and, according to Anna, does not deserve to be involved in such a difficult situation, now that she is old and should be leading a peaceful life. Also with her siblings there are problems; they behave as they have always done. She is the eldest and has always had a role of supremacy. It was she who acted as mother when they were small, and she continues to do so, even though now she would like it if the roles were reversed and her siblings took care of her, instead of continuing to take advantage of her availability.

She does not have friends outside the family. Her husband was a Don Juan and after having discovered him in an unpleasant situation with some of her women friends, little by little, she has isolated herself. Very active in an association of parents of children with Down's syndrome, she is often called to participate in planning the teaching programs in her younger daughter's school, where integration is practiced. In her relationships with the mothers of the "normal" children who attend the school, she says that she is often upset by their absolute lack of sensitivity, speaking of their "normal" problems, without realizing "who she is" and "what she is going through at this moment."

In reality, everyone at the school appreciates her daughter's sympathy and affection, inviting her to birthday parties in their homes and complimenting her on her good manners, but they do not go beyond these formalities. In brief, Anna feels she is not understood and is developing the idea that "the others are cold and unkind," distant from her and from her situation that is so different and "abnormal," as different "as the earth is from the moon."

THE ATTEMPTED SOLUTIONS

Anna would like others to help her spontaneously, without her having to make specific requests: she would like it if others wanted to help her. She says that each time that she has helped someone, she has done so without it being requested specifically, because she is generous and knows how to recognize the needs of others. If her sister, for example, does not help her as she would like, this is because the sister does not want to and if she does not want to, there is nothing else to be done but realize that she is insensitive. "It's useless to expect something that does not happen–better to pretend you have noticed nothing and maintain a dignified attitude."

In brief, she is always increasingly angry with everyone and acts in such a way as to drive away even those who would like to give her a hand. Among these are her mother whom Anna accuses of spending time more willingly with her other children than with her. Thus, day after day, she cultivates an obstinate rancor. She complains continuously of everything, does not succeed in looking after herself, and is profoundly discontented with herself.

THE INTERVENTION

It seemed useless to propose an intervention to Anna, without using all the rancor inside of her, so, I advised her to "test" her sister. She could take advantage of the first time they happened to speak on the telephone, to say she was disappointed at not being invited to her last party. I tried to convince her to be just a little melodramatic, saying, "Since my husband left me, I've been feeling very alone and I need help." At first she refused to do anything of the sort because "her sister knew very well that she was lonely," and "she had no desire to humiliate herself in this way." I said that it was only a performance, insinuating that this was a sure way of finding out if her sister was really as insensitive as she thought and pointed out that if her sister did react as coldly as usual, it was not the end of the world since she was already used to it. There could be no disadvantage in clarifying this situation which she felt very deeply about and it was worth trying. Anna agreed. She was very convincing on the telephone, because her sister, in tears, confessed that she had been worried about her for some time and had tried to get close to her on many occasions, but it always seemed that she did not want this and she "was too proud to accept the help of her little sister." The sister said she was available to help her with the younger daughter and would be happy to have her to supper at her home as in the old times. Anna's satisfaction at this first success was so great that between one session and the next, she found herself saying the same thing to her adolescent daughter during a squabble. Her daughter's reaction was even more surprising than her sister's. The girl tidied her room quickly and was home in time for supper, which had not happened for a very long time. She also wrote Anna a letter apologizing for having made her desperate and said Anna should not feel alone because she was now there at her side.

Meanwhile, Anna was also changing physically; she looked better and smiled. The time had come to think of how she could improve her relations with "the others." Anna felt uncomfortable talking to the parents of "normal" children because they seemed embarrassed or frightened of her difference. Neither did they understand how much stress she was under because of the health of her younger daughter who has a heart malformation which at more or less regular intervals leaves her gasping for breath. For Anna, it was a relief to participate in the meeting of the association of parents of children with Down's syndrome; they knew what it meant to be in an intensive care unit, waiting, possibly for weeks, for all to end well. But, incredibly, sometimes she felt uncomfortable there also, since only a few parents in the association also have a healthy child.

Her situation is paradoxical: there is always something different about her as a mother. When with parents of healthy children, she is different because she has a handicapped daughter. When with parents of handicapped children, she is different because she has a healthy daughter. This is the problem to resolve–she must change her point of view completely. Her experience outside the normal and ordinary is in fact, extraordinary. She can communicate her extraordinary experience in all the environments in which she lives, if only she remembers all her resources. She can reduce the distance and the sense of fear of "different" people felt by the parents of the school, sensitizing them to the problems that she lives with, as the mother of a daughter with Down's syndrome, paving the way for greater reciprocal integration and solidarity. In her association, her resources may be made available to the more discouraged parents.

She is also able to realize the positive benefit of an education towards true autonomy, because of her older daughter.

Therapy was finished in nine sessions, but we agreed to meet again two months later for a check-up. At that time she had stopped complaining, and realized her experience could be of real use to others. She had decided to change jobs and found the funds enabling her to be taken on the staff of the association. She was finishing a preparatory course, and had decided to take responsibility for receiving new parents–those who have just had a diagnosis of Down's syndrome for their child. It seemed to her that doctors who normally did this were too pessimistic. Anna certainly does not intend to hide the difficulties facing the parents, but wants to communicate to them that it is a rich and a most extraordinary human experience.

Chapter 6

Brief Strategic Therapy of Phobic Disorders: A Model of Therapy and Evaluation Research

Giorgio Nardone

The application of a strategic therapy model leads to a brief therapeutic intervention with its main aim consisting of the resolution of the problem and the elimination of the symptoms presented by the patient. During treatment, we refer to the present living condition of the clinical subject. Information from the patient's "clinical history," is useful only to set up the best strategies to solve his problems.

We believe that the solution of each problem first requires the breaking of the circular system of relational feedback which preserves the clinical situation. Afterwards, it will become necessary to substitute the dysfunctional behavioral patterns of the patient (the so-called "attempted solutions") with more functional ones. Such a substitution, if well applied, will lead to a deep psychological modification in the patient, in relation to his perceptions, conceptions, and his view of the world, which were the "cause" of his "psychopathological" behavior. The model we are referring to is a pragmatic one; during treatment, the formulation of the therapeutic strategies is based on:

A. Direct observation of the problems presented by the clinical subject;
B. Consideration and evaluation of the following questions:

(1) *which* are the characteristics of the interaction of the patient with himself, with the others, and with the rest of the world?
(2) *in which way* are these interactions dysfunctional?
(3) *how* is it possible to modify the problematic situation in the fastest and most efficacious way?

This therapeutic strategy seeks to answer the abovementioned questions and plan with the patient the aims of the therapy. Usually, if therapeutic treatment works out, we can observe, from the beginning, a clear decrease of symptoms and a progressive change of the patient's perception of himself, of others, and of the rest of the world. This means that the patient will gradually shift from a restricted outlook of the world, which was the kernel of its problematic conditions, to a wider perceptional aptitude towards reality. This will lead to an increase of self-esteem and personal independence.

The therapeutic process develops in two different phases. First, a modification of the patient's behavior and actions takes place. Consequently, in the second phase, the patient's conceptions and emotional dispositions will be modified. In this sense, the traditional psychotherapeutic procedures are reversed. According to the traditional procedures, in fact, the therapist should induce a cognitive insight in the patient (relative to the specific clinical problem) and only afterwards should work towards the modification of behavior and social interactions. They are longer, more difficult, and, indeed, have the opposite effect. In fact, it makes the patient resist the change that a primary insight causes. We believe, on the contrary, that a cognitive reframing of the problem and of the clinical condition could be a useful subsequent stage of the therapy when the patient's behavior has been already modified.

PART I: THE RESEARCH

The Treated Phobic Disorders

This chapter deals with the brief treatment of serious phobic disorders like agoraphobia, panic attacks, serious anxiety attacks, or recurring immobilizing fear situations. From a diagnostic point of view, the following therapeutic program can be divided into two clinical groups. The first group refers to the *very serious* phobic disorders; the second one, refers to the *less serious* phobic disorders. At this point, we would like to précis the concept of *very serious phobic disorders*.

We can say that a serious phobic disorder is a psychological condition in which the patient "fears to fear." He is so scared that he cannot initiate any activity requiring engagement, responsibility, or personal involvement such as sports, hobbies, parties, work, etc. He is also unable to go out or stay at home by himself. Every environmental stimulus is transformed by him into an alarm signal rousing terror. A similar terror is also determined by proprioceptive stimuli which are felt as symptoms of disease. The situation becomes unbearable both for the patient and for the people living around him (family, friends, relatives, etc.) who cannot leave their relative alone and have to bear his obsessions.

The phobic disorders belonging to the second group are less serious. In fact, the patients suffering from such disorders can fulfill their working or domestic duties, even if they find great difficulties in doing them and their productive level is very low. In all these patients, the manifestation of paralyzing fear attacks is very frequent and a phobic reaction is not apparently determined by any external stimulus. In these particular situations, the patients were completely unable to do anything about solving their critical condition. Moreover, the patient would start having more numerous symptoms more frequently.

In all the patients of the first and second group, somatic indicators of very high anxiety level have been very evident. Most of them had suffered from psychosomatic disorders for a long time. In almost all cases, psychiatric pharmacological therapies had been tried without result. A few patients improved, but after some time, they presented the symptomatology again. Some of them decided to turn to psychoanalytical therapies, even for a long time, but with no benefits. Three patients reported to have had paralyzing dread attacks and had been treated with behavioristic therapy by the same therapist. Symptomatology disappeared for a period of three to six months; then reappeared with psychosomatic disorders such as alopecia, dermatosis, and sexual problems. The original disorders then reappeared in addition to the new ones.

Methodological Criteria and Sample

Our sample is made up of some patients, treated by the author in the last three years of professional activity in Arezzo (Italy), who suffered from phobic disorders. All of them have been treated following the brief therapy model. The patients selected are only those who, in addition to the release of the symptoms, also presented a positive follow-up (three to six months and one year).

The follow-up has the function of measuring relapse if any, after the treatment. Relapses are sometimes frequent in brief therapy treatment and subsequently, many therapists consider brief therapy a superficial intervention.

Following the abovementioned criteria, *41 successfully treated cases* were chosen and the whole series of follow-ups has been completed. All the other cases treated by the author, are not to be considered completely solved, even if they have positively passed the first and the second follow-ups and even if the results of the therapies have been the same as with the other 41 patients.

According to the author, these cases cannot be considered solved. In fact, we believe that it is only after having gone through the first year of follow-up, that the patients have few possibilities of a future relapse. So, only after the first year of follow-up do we consider the therapy as completely accomplished and not as a superficial symptomatic treatment, but as an effective "change" of the patient's conditions.

Follow-up interviews have been done taking into consideration not only the patient, but his whole family. The standard interview focused on possible relapses or new symptoms and on the patient's behavior, mood, and interpersonal relations. The group of patients who have been treated by the author is formed of 24 women and 17 men of different educational levels (elementary school, high school, or college); ages range from 18 to 71. The sample includes housewives, medical doctors, professionals, and different kinds of employees.

RESULTS

Effectiveness

Therapy has been completely successful with all 41 patients. This means that the symptoms and disorders presented when the patient came for the first time gradually disappeared and at the last session, were completely extinguished.

A year after the end of therapy, only in nine cases did the patients suffer again from some anxious crisis or light dread episodes. Nevertheless, most of these reported that they had not paid any attention to these episodes and that they continued their activity thinking that the trouble would disappear after a short while (in fact, this is what happened). Only two among the nine had to be treated a gain for a few sessions. Thus, we can affirm that in the other seven subjects the phobic mechanism reappeared, but was immediately reduced and extinguished by the patient's new behavior.

In summing up, after a year following the therapy, we can say that among the cases, 32 have been completely and successfully treated, seven have improved their problematic condition and the last two patients have improved, but not fully recovered from their condition.

Efficiency

In all cases, treatment in the beginning consisted of weekly sessions followed by bimonthly sessions and finally, by monthly sessions. The average length of treatment has been 15.6 sessions, from a minimum of six sessions to a maximum of 34 sessions. More precisely and clearly, we can gather these data in four groups of length and show the percent of cases as follows:

Percentage of Cases	Length of Therapy
19.2%	from 1 to 10 sessions
61.5%	from 10 to 20 sessions
3.0%	from 20 to 30 sessions
15.3%	from 30 to 34 sessions

Approximately 80% of the cases have been solved within 20 sessions. To sum up the research section of this chapter, we can report that considering the seriousness of the treated problems, and the literature on this specific kind of psychological disorder, the results appear really astonishing.

PART II: THE THERAPY MODEL

Preliminary Remarks

At this point, it is useful to state that:

(1) The therapeutic process and strategies applied have been the same in all cases;
(2) The applied treatment has been an individual-strategic one.

As far as the first point is concerned, we can say that for each case, a pre-fixed procedure of therapeutic actions and prescriptions has been followed. The only thing changed for each single case was the therapeutic communication and the framework of therapeutic actions and prescriptions.

The strategic therapist's first task is that of "learning and speaking the patient's language," thus adapting the intervention strategies and techniques to the particular individual reality. Nevertheless, the pre-fixed goals and the applied strategies have not been changed. Rather, they have been creatively adapted to each patient's reality. In other words, the format of the same prescription or action has been adapted to each single patient, but the structure and function have not been changed.

For example, each reframing applied to a single patient has been different in its communicational form, but its function and structure have not been changed. We believe that the procedure followed causes the same effects in different situations and on patients with different personalities, who are sharing the same psychological disorders and symptoms, and that it is very useful both for the etiology of the symptoms and the setting up of new and better psychotherapeutic tools. What is most important is the repetition of a valid means of intervention which, due to its application and its effects, allows researchers to prove the validity and reliability according to the criteria of contemporary epistemology.

The second peculiarity of our work is that we have dealt individually with the phobic patients; their relatives or acquaintances have not been directly involved. But, obviously they have been indirectly. In agreement with Weakland (1974), we believe, that according to the systems theory, within a system of relations, even if the smallest particular is changed, a change starts a chain reaction in the system.

The model of treatment, therefore, has a systemic interactional perspective, but an individual therapeutic strategy employed has been most effective. The choice of "apparently" individual treatment has been motivated by observing and taking into consideration the interpersonal relations of each single patient treated. Such patients usually have a rather close relationship and great social support from their husband/wife, relatives, friends, or other people around them who give them a feeling of protection and peacefulness as soon as help is requested or they are in a crisis. This social support acts as "the attempted solution which maintains the problem" (Watzlawick, Weakland, and Fisch, 1974); this means that this attitude and social behavior, instead of helping the patient overcome his fears, contributes to the maintenance of the problem.

The first step of the therapy should be the breaking of this dysfunctional system which maintains the problem. The strategy which was chosen was the one of "reframing" the patient's position during the first session. The patient is told not only that he cannot count on the support and protection of other people, but that he has to begin to consider it as harmful and dangerous because it maintains the problem and it can make it worse. Moreover, he is told that the people around him are an integral part of the dysfunctional system and since they are so involved, there is nothing they can do to change the situation. The initial strategy, therefore, is to create a reframing of the situation through which the patient realizes that his present relations are not only dysfunctional, but also dangerous. By using his own fear, his collaboration can be obtained towards change. Furthermore, the power of the disorder is channeled towards its elimination.

People around the patient are not asked to pretend that they are not able to support him anymore, give him the requested protection, or to pretend that they themselves are in a crisis. The patient himself is led to modify his interactions. This strategy has been chosen, because, due to my experience, whenever I tried to involve the people around a phobic patient in therapy, usually I obtained two different reactions which had opposite effects:

(1) The people around the patient could not really change their attitude and behavior, ended up being overprotective, thereby reinforcing and making the problem more complex.
(2) If those involved with the patient maintained a different attitude and behavior, the patient usually reacted by looking for support from other people or building up a refusal of the therapy which gave him anxiety and which was the cause of this unwanted change. Consequently, the patient becomes rigid toward the therapist and very often gives up the therapy. If instead, the tactic used is the one mentioned above, the patient is willing to do what is suggested and accepts the help of the therapist as his only true support. By so doing, the patient himself works against the dysfunctional interactions.

I believe it is possible to reach the first goal for a brief therapy (i.e., the breaking of the restrictive response system which maintains the problem), by this a kind of perspective change. In other words, our attention should be focused on how to change the relation between the patient and his "self" and then to reinforce his new perception with the interaction with significant others and the rest of the world. Often, following therapy, it was necessary to have an interview with the husband/wife or the members of the family who were confused by the change in the behavior of the patient.

Treatment Description

We can now present a detailed exposition of the treatment sequence. This sequence will be divided into four successive stages which represent the different phases of the treatment.

Resuming Treatment File Card

First stage: From the first to the third session.

> *Goals:* (a) obtain cooperation and trust; (b) break the rigid system of perception of reality; (c) demonstrate practically that the change is possible.
> *Strategies:* (1) speak the patient's language; (2) reframe the problem; (3) indirect prescription; (4) reframe prescription effects.

Second stage: From the third to the fifth session.

> *Goals:* (a) reinforcement of the capacity to change; (b) actual change of the situation; (c) cognitive reorganization.
> *Strategies:* (1) reframing; (2) paradoxical prescription; (3) "go slowly" technique; (4) reframing of prescription effects.

Third stage: From the fifth session on.

> *Goals:* (a) help the patient experience the gradual overcoming of the problem; (b) redefinition of the patient's perception of "himself," of other people, and of the world.

Fourth stage: Last session.

> *Goals:* (a) final incentive to personal autonomy and its consolidation.
> *Strategies:* (1) detailed explanation of the work developed together and the techniques utilized; (2) conclusive reframing of capacities the patient shows in facing and solving the problem.

First Stage: From the First to the Third Session

The first session represents an extremely important phase in strategic therapy. During the meeting, the therapist's attention is directed to establishing a proper and cooperative relationship with the patient. To reach this goal, it is necessary to carefully listen to the patient, learning his language and way of perceiving reality. At the same time, we proceeded with the first important therapeutic step: the reframing of the patient's actual condition,[1] which consists of telling him that there is no doubt that his problem, as well as any other psychological problem, has a deep effect on his relations with other people.

Moreover, if we really want to solve his problem, we must start by ascertaining from the patient that the help given to him by other people can only damage and not improve his actual condition. Thus, the focus of the treatment is placed upon the patient's way of perceiving reality and on his reactions. As we have already said, the reframing plays to the fundamental role of interrupting the system of supports from other people which prevent the patient from being able to react in a personal way. If the help given to the patient by others is considered harmful, we can channel the patient's phobic power to obtain a change in his condition and his cooperation in behaving actively.

After this first therapeutic action, which usually takes most of the first session, we carry out the first prescription. We tell the patient that we still are in an investigation phase and that the prescription must be considered as a survey technique useful to reach a better understanding of his actual condition.

The first prescription has been presented as follows: "every time you get into a crisis, or you have a panic attack, or your anxiety grows, even if it happens one hundred times a day, you will take this 'journal' I am giving you now, and you will note in it everything that happens to you. You must follow my instructions and you must fill out each part. The next session, you will give me the pages related to the past week and I will study them."

The journal is a notebook given to the patient with the first prescription. In each page, there are ten columns to write the date, place, situation, thoughts, symptoms, etc. The compilation requires more or less five minutes each time, and it is very boring.

In all cases here presented, the effect of the prescription has been more or less the same; during the second session, the patient starts the conversation by saying: (a) "Excuse me, doctor, I did not fulfill your prescription. It might look strange, but the past week, I did not have any crises"; or (b) "Doctor, I surprisingly felt better; I had some difficult moments, but they were not so serious as to be noted in the journal"; or (c) "Doctor, I have fulfilled your prescription and while I was writing down my feelings in the journal, my anxiety and fear disappeared without apparent reason."

What has happened? How is it possible that such change could happen? The strict system of perceptions of reality which forced the patient to give certain dysfunctional responses, has been broken. The enchantment has been broken. The best explanation of this phenomenon has been given by Watzlawick[2] who asserts that the power of this kind of prescription is forcing the patient to behave differently and to forget the attempted solution to his problems–for instance, by trying not to think of what we feel, or to look for somebody else's help. Having to note in the journal events and ideas makes the patient react to fear in a completely different manner.

Usually, these prescriptions are embarrassing and it is also embarrassing to give the journal back to the therapist. Thus, the phobic patient escapes from such embarrassment and, in so doing, he skips his usual response. In other words, embarrassment takes the place of fear and blocks it. So, once again, we use the power of the symptom in order to destroy it.

In the second session, after the patient reports on what has happened during the week, the therapist continues with the *reframing*. Thus, we tell the patient: "The problem was not as big as it looked in the beginning. In fact, just a simple prescription has modified your condition. Your 'physical disorders' are not unbeatable and unavoidable: you have proved you can change in the past week."

During the second session it is useful to insist on this reframing of the problem. By doing so, we obtain the breaking of the dysfunctional response system and, at the same time, we can reinforce the patient's self-confidence. In other words, we actively work to change the patient's point of view, shifting it from a restricted to a more functional perspective. To this point in therapy, we have followed two different pathways, according to the kind of results obtained during the previous sessions. If the patient's response to therapy has been positive then, at the end of the second session we can shift to the second phase of the procedure. Otherwise, we give the patient the same prescription again, proceeding with another framing in the third session.

Second Stage: From the Third to the Fifth Session

At the end of the second or third session we give all the patients a new behavioral prescription, paradoxical in nature, such as "be spontaneous." The typical paradoxical prescription we give is framed as follows: "During the past weeks you have been very capable in fighting against your problem. Thus, I want to assign a task which may appear even more strange and absurd, but you must carry it out. Find a very noisy alarm clock. Every day, at the same time we will decide on later, I want you to wind up and set the alarm clock so that is will ring one half hour later. During this half hour, I want you to sit in an armchair and try to feel bad. Concentrate on the worst fantasies you can think of concerning your psychological problem. You should think of the worst fears you can, up to the point of voluntarily provoking an anxiety or panic attack. When the alarm clock rings you will interrupt the exercise forgetting the thoughts and sensations you created. Then go on with your usual daily activities."

Such a paradoxical prescription usually leads to one of two kinds of response. (a) The patient reports something like: "Doctor, I did not succeed in carrying out your prescription. I made an effort to do it–everything seemed so funny that I would even start laughing!" In relation to the second kind of responses, (b) the patient said: "Doctor, I carried out the prescription so well that I felt the same sensations I had before starting the therapy. I suffered very much, then the alarm went off and it was all over!"

In both cases, it is important to notice that most of the patients, aside from the prescription time, have not had any crises; only a few of them had some occasional anxiety crisis, which was easily manageable.

In the subsequent session, after the patient's report on the effects of the prescription, we reframe the situation again. In relation to the first kind of responses, we have adapted the following reframing: "As you could observe, your problem can be eliminated intentionally. It is certainly a form of paradox, but, as you know, sometimes the human mind works more by paradoxes than by logical inferences. You are learning not to fall back in the trap of your problem and related attempted solutions which make your problem more complex instead of solving it. This was the topic of the session. With the second kind of response, the reframing was: "Very well, you are learning to handle and control your disorder. You're able to provoke the symptoms intentionally as well as to reduce and to eliminate them–this was the topic for the whole session.

In both cases, the reframing focuses on reinforcement of the patient's awareness and confidence in the change, and in the complete solution of the problem. The patient has indisputable proofs of the effectiveness of the work he is doing with the therapist which leads to exceptional cooperation and readiness for further progressive change in his perception of reality.

We have been very careful to place responsibility for changes with the patient. The therapist uses particular techniques to bring to the surface capacities the person has but does not know how to use. This observation gives great incentive to a person who considers himself a good-for-nothing and this firmly held belief has been confirmed by the behavior of people around him. Therefore, our attention focuses on the patient's self-confidence and self-esteem.

After only a few weeks of therapy, the situation has changed drastically in the cases considered in this paper: Symptoms disappeared. Nevertheless, it cannot be stated that the patient gets rid of the problem. It is extremely important to reduce the patient's euphoria, in this phase, making the person aware of the danger of the symptom disappearing too quickly.[3] The necessity for going slow is emphasized. In fact, if we go too fast, it is easy to fall back into the problem. At this point, it is important during this phase to strengthen the progress made thus far.

Third Stage: From the Fifth Session On

At this point in the therapy, we have programmed direct prescriptions of behavior following a progressive scale of anxieties to which the patient would be exposed. We follow the same procedure used in "systematic desensitization," but in our case, for every direct behavioral prescription, a *suggestion* is added. The suggestion inevitably leads the person to fulfill the anxiogenous task. For example, a 33-year-old woman, at this point of the therapy, chose as her first exercise of anxiety, to drive her car. She was asked to describe in detail a panic attack she had while in her car. The woman said that sometimes before, while driving on a country road, she had such a terrible panic attack that she was forced to stop and ask for help. A driver helped her and took her to the nearest hospital. After this episode, she was unable to drive anywhere but in town.

I prescribed her the following: "Well, I believe that if you follow my instruction, after what you were able to accomplish in the past weeks, you will be able to overcome this first test. But, as usual, do exactly what I ask you to do. Tomorrow, after lunch, go to the garage, start your car, and drive on the same road you were on when you had your panic attack. Instead of driving in the same direction, do it vice-versa (first suggestion). You know that more or less half way on the road, there is a detour leading to a store where farm products are sold. I love apples, therefore, you will take that direction and you will go and buy me the biggest and ripest one you can find in the store then take the apple straight to my office. I will be busy and you have no appointment, therefore, you will knock at my door, give me the apple, and I will see you at our next meeting" (second suggestion).

The next day, the woman knocked at my door; she was happy and she handed me a huge apple. The following week, when we met, she told me enthusiastically that every afternoon of the past week, she had driven around, always venturing farther away without fear.

We must point out that we gave the patient an anxiogenous task fitted between two suggestions: the first one concerned the task itself, the second referred to an independent task whose execution depended on that of the first one. By so doing, the attention of the patient focused on the second task instead of on the first (the real anxiogenous one). The patient realizes she has overcome her fear.

She understood the trick, but she also proved herself to be able to overcome her own fears. Traditional behavioristic desensitization very often does not work because the patient refuses to execute the direct behavioral prescription. Suggestions we have used are analogous to those presented by Milton Erickson. Contrary to behavioristic desensitization, we use a "beneficial trick" (the abovementioned suggestions) which is the only means used to have patients follow the prescriptions. Within the third stage, the therapist presents to the patient a direct behavioral prescription related to those anxiogenous problems on which therapeutic attention has been focused.

After the patient has followed each prescription provided, as was done in the first stages of the therapy, we then work on reframing the ability of the patient to overcome those situations that had previously provoked a psychological crisis. Usually we reached a point in which it is the patient himself who declares he is able to face any situation without problems which was anxiogenous before. At this point, we can move to the last stage of the treatment.

Fourth Stage: The Last Session

The goal of the last session involves strengthening the personal autonomy of the patient. To reach such a goal, we have formulated a summary and an explanation of the therapeutic process applied, and of the strategies which have been used. We offer to the patient the tools useful to grasp the meaning of all the techniques used during the sessions of the therapy (paradoxical prescriptions, suggestions, indirect orders, etc.). We believe that the personal autonomy of the patient can be strengthened only when he is really aware that his mind and behavior have been changed thanks to a specific and systematic intervention, and not as result of the practice of magic.

Furthermore, it is very important that the patient is aware that during the therapy we have used some of his natural characteristics which he did not know he possessed before the therapy and that he is now able to use. Nothing has been added other than what the patient already possesses. The patient, thanks to the experiences guided by the therapist and using his personal characteristics, has learned a different way to perceive and to react to reality. He is now able to behave more autonomously.

CONCLUSION

We believe that the therapeutic model and results presented clearly show that it is possible to treat briefly and successfully those psychological problems which, in order to be solved using traditional techniques, usually require long-term treatment. It has been our experience that traditional behavioristic techniques definitely do not solve phobic disorders. The most important characteristics of our model are the following: (a) *heuristic effectiveness*; (b) *the repeatability and efficiency of its techniques*; (c) *its competitive capacity for achieving good results in a short period of time*. These characteristics support the empirical efficiency of our psychotherapeutic model. Nevertheless, the reader who believes in traditional conceptions, could try to escape the pragmatic consequences of our model. He could follow L. Salzman (1968) who argues: the disorders we have referred to are not *real* phobic disorders, if for no other reason than they have been treated using a small number of therapeutic sessions. According to this point of view, phobic disorders cannot be treated in a short period of time. It is clear that Salzman's argument does not have a logical consistency. We cannot deny the empirical results we have obtained in brief treatment of phobic disorders. A theory must be supported by empirical evidence; and in the case in which empirical evidence contradicts a theory, we should not deny such evidence. We should change the theory in order to make it compatible with empirical data, not the other way around.

Following Salzman's point of view, it is better to maintain a theory than treat the patient and make progress in scientific research. We think to consider psychotherapy a scientific discipline, the approach must be very different. The effectiveness of a psychotherapeutic model does not consist in its theoretical structure; but in its heuristic and predictive utility, and its effectiveness for achieving the goal that we like to pursue (i.e., the solution of specific psychological disorders). Our clinical work has followed this epistemological approach.

NOTES

1. See (2) of the preliminary results.
2. Personal communication, June 1988, Palo Alto, CA.
3. "Go-slowly" technique in *Brief Therapy*, see Watzlawick, Weakland, and Fisch, 1974.

Chapter 7

Implementing Brief Strategic Therapy Within a Psychiatric Residential/Daytreatment Center

Terry Soo-Hoo

In this technological age, few would dispute that scientific knowledge has been advancing at a remarkable rate. Yet how institutionalized theories and concepts evolve and transform is rarely clear. This is especially true in the field of psychology. It seems that once a psychotherapy theoretical orientation has been implanted in an organization it is extremely difficult to alter it or add a new innovative method in conjunction to it. It is particularly difficult if the proposed new theoretical orientation is based on vastly different premises and assumptions than mainstream psychotherapy such as Brief Strategic Therapy (Watzlawick, Weakland, and Fisch, 1974; Fisch, Weakland, Segal, 1982). Brief Strategic Therapy as practiced at the Mental Research Institute (MRI) has been applied to many settings by numerous theorists and therapists oftentimes with some difficulty. However, despite much verbal discussion about the prevalence of such difficulties, the literature concerning how such an innovative method can be implemented in these diverse settings is quite sparse. This article is intended to contribute to the discussion of this important process. I will attempt to outline some of the difficulties I have faced in implementing a Brief Strategic Therapy approach to a particular community mental health setting and some basic principles that I have found to be of some significance in this process. The agency in discussion is a psychiatric residential/daytreatment facility. There are unique difficulties presented by the particular characteristics of residential and daytreatment settings which offer a formidable challenge above and beyond the more typical outpatient setting. In addition, since much of psychotherapy theory is based on individual or family therapy within an outpatient setting, adapting a theory (including Brief Strategic Therapy) to a residential/daytreatment setting requires some innovation. There are also a number of difficulties one faces in implementing a novel clinical approach in *any* agency. A brief discussion of these general issues should provide a foundation for the more specific issues related to the implementation of the Brief Strategic method to a residential/daytreatment center.

ORGANIZATIONAL STRUCTURES

When attempting to introduce elements of change in an organization, a brief organizational analysis is oftentimes very useful. In keeping with the general intent of brief family therapy that of getting to the heart of a problem and not delving too deeply into the structures and dynamics of a family system, the discussion will be kept brief. However, even in brief family therapy there are times when it is helpful to discover which family members have the greatest influence and which members are presenting substantial obstacles to change. In this vein there are three elements of an organization that may influence its receptivity to introduction of a new clinical approach. These are the *Power Structure, Social Structure,* and *Culture.*

Power Structure–refers to the hierarchy or chain of command in an organization and how decisions are made, who sets the policies and rules. There are certain advantages as well as disadvantages in introducing change at the highest level of the power structure versus the lowest level. For instance, if change is introduced at the line staff level other line staff may be more receptive because the ideas are from one of their own rather than some authority figure dictating new ideas down to the lower level staff. On the other hand, it is also possible that other staff members will resist new ideas even if it comes from their fellow colleagues because these ideas are not congruent with theirs. Furthermore, some line staff may even feel that fellow staff members should not hold special status or position and that only supervisors should introduce major changes. However, the greatest difficulty in introducing new ideas at the line staff level is the possibility that if the supervisors and directors of the agency do not support them, they will simply reject these ideas and block their implementation. Even if the administration does not overtly reject the new method, passive non-support can serve to hinder implementation. In general, administrative support is usually crucial for successful implementation of any new method, although support or even directives from the administration do not always translate into acceptance or even compliance from the larger staff. Just administrative support alone is insufficient to guarantee success.

Social Structure–refers to the social relationships within the organization, how staff members interact with each other. Group membership is one aspect of an organization's social structure. There are pressures to become a member of the group, to adapt the culture (or group norms) of the organization. Group membership is a factor that influences one's professional credibility within an organization. An organization also has a social hierarchy in which certain staff members have social and/or political power. To maximize the possibility of success, one should consider how introducing change will effect the social structure of the organization. For example, if there are staff members that hold special social power and command respect both personally as well as professionally, they may have as much or greater influence than the identified supervisors or administrators in deciding whether to adapt or reject any new ideas. The task then becomes not only to gain support from the administrators and supervisors but also staff members who have key positions of social or political influence. In some ways this can be analogous to family therapy in which the therapist forms a therapeutic alliance with family members who have the greatest influence in the family and thus, may assist in inducing therapeutic change.

Culture–is the third factor and it refers to the set of values, beliefs, assumptions, and goals that an organization or agency develops over the course of time. Particularly in human services organizations the culture often includes a stated or unstated "mission" or "mandate." These missions or mandates usually involve statements to the effect, for example, "To provide psychiatric treatment to those in need of such services, thereby reducing human suffering." The culture can also involve clearly stated overt values and beliefs such as "We believe in helping clients to become more independent and self-reliant." Or they can be unstated such as "But only if the clients obey the rules and follow staff instructions. If they do not obey, then the clients are not behaving in an acceptably independent manner." One might notice the potential paradox for there are times when a client's defiance of staff rules can be seen as healthy independent behavior. It is the unspoken values, assumptions, and beliefs that cause the greatest difficulties because they are rarely challenged, evaluated, or even discussed thus not opened to direct conscious revision. Oftentimes, a culture bearer of an agency will communicate either verbally or nonverbally that "This is the way that it is done and it has always been done this way and it will always be done this way!" Over a period of time, no one even remembers why it was originally done this way or that it ever had a reason at all. Theories of psychotherapy are frequently based on assumptions that are rarely tested or evaluated, yet they are revered as truths.

These general factors are present in all organizations, although how they are manifested may be unique to each agency. Beyond these organizational factors, there are characteristics of the residential and daytreatment settings that compound some of these problems and add even greater obstacles to implementing change. The agency I will discuss has many characteristics in common to other residential and daytreatment centers. It also has many unique qualities. The next section will describe some of these characteristics.

THE AGENCY

It should be noted that although I am no longer involved with the agency that is the focus of this chapter, I still have very fond memories of my six years there. This is true even after many personal and professional struggles to implement change in the agency. The agency has been a model of its type since its inception in the early 1970s and has provided excellent psychiatric services to perhaps thousands of clients who would otherwise have nowhere else to go for such treatment. Unfortunately, since the purpose of this chapter is to examine the process of implementing a new method to this agency, space does not permit the discussion of the particular strengths and positive qualities of the agency. It is possible that in the process of describing the difficulties in implementing the strategic method, the reader might interpret some of the discussions as critical of this agency. It is not my intention to criticize the agency as a whole, but only to point out how aspects of the agency made it difficult to implement the strategic approach. In fact, I have great respect for the high caliber of the staff and the equally high quality of services provided by the agency. However, even the finest agencies have room for improvement. Indeed, progressive improvements evolved over my six-year tenure there. Conceivably some of these improvements may have been the results of my efforts, others were probably due to various separate factors. At the point of my departure the agency was still going strong and still evolving with plenty of room for improvement.

The agency that I am referring to is the only agency that I am familiar with that has a combination of a 35-bed adult psychiatric residential program, as well as an 80-client capacity psychiatric daytreatment program within one agency. All residential clients attend the daytreatment program. The remaining clients who attend daytreatment live either independently, with families, or in some halfway house or cooperative living program designed specifically for psychiatric clients. These clients only attend from the hours of 10:00 a.m. to 3:30 p.m. In this type of residential/daytreatment program, the primary treatment approach is called Milieu Therapy or Therapeutic Community. The principle of this approach briefly rests on the assumption that psychiatric problems are a major factor with some dysfunctional interactions with others. Consequently, whatever the original cause of the psychiatric problem, the clients' difficulties relating to others are currently hampering their ability to lead productive and satisfying lives. It then follows that a great emphasis is placed upon the use of groups, both group psychotherapy as well as other less verbal and more activities oriented therapy groups. In addition, there is great emphasis on "client as helper" and resocialization as a process of relating and interacting with a community of one's peers. However, despite the fact that the members of the staff come from diverse backgrounds, the majority of the staff from the director down have been primarily trained in various psychodynamic or intrapsychic forms of psychotherapy. The intrapsychic approach frequently had an uneasy coexistence with the Therapeutic Community concept. The administration included the Director, Associate Director, and Residential Director. The staff was organized into three teams. Each team consisted of a multi-discipline staff with a clinical supervisor in charge of the team. Clients were assigned to each team somewhat analogous to having a homeroom in school. Thus, each team was primarily responsible for the treatment plan of their clients assigned to them. However, since the agency operated in a therapeutic community and clients were assigned to various therapy groups across teams, the whole staff was responsible for the entire client population in the agency.

OBSTACLES IN IMPLEMENTATION

Perhaps one of the most unique factors in such a residential/day-treatment setting is the issue of staff responsibility. Although clients were assigned to a particular team and to an individual staff member in that team, ultimately the entire staff had clinical responsibility for every client. This situation led to periodic difficulties in clinical agreement or consensus. In a staff with a wide range of professional backgrounds, it was not unusual to have as many diverse opinions concerning any clinical situation as there are staff members. In fact, one of the impressive aspects of this agency was the ability of the staff to formulate a coherent treatment plan for a client taking into account these diverse clinical opinions. One might hypothesize then that such diversity would allow for new theories such as Strategic Therapy. Unfortunately, this was not the case, especially in the early stages of introduction. In many instances the range of diverse opinions did not extend to anything as different as Strategic Therapy which ran counter to some of the staff's basic assumptions.

Also, as can be inferred, in such a communal setting there is much public scrutiny of one's clinical work. The majority of clinical interventions or staff actions are subject to review and comment by other staff members and the administration. Consequently, staff tended to be somewhat more cautious in implementing interventions that are more controversial, especially some strategic interventions that may seem odd or unusual in part due to their unfamiliarity. This public scrutiny is in marked contrast to a typical outpatient clinic in which an individual clinician may discreetly, in private, select and apply his or her therapy approach for a particular client.

Another factor that has complicated the implementation of Brief Strategic Therapy in this setting has been the conflict over the individual versus group approach. As referred to earlier, despite the stated position that the concept of therapeutic community (or milieu therapy) was the major clinical approach of the agency, many staff members were trained in individual psychodynamic and intrapsychic therapy. Therefore, these staff members advocated using individual intrapsychic methods in contrast to those who emphasized group therapy methods. The group therapy approach included not only traditional verbal group therapy, but also drama therapy, music therapy, dance therapy, activities therapy, art therapy, arts and crafts, exercise therapy, social skills therapy, and many other therapies that are group oriented as opposed to individually oriented. It is conceivable that both methods could be integrated together and in fact, both were done in various degrees depending upon the individual staff member. However, there was persistent pressure to officially delete the individual approach and apply a strictly group approach for theoretical as well as economic reasons. The strategic approach is based upon systems theory and as such, interventions can be made anywhere along the system whether in a group setting or with an individual. Regardless of this, there are still many strategic interventions that involve one-to-one individual communications with clients. This pressure to restrict all clinical activities to group contact added another obstacle to the strategic method.

The client population also contributed to the particular setting. Many of the clients might be called "noncustomers." Some clients were referred from the criminal justice system and were on probation. Others were referred from hospitals and psychiatric emergency centers because they had nowhere else to go for treatment even though some clients exhibited very little motivation for such treatment. Many of these clients had what was called "dual diagnoses." They had both substance abuse problems, as well as psychiatric problems. One of the greatest challenges facing community mental health centers has been how to deal with clients who for numerous reasons are not invested in therapeutic change, but continue to be in some distress or are behaving inappropriately in the community. Many of these people get placed in residential and daytreatment centers. A common pitfall is trying to pressure noncustomers to admit they have a problem when they are communicating they do not have a problem that they want to *actively work on*. A frequent phenomenon is the client who complains that he is in much distress and needs help desperately, but once he is admitted to the program, he refuses to get out of bed to attend his therapy groups. One might assume that the threat of discharge or similar consequences would encourage him to be a more willing participant. In fact, this usually only aroused further struggles, with the client complaining that he was not getting what he needed. Even if the client finally gets discharged, he usually returns to the community in the same state, perhaps to return periodically to the hospital or even the residential/daytreatment center. Complicating matters more were external pressures from the county to serve larger and larger client populations, regardless of whether these clients were invested in therapeutic change or not.

A large number of clients have had many years of professional psychiatric contacts and were considered chronic, long-term, and severely disturbed. Oftentimes, these clients were at best highly conflicted about wanting to face some of the horrendous traumas and experiences that led to their serous long-term illnesses. So it was no surprise that they tenaciously resisted attempts at traditional insight oriented therapy. Moreover, many of these clients were noncustomers because they had come to some uneasy adjustment to their illnesses (though they may still appear to be in some distress) and were reluctant to open old wounds and face their old fears after years of fruitless therapy attempts. It is understandable how these clients can be viewed as unresponsive to psychotherapy and therefore, should be maintained and stabilized at a minimum level of functioning by providing external structure and psychotropic medication. Furthermore, even if some of these clients were able to benefit from traditional psychotherapy it would take many years for psychotherapy to produce noticeable results. Nevertheless, despite the generally poor prognosis given to these clients, I have observed significant improvements in a number of them in response to a shift in clinical perspective. Yet, this shift in perspective was extremely difficult to achieve with both staff as well as clients, myself included, since I was also part of the system.

One last factor to consider was the issue of staff control. Another difference between an outpatient clinic and a residential/daytreatment center is the issue of limits setting. In an outpatient clinic, a client comes to see a therapist for 50 minutes to an hour and departs. Whereas in a daytreatment setting, the client is in contact with the therapist for most of the day and in a residential setting, most of the night as well. In many circumstances, these clients tend to replicate their own family systems within the treatment setting. It is quite common for the clients to relate to the staff as authority figures similar to their parents and play the role of acting out children in a dysfunctional family. Under such circumstances, the staff oftentimes get maneuvered into playing out the role of concerned parents who are highly focused on staff (parental) control or setting limits. However, the most commonly used methods for setting limits tend to replicate the way the clients' parents have attempted and are usually as ineffective. Since a residential/daytreatment center is a family system (even more so than an outpatient clinic), it is very difficult to realize a shift in perspective toward this problem. The tendency is to continue to apply the familiar traditional methods but with more vigor. Even though a strategic approach to this problem might be very effective, the concern about staff control and ability to maintain limits over inappropriate client behavior, inhibited consideration of such disparate ideas. These strategic ideas were frequently seen as relinquishing critical control despite the fact that such controls were largely ineffective or counter-productive.

OVERCOMING OBSTACLES

It is evident that a residential/daytreatment setting presents many difficulties and obstacles to the implementation of a Brief Strategic Therapy approach. There were times when I questioned the wisdom of taking on this type of challenge. However, after much effort and many mistakes, some noticeable progress was made in implementing certain strategic ideas and concepts. From this experience, it became apparent that certain approaches were more effective than others in introducing such a therapy method. The following is a discussion of certain basic principles that are of some importance in the introduction of the method to this agency and how these principles were able to overcome at least partially, many of the obstacles described previously.

Gaining Organizational Support–Needless to say, a positive working relationship with one's colleagues can be of great help in gaining acceptance of any new method. However, if that is not possible, an important principle in Strategic Therapy is not to struggle with those who present differing opinions and to avoid as much as possible an adversarial stance. It was fortunate that despite some disagreements, I did have positive working relationships with the administrators. I perceived that if change was to occur, it was optimum to work with them rather than against them. My first job was to understand how the agency worked. I entered the agency at the line staff level and after one year, was promoted to clinical supervisor of one team. As a line staff, I had the opportunity to learn about the structure of the agency from the ground up, and gain some understanding first-hand how line staff felt about the existing clinical methods and how they felt about altering these methods. My initial mistake was to naturally be open and receptive to innovative ideas from a new and unknown entity. This was especially naive since as a new staff member, I had not "paid my dues" nor even been acculturated to the agency. A further hindrance was the fact that even though I had some theoretical understanding of the strategic method from my courses at the University of California Berkeley (courses offered by a professor who unfortunately has since left), and at the Mental Research Institute (MRI), I had little practical experience applying the method. At the time I was receiving intensive training at MRI. As is common with people who are engrossed in a fascinating and exciting new type of therapy, I was overzealous and excessively confident in my presentation, which tended to arouse more resistance.

In the initial stages, I had the tacit support of most of the administrators, but not of the team supervisor. Tacit support usually meant verbal support, but often did not translate into endorsement of divergent treatment plans or clinical interventions that deviated too substantially from the norm. My first year as a line staff was fought with many skirmishes over these treatment plans. Soon I realized that for this method of therapy to be more accepted, I had to assume a lower profile. It also became clear that I had to become a part of the staff (a team player) before I would be allowed to be unique and different from them. Being part of a team is probably even more central to a residential/daytreatment center than to an outpatient clinic. The social structure of the organization made it very difficult for an outsider to have any credibility. The focus then was to develop social relationships with my fellow staff members and to learn to appreciate their perspectives on the clinical work. This was not strictly a ply to achieve an objective. In fact, work was much more pleasant and enjoyable once I joined with the staff and shared their common experiences, to commiserate with them about the frustrations and emotional stress inherent in this line of work. In this type of setting, mutual staff support was vital, especially since the possibility of serious crisis was ever present. The term being on "the front lines" was very applicable. In public, I toned down many of my own very divergent clinical views. Fortunately, there were opportunities to experiment with the strategic method, but usually in a somewhat discreet fashion.

My second year at the agency was a significant improvement over the first. Since I was promoted to clinical supervisor of my own team, I had a new role and position in the agency. My professional and clinical credibility in the agency had substantially improved not only due to my elevation in position of responsibility, but also as a result of paying some attention to social working relationships among fellow staff members. I was now one of them (a team player) and shared their perspectives and appreciated their points of view and the struggles they faced in handling difficult clients and situations. Thus, when I spoke it was with the authority of someone who clearly understood both the client's and staff's experiences as well as their positions. This does not imply that from this point on, the process of introducing the strategic method was then easy or simple. Rather, at least then I was no longer an outsider who was seen as introducing something quite alien as previously thought. The fact that some of the staff had heard of, or had passing acquaintance with the method (i.e., read articles and books about Brief Strategic Therapy) seemed not to be a deciding factor in staff receptivity. As clinical supervisor of a separate team, it was now possible to provide more extensive training (although up to a point) to the four staff members and two interns on my team. Discussions about alternative methods could be carried out in a more comfortable setting of team staff meetings without having to justify suggestions for clinical intervention to the entire staff until after the fact. In addition, I was becoming more experienced with the strategic method itself as well as how to introduce it to the staff. After some years experimenting with the strategic method at the agency, many clinical issues began to coalesce into a more organized theory of how the method can be effective in this setting. As a result I was better able to consult and supervise other staff in a wider range of clinical situations.

Another factor related to organizational structure involved staff turnover. Over the course of six years, a number of staff members left the agency, primarily for higher level positions in other settings, and were replaced by new, usually less experienced therapists. These new therapists obviously had not been indoctrinated into the social structure or the culture of the organization as yet and therefore were less biased toward a certain view of therapy in a residential/daytreatment setting. Some of the new therapists were more experienced and naturally tended to have more set opinions about therapy. However, as a whole, the majority of the new therapists were in the early phases of their careers and exhibited greater willingness to consider new alternative therapeutic approaches. Subsequently, over a period of time a number of new and more open and receptive therapists joined the staff and contributed to the gradual shift in the social structure and culture of the organization. This does not imply that the shift was all in the direction of greater acceptance of the strategic method, only that the staff was at least more open to considering new clinical approaches in addition to contributing their own approaches.

Gradual Introduction–Institutions generally resist change. Like family systems, institutions (e.g., mental health agencies) tend to have their own homeostatic mechanisms to maintain the system at equilibrium or sustain the status quo. To accomplish this, institutions apply direct and/or indirect pressure on the deviant person to conform to the culture and social structure of the organization. The more deviant the ideas and behaviors, the greater the pressure to conform to the norms. If change is to occur, it is most likely to occur slowly. Pushing for rapid change may lead to two possible outcomes in most institutions. One possible outcome is the arousal of massive resistance with the ultimate threat of ostracism or rejection from the organization for the one pushing. The other possibility is that even if one gains some success in changing the institution rapidly it is likely to generate significant organizational disruption, the more dramatic and profound the change, the greater the possibility of disruption. In a community mental health center the disruption of quality psychiatric services to clients who are in some need can have human costs. Although this may not always be the case, I have seen this pattern sufficiently to be concerned. To avoid these and other undesirable possibilities a more gradual introduction of new ideas to an organization is preferable. Certainly my first year at the residential/daytreatment center confirms this. After a number of months of energetic attempts to convey to everyone how "wonderful" the Brief Strategic method was in handling many of their most difficult cases, it became apparent that the agency was reluctant to accept an unconventional approach from an untested stranger. Unfortunately, my high profile presentation contributed to the problem. It was only after I adapted a more gradual and less exuberant approach that the proposed changes occurred at a reasonable rate.

From my experience, it seems that the strategic method can be introduced as a broad and general theoretical perspective or as a way of thinking about human problems. As such, it can be applied in a number of ways and situations. The primary intent is to search for successful means of helping individuals change those behaviors that are not effective for them. Whatever piece of the theory one wishes to try out and apply at whatever level, should be supported. One can also convey that although the theory is broad and general, it is not all encompassing and is not intended to replace that which the agency already has in place. Rather, the theory and method can be seen as a supplementary alternative, in addition to what the staff is already practicing.

The initial endeavor to assist a fellow staff member in attempting a strategic intervention may take some careful studied effort. If a staff member presents a clinical situation of some difficulty, and it becomes evident that what has been tried has not worked, it is important not to offer a solution too quickly. In such a circumstance, it would be helpful to clarify what position the staff member is taking. Is he asking for help, or is he primarily complaining? Perhaps he is seeking emotional support for facing such a difficult case, but is not asking for suggestions. Only if it becomes clear that the staff member really is asking for some specific assistance with this case, should one proceed. At this point, the usual approach is to assess what has been tried that has worked as well as what has not worked. After this, the challenge is to find a significant step that the staff member is willing to take that would provide a shift in perspective for the staff member as well as the client. This could take the form of some reframing or some specific behavioral assignment. What seems most effective are suggestions that do not challenge directly someone's basic theoretical assumptions, but instead, subtly and perhaps indirectly shift his perception of the problem. For example, in situations where a client is acting inappropriately and violating agency rules like an acting-out teenager in a dysfunctional family, the usual methods of setting limits tend to generate a power struggle between staff and client. It was not suggested that all limits be abandoned in favor of a more paradoxical approach which would have challenged the staff's need for social control. On the contrary, it was suggested that limits need to continue, but the way it was presented may be shifted slightly. Instead of presenting limits as threats and punishments, or the application of social control, it could be presented as unfortunate consequences to behaviors the client himself chooses. In other words, the client is told that only he has control over his behavior, and the staff, in fact, is powerless to stop him from misbehaving. All the staff may do is either discharge him, or apply some other equally ineffective consequence. They need to do this because they are obliged to follow these rules and not because these rules are seen as effective in controlling his behavior. The client's behavior is defined as a conscious choice concerning self-control instead of a reaction to staff applied controls.

At times, it may be preferable not to attach a label to a clinical intervention. Instead, using the language of psychodynamic therapy can provide a common frame of reference. For instance, someone presented a problem concerning a client who was avoidant and resistant to talk about why he was reluctant to face his problems. It was proposed that instead of pressuring him to talk, why not suggest to the client that there were probably many reasons why he should not talk about such things and that he perhaps needed to protect himself from such consequences. The staff quickly labeled this "going with the resistance," a psychodynamic term. Once having labeled it such, the staff was free to apply it to their own work without thinking they were using a mysterious or controversial concept such as paradox.

Flexibility is an exceptionally beneficial and desirable quality to possess in this work. There were many circumstances that tended to hinder strategic interventions. The conflict between the individual versus the group approach was an ongoing struggle. From the strategic perspective, it was often preferable to address the clients individually. However, instead of struggling with other staff members over how often and when this contact should occur, it was possible to reduce the number of individual contacts (but not eliminate them completely) and focus more strategic interventions in group settings. This required some creativity and concerted effort, since very little has been written about applying the strategic approach to groups. Moreover, some may have the notion that treatment modalities such as psychodynamic therapy, group therapy, or drug therapy are incompatible with Brief Strategic Therapy in a residential/daytreatment center. This is based on rather rigid thinking which may not be practical in most community mental health agencies. Although the Brief Strategic Therapy presented at MRI advocates a certain theoretical purity, in practice the approach needs to be adjusted to each unique setting and circumstance. Drug treatment, in particular, on the surface may appear to be in conflict with strategic assumptions about the cause and maintenance of psychiatric problems. However, in practice, it was possible to integrate the two approaches with some adjustments on both parts. This is of some importance since drug treatment is a major part of most residential/daytreatment centers and would be difficult to eliminate completely.

Another important point is to accept small steps. When individual staff members practiced an intervention or some shift in conceptual thinking or perspective that was close to strategic thinking, it was important to validate and support such behavior. Even when these steps were small, they were signs of progress in the right direction. Although Brief Strategic Therapy is rather systematic, and the parts are interrelated, it does not mean that one could not try out some piece of it even if you are working from a different model (e.g., intrapsychic model). At times, it is valuable just to get clear *what is the problem* from the client's point of view. Another substantial point was to acknowledge that it was feasible for staff members to focus on the intrapsychic process of discussing a client's internal feelings as well as discussing what small steps he was wiling to take to alter his ineffective behavior and how to promote that change. As the staff gained more success in these areas, they were then free to try on more parts of the method. Since public scrutiny was a fact to be considered, staff needed to be able to explain the rationale for their interventions. Small steps were easier for staff to explain and tended to reduce the chances of public disagreements.

Handling Resistance–One of the most difficult issues that arise in the introduction of a new method to any agency, is the issue of staff resistance. Beyond the previous discussions of social structure and culture, there are other strategic considerations. The greatest strategic principle when one encounters resistance is to restrain from pushing harder. It is advisable to disengage and reassess what is the nature of the difficult. What is underlying this person's reluctance to accept this idea? Are there other people involved in this? How is it being proposed? How can I propose it in a way that can be heard better? Resistance tended to be stiffest around interventions that were seen as high risk. For instance, depressed, suicidal clients (of which there were always a number attending the agency), presented extremely difficult clinical issues. These clients played out the "Yes, but . . . " game so effectively that they often thwarted the majority of conventional therapeutic interventions. However, when certain paradoxical interventions were suggested to circumvent this game, there was much resistance. In part, this was due to some suicidal clients' abilities to hold themselves hostage. The threat is if the therapist does "not do what I want of him, I will kill myself." This threat at times, served to immobilize even experienced therapists. It is understandable that a therapist would be more cautious in implementing interventions he is not totally familiar or comfortable with since a serious error could be catastrophic. The task then was to explore other less paradoxical and lower risk interventions, interventions that the staff would be more comfortable with. One such technique was to shift the focus away from the negative presentation of the client and instead focus on the client's strengths. More specifically the emphasis can be on how has the client survived the horrendous experiences he is describing. What has kept him going? There must be something inside of him inherently strong and capable to help him survive. One might notice that this shift in focus or reframing can also be considered somewhat paradoxical. Yet since it was presented as "pulling for one's strengths" and was low risk, most staff members gravitate to this intervention enthusiastically.

If the resistance is staunch further pushing could lead to confrontation. Confrontation is a very common approach in handling disagreements among staff members. It is possible that at times confrontation can produce results. But how does this approach produce results? One element of confrontation is intimidation or show of force which may hold many risks including the possibility of creating hostile responses. Another common procedure in confrontation usually involves pointing out all the negative aspects of the opponent's arguments, all the faults in his thinking and actions in contrast to the superiority of one's own arguments. The effect is that one person needs to back down. Backing down involves losing "face" and has particular significance if it occurs in public (such as a staff meeting). If no one backs down then, there is a struggle over who is going to back down. In other words, confrontation produces a winner and a loser. In such circumstances the loser is typically quite resentful. He may hold residual negative feelings from the struggle which may in turn hinder future cooperation. Of course, one might argue that this is not always the case, that confrontation if done correctly can lead to productive outcomes. Confrontation airs out diverse opinions and even if an agreement cannot be reached the parties can agree to disagree. This in fact has not been my experience. Usually when differences are aired out in a confrontative manner it leads to both sides taking an adversarial stance towards each other.

Often it is necessary to accept divergent views. Even if there is no direct confrontation one of the most common communications in a disagreement among staff members is the message that "I am right and you are wrong." This type of communications tends to stiffen resistance and leads to greater resolve to prove that you are wrong and he is right. Particularly in the field of psychotherapy there are few if any absolutes. There are many ways to approach a problem. Even if what someone is practicing is not overtly working, struggling with him to convince him he should change his approach is not likely to be effective. It is more likely to produce an adversarial stance which is generally unproductive. If a decision needs to be made and a consensus arrived at, it is preferable to negotiate a reasonable compromise with the possibility that more can be implemented at a later date.

Related to avoiding an adversarial stance is the concept of "face." Although the concept of "face" has been particularly attributed to various Asian cultures, in fact, it has its equivalent in most cultures. Some might find similarity with the concept of ego and how one behaves to protect one's ego or self-image. Face may have a larger social significance than the concept of ego, which is more internal. Even though "face" may have a more central role in Asian cultures, nonetheless, mental health professionals would do well to comprehend this concept and learn to apply it with some skill. Diplomats universally have devoted much attention to developing the skill of expressing their opinions without offending or violating one's sense of "face." Negotiation is possible only if this concept is taken into consideration. In essence, the skill involves the ability to present one's ideas in a manner that conveys respect and appreciation for others. One may ask if there is ever a time when it is advisable to take a strong stance and hold firm to your position. Certainly in psychotherapy there are situations when a therapist takes a firm position and chooses to convey this to the client. However, this is done with much forethought and careful consideration of the intent and consequences of such an action. This is no less true in working with one's colleagues in implementing a new method.

One should choose his/her battles carefully and continuously assess how successful this method is in achieving his/her goals.

RESULTS

After six years of effort it can be concluded that certain things were achieved. Since I was not the director of the agency, it was not possible to establish (as a general policy) Brief Strategic Therapy as an agencywide therapy approach. The alternative was to propose gradual shifts in perspectives and alternative interventions to various clinical situations. While it would be unrealistic to expect the staff to embrace the strategic method completely, most of them were in fact flexible enough to try some strategic interventions. Indeed, it was eminently satisfying to observe that a number of these interventions were quite effective in helping clients break out of many of their usual patterns of maladaptive behaviors. The greatest difficulty in this residential/daytreatment center was in handling client resistance and avoiding power struggles. Although this was to be an ongoing struggle up to the point I departed the agency, there was noticeable improvement in this area. Conceptualizing the agency as a family system in which staff played out the role of caring and controlling parents provided a useful perspective. However, a shift in perspective is not always complete, permanent, or readily transferable to their circumstances. At other times this was much more difficult. What makes this perceptual shift difficult is the fact that we are all bound by our own perceptual fields. Similar to the nine dot problem, we assume the solution rests only within the framework of the nine dots and do not consider that the solution is possible only if we see beyond the perceptual field of the dots themselves. In time with John Weakland's helpful consultation at MRI, it was more possible for me as well as other staff members to look beyond the perceptual field and generate new alternatives to those interventions that were ineffective. However, in a mental health agency like this, even if one solves a problem by achieving a shift in perspective, the structure of the institution applies pressure to return to the conventional viewpoint. Therefore, it is a never-ending struggle to sustain the fresh new perspective.

Handling noncustomers continued to be a problem but at least staff were willing to attempt new methods. One method was instead of pressuring the noncustomer to become a customer the staff would question *why* the client wanted to be in therapy since therapy was adding even more stress to his life. This approach got to the "bottom line" much more rapidly without a struggle and indirectly coaxed the client to discuss some of his fears without external pressure. It was more effective in assisting the client to understand how difficult treatment might be and subsequently to decide whether he should be in treatment. Becoming more problem focused was an easier task because many of the staff had some familiarity with various forms of behavior therapy and were already taking this approach. The Brief Strategic approach added a slight shift in focus and intent. It also expanded the traditional behavioral techniques by introducing the concept of how the underlying function of the problem behavior sustains the behavior. To successfully change the problem behavior one needs to circumvent its function.

Of all the concepts and techniques introduced, reframing was perhaps most positively received. This was due in part to the similarity at times to the technique of interpretation, although it has quite a different intent and purpose. Reframing also provided a highly useful tool to reach very difficult clients who were resistant, rebellious, and oppositional. It was also seen as a positive phenomena, to transform a client's negative presentation to a positive strength. The opposite direction was much more difficult, to reframe in the negative direction in order to stimulate change by eliciting paradoxical defiance in the client. The concept was not always easy to understand nor was the application readily mastered. Another factor that might have contributed to the popularity of reframing had to do with the disassociation from the concept of paradox. Even though reframing, in fact, can be very paradoxical most of the staff gravitated to reframing because they preferred to try some strategic interventions that were not paradoxical. If reframing had the greatest acceptance, then the concept of paradox elicited the greatest resistance. Frequently when paradoxical interventions were introduced it was greeted with great confusion and controversy. Admittedly, by definition paradoxical interventions are quite out of the ordinary (or orthodox) and require a major shift in perspective. This shift often challenges our primary assumptions about behavior and psychotherapy. It is understandable why the staff would be leery of the technique. I learned rather quickly that this was not to be pushed. Interestingly, as some of the previous examples highlight, if suggestions were presented as a reframing of a problem rather than a paradoxical intervention (even though the reframing was in fact paradoxical), it was much more likely to be favorably received.

There were other positive signs that the staff was beginning to be influenced by this method. These included staff implementing strategic interventions on their own and presenting them as natural courses of action that required no discussion. In fact, there were incidents in which some staff members presented strategic concepts as their own ideas not even thinking they were strategic ideas. These are signs of the method or at least aspects of the method becoming institutionalized or becoming part of the culture of the organization. It is only when a method becomes integrated into the culture of an organization separate from and independent of any individual is the method truly on the road to organizational acceptance.

In summary, clearly introducing Brief Strategic Therapy to this residential/daytreatment center was not easy. There have been a number of obstacles that hindered the implementation of this method. I have also made a number of errors especially in the initial stages of this process. These errors were quite enlightening and allowed me to modify my approach. Subsequently, this modified approach was more effective in engendering acceptance of the strategic method. Some of the major principles of this approach can be summarized by the following: (1) Gain organizational support: to do this one needs to consider the power structure, social structure, and culture of the organization; (2) Introduce change gradually: propose change in a flexible manner with small steps and a low profile stance; (3) Handle resistance in a strategic fashion: avoid pushing harder against resistance, avoid an adversarial stance, handle disagreements diplomatically, assess the nature and source of the resistance and generate alternative suggestions. Although it cannot be said that the agency was transformed to a Brief Strategic Therapy orientation, it is fair to say that the strategic method had significant influence on the staff and the agency as a whole. In discussing the implementation of the method I have also pointed out many challenging clinical problems facing a residential/daytreatment center and have suggested that there are strategic alternatives to how they can be approached. Since space does not permit a more detailed description of these alternative approaches, a more thorough discussion of this topic will be presented in another article.

Chapter 8

Outpatient Clinic Effectiveness with the MRI Brief Therapy Model

Hendon Chubb

Although the MRI's Brief Therapy model is well known, little has been written about its use in clinic practice (Chubb, Nauts, and Evans, 1984). This chapter contrasts statistics for the years 1985-1986 of Kaiser-Permanente's Pleasanton, California, psychiatric clinic, which adhered to a MRI Brief Therapy model, with other Kaiser-Permanente clinics that used psychodynamic-eclectic models. In 1983, the Northern California Region of the Kaiser-Permanente HMO, as part of a drive to reduce escalating outpatient psychiatric costs and improve service by unconventional approaches, opened a clinic at their new Pleasanton medical offices which was to base its approach on the MRI model. Headed by Eldon Evans, MD, a member of the MRI Brief Therapy Research Project, and staffed by two graduates of the MRI Brief Therapy Intensive, Phyllis Nauts, LCSW, and the author, it strictly adhered to the Brief Therapy approach except for sparing use of medications.

This chapter compares certain 1985-1986 statistics of the clinic to those of other Kaiser-Permanente Northern California psychiatric clinics, which generally followed a psychodynamic-eclectic model. The principal statistics on which it is based are detailed and summary computer reports by clinic of the number of patients seen classified by total number of sessions during the two-year period. As an example, the detailed report for Pleasanton showed that 1963 patients, or 48.0% of the total, were seen only one time while 27 patients, or 0.7% of the total were seen exactly nine times. The summary report showed that 89.9% of Pleasanton patients were seen for five or fewer sessions and 97.5% were seen for ten or fewer. By contrast, the equivalent figures for another and more typical clinic were 69.5% and 89.3%.

While these differences are striking, they fall to highlight the impact of longer-term therapy on clinic operation. A therapist can serve five four-session clients in the time it takes to see one 20-session client. At the comparison clinic, 29.7% of all therapist hours were spent on cases that had already run at least ten sessions. The equivalent figure for Pleasanton was 4.0%. Had the comparison clinic (which, it must be emphasized, was typical and not an extreme case) been able to achieve the Pleasanton pattern for its longer cases, it would have been able to free 25% of its therapist time for waiting list cases and ultimately handle the same case load with a quarter less staff. A detailed analysis of the figures has been offered elsewhere (Chubb and Evans, in press), but a few highlights may prove interesting. Pleasanton averaged 2.5 sessions per patient and 834 different cases per therapist over the two-year period. The equivalent figures for the clinic with the next most patients per therapist were 3.7 and 742. Regional means were 5.4 and 456; and of course about half the clinics did worse than this.

Therapist productivity in a setting with limited resources is best measured not by contact hours per week but by number of clients served. Therapist efficiency is in the interest of both the clinic and the clients; the latter want to be seen fast and, as Pekarik (1985) notes, not only desire but expect therapy to be brief.

There is no evidence the Pleasanton clinic's efficiency was achieved at the cost of quality. Several user surveys revealed client satisfaction was high. Since there was never a waiting list during the two-year period, complaints about accessibility, a severe problem at other facilities, were nonexistent. Immediate access is an element of high quality service as some problems can be nipped in the bud if dealt with quickly. Another indicator of service quality is flow between nominal catchment areas. Kaiser subscribers are encouraged but not required to go to the clinic nearest them. A flow away from a clinic could suggest problems, but as far as could be determined net flow is substantially inbound. Hospitalization rates may be an indicator if clinic clients rarely require hospitalization. Outpatient care was lowest in the region and two-thirds the average.

MRI Brief Therapy has been widely used but little-studied. Other than Weakland et al. (1974), which lacked control groups, the author knows of no outcome research. The Kaiser-Permanente data constitute a natural experiment. While lacking random assignment (although one geographically close clinic with an almost identical socioeconomic mix had figures at almost the opposite extreme) or true outcome measures, results strongly suggest the effectiveness of the model and the desirability of well-designed outcome research.

Chapter 9

MRI Brief Therapy Training: An Introduction to Cybernetic Thinking

Ray Storts

In 1982, Lynn Segal began a series of seminars and training experiences for Family and Children's Services in Tulsa, Oklahoma. The agency had explored the "structural model" during the previous year and was enthusiastic about continuing to explore systems paradigms that might lead to our increased effectiveness in our work with clients. At that time, systems models were not in wide use in our community and like many new ideas, MRI ideas received mixed reviews from the more conservative clinicians on our staff. The remainder of the staff embraced these ideas and Mr. Segal was asked to return no fewer than three times to train the staff. The facilities for "live supervision" were in place at the agency and were used in the training as well as video tapes and lectures.

The effects of this training experience on most of the staff were profound and extremely varied (too varied to detail here); however, a few should be mentioned. Gradually at first, then increasingly, staff discussions of case materials moved away from the concept of "pathology" including the implied pathological structures inherent in our previous model. Staff now found itself with a model that helped it decide what to pay attention to and what to ignore in planning interventions. Additionally, criteria for the successful outcome of a case were established early. In short, we began to enjoy the benefits of a focused, nonmedical, nonpathological, nonlinear model of therapy. We were provided with a map to follow.

At this point in the discussion, the *general* must be abandoned in favor of the *specific*. I am really not able to speak with any great authority on the experiences of the other members of the staff, so I will confine myself to a discussion of two areas of my own experience. These are the effects of MRI brief therapy training on (1) my practices with clients and, (2) my system of personal beliefs.

EFFECTS OF MRI TRAINING ON MY PROBLEM-SOLVING STYLE

Prior to my exposure to the ideas presented by Mr. Segal in 1982, I had no "conceptually tight" theory of problem formulation and problem resolution. I had done my undergraduate work in languages and psychology and had received my MSW in 1979. Most of the theory I had learned was descriptive and personality oriented rather than predictive and behaviorally oriented. I had inherited more than my share of psychodynamic and ego psychological concepts from the culture at large, my schooling, and from work experience in a mental health center. It is difficult now to recall even the "conceptually loose" framework I may have had related to problem formulation and resolution, so all that follows is representative of the learnings and changes in my problem-solving style as a result of MRI training.

MRI training requires several distinctions be made early in the conduct of treatment. One of the first is to determine the nature of the concern the client brings in and whether or not it is an appropriate concern for the psychotherapist's consulting room. Many people seek the counsel of a therapist who are in need of assistance of other professions such as law or medicine. These people should be referred to the appropriate professional. Additionally, those who believe the solution to their problem for which they seek help lies in the practice of another profession should be referred. This spares the counselor and client needless frustration and expense.

Another early distinction to be made is the decision as to whether the complaint is a "problem to be endured and lived with" or a "problem that can be solved." Those, for example, who complain that getting old is depressing cannot really expect a counselor to provide a solution to aging. Understanding and discussing this early in treatment helps both the therapist and client avoid entering into contracts to solve unsolvable problems. Those who opt to work toward minimizing feelings of depression about aging or toward enjoying their "golden years" may be candidates for continued sessions, ready to consider the depressing possibilities of *not* getting older.

It can be seen that the "conceptual tightness" built into this way of thinking provides a map for avoiding pitfalls in treatment from the very beginning. After the initial distinctions are drawn and, providing the client's issue of concern fits with what a counselor can help with, a clear, behavioral definition of the problem is solicited. This is done to establish a clear and limited definition of the problem. Often complaints are a combination of poorly-defined concerns and, when this is the case, it is important to move slowly and work toward defining which concern the client wishes to address first. A clear definition of the problem allows the counselor and the client to arrive at criteria for the successful outcome of treatment. This enables both to imagine the client's situation once the problem is solved.

Once the problem is defined, both in terms of its presence and its absence, the client's beliefs surrounding the problem are explored. A brief exploration of the historical context is solicited and the client is asked to speculate about the problem's origins and describe its effects. The client is prompted to describe what he expected treatment would be like and asked about any previous experiences in treatment. This is done to learn the client's theory about the cause of the problem and his theory about the possible form solutions might take if treatment is successful. Many people come into treatment with clear expectations as to how things should go and are disappointed if the therapist does not seem interested in these expectations and makes no attempt to take them into account.

Once the client's theories related to the problem are known and his expectations for treatment explored, attempted solutions must be explored. Questions that invite the client to relate his previous problem-solving attempts are asked. Often the client has engaged in several activities in an attempt to resolve the troublesome issue. Close examination of these attempts usually reveals that they fall into the same class of attempted solutions, and are based on the client's theory of the cause of the problem. For example, a parent who presents a concern about his child and who believes the child is misbehaving will have tried activities that fall under the rubric of punishment. If the parent's belief is that the child is psychologically troubled, the attempted solutions will be to get the child to "open up" and reveal his "true feelings or inner conflicts." In either case, the parent will have attempted solutions that conform to his theory of cause. It is useful at this point to decide who is the most troubled by the problem and therefore the most likely to be willing to make a change to solve it. This "most impacted" person can be described as the *customer*. Interventions are directed to the customer since he is the most likely to make use of suggestions.

The strategy for designing interventions that MRI brought to our agency are as "conceptually tight" as the preceding stages in therapy, and are based on a very simple idea which could be stated as, "If what you are doing to solve your problem isn't working, try something radically different." The solution the therapist suggests should be as nearly as possible 180 degrees away from the client's original attempted solutions. This would seem at first glance a very difficult operation to accomplish, since the client's attempted solutions are immanently logical to him, and in fact, were the best he could come up with based on his universe of possibilities. How to accomplish this was one of the "grand revelations" of the MRI method.

The form of the intervention has already been determined in that it will deviate from the client's attempted solutions by 180 degrees. The manner in which it is presented must carry within it the probability that the client will not only hear the suggested change in direction, but employ it. To accomplish this, we were taught to listen closely for the logic, language, and beliefs on which the client based his attempted solutions and to employ the same logic, language, and beliefs in suggesting a radically different solution. The rationale for the change in direction needed to be as isomorphic as possible with the client's original rationale. The idea of calling forth radically different solutions from identical or nearly identical rationales was a new idea for most of us in 1982, and those of us who learned to do this were delighted with the results.

The Agency has continued to bring in trainers with new ideas, and continued to grow and evolve in its thinking, but it is my belief that our experience with MRI training constituted a turning point and a direction in which to move. The ideas we were introduced to are now implicit in the Agency's thinking and are still regularly used, sometimes in their original form, sometimes in modified ways. We gained a point of comparison by which to evaluate other systems of thought dealing with problem formulation and resolution.

EFFECTS OF MRI TRAINING ON MY PERSONAL BELIEFS

At the time of Mr. Segal's initial visit to Tulsa in 1982, I had very little training in, or understanding of, systems thinking. The little I had in my social work training seemed primarily descriptive and seemed to me to be of little value as a guide to treatment. My agency had brought in a trainer several times in 1981 to promote our learning Structural Therapy and I had begun to understand those concepts. I had read Salvador Minuchin's work but certainly was not feeling in possession of a clear model for doing therapy. I was, after my first year, working as a therapist, unsure that therapy could ever be taught, at least in the way that mathematics could, and that it was perhaps a vague art that could be learned well only as a result of years of supervised practice. My first experience with MRI training left me rethinking this conclusion.

The immediately attractive aspect of this method of therapy was the clarity with which its concepts could be communicated. We were directed toward gathering specific kinds of information from clients, offered a way to sort through what we had gathered to decide what was important information and what part of it was merely incidental. The direction of the solution we were to suggest was already determined in that it would be 180 degrees away from the category of solutions already attempted by the client. The means whereby such an intervention might be rendered sensible enough to the client for him to use it were more difficult to grasp, but clear guidelines even existed for doing this. I came away from this experience believing that a clear and learnable way of doing therapy existed and that I should set to work to learn it. The next step was to find written material to study before Mr. Segal returned. I bought a copy of *Pragmatics of Human Communication* (Watzlawick, Beavin, and Jackson, 1967) and began my introduction to nonlinear thinking. As a consequence of learning to think of problems as loops of behavior that operated in a self-sustaining way, I began to look for patterns in my own personal relationships and began to experiment with altering these and examining the effects. The method proved to be at least somewhat personally verifiable. Gradually I began to shift from a view that placed the problem within individuals to one that placed problems in interactional loops between people. My concept of "psychopathology" in the psychodynamic sense began to dissolve and become useless, not because I had decided "psychopathology" didn't exist (I still don't know whether it exists or not), but because the treatment model I had decided to verify and use was not based on such a concept. Communication in all its forms became the unit of analysis and the basis for understanding behavior.

Some time later, Lynn Segal's book, *The Tactics of Change* (Fisch, Weakland, and Segal, 1982), came out and was very helpful in clarifying concepts subsumed in the MRI method. Our agency has had many trainers visit since 1982, but I doubt any of the ideas they brought had as much impact on me and my understanding of people as did MRI ideas. This is because these ideas pointed in a direction, at that time a radically new direction to me, and I find myself still headed in that direction. I see MRI training as the event that created the *conditions of possibility* for me to head in this new direction, toward a cybernetic understanding of people, events, and history. The seeds of recursion as a means of understanding phenomena are embedded in MRI concepts and were first made known to me through the teaching of these concepts. Nearly everything useful I have learned since has been an elaboration of my original introduction in 1982 to the concepts of loops, circularity, and recursion.

It is difficult if not impossible to isolate, in all its particulars, the impact of MRI ideas on my personal beliefs because the influence of these ideas has been so pervasive. Seven years is a long stretch of time to recall in any detail (though I thought it would be easy when I started this chapter), so I may have entertained too difficult a project. Following is a list of some of the most useful ideas I have gained, all of which represent a substantial change or new awareness in my beliefs since 1982.

1. Complaints must be examined and a determination made as to whether they are problems to solve, or conditions to be lived with. If the complaint deals with a person's interactions with others or with his interaction with himself, it may be appropriate to examine further in therapy.
2. Many complaints are the result of continuing use of failed solutions which are intensified with each failure, causing the complaint to seem progressively more serious.
3. Language is of paramount importance in therapy, in that problems are all communicated in that medium and all discussions of solutions also take place in the form of language. Many, if not most, people relate to their verbal descriptions of problems as if the description were a totally accurate representation, complete in every way. The client's description is important in understanding his understanding of the problem, but it is usually also a very fragmented and limited picture of the problematic process troubling him. Language is a linear string of words timed together in a process governed by linguistic rules, and usually presents a linear view of the problem. By its form, communication almost implies cause and effect. This is an artifact of language and must be overcome by attempting to formulate circular process descriptions of the problem.
4. When circular descriptions of the problem can be mapped which are roughly isomorphic with the details of the client's description of the problem, it can be seen that the language that describes the theory of the "cause" of the problem can be used to describe the theory of the "solution" as well.
5. Many problems result from the paradoxical use of language as described in the book *Pragmatics of Human Communication.* Some understanding of the paradoxical use of language is helpful in resolving these kinds of problems. Sometimes another paradoxical use of language is needed to aid in resolving the problem.
6. People cannot attempt solutions they cannot think of and, if such a solution occurs spontaneously, it is difficult to repeat. People like to solve their own problems. Solutions that the therapist can imply in such a way that they later become the client's own idea are often more powerful than directives.

There are many more useful ideas for which I am indebted to MRI thinking–too many to list here. In the past few years, the agency has brought in thinkers like Karl Tomm and Michael White who have helped us add to our knowledge and skill as therapists. These, too, have been good experiences and, building on my MRI training, have led to new ideas. None of these ideas, however, have been as radically new to me as my first exposure to MRI thought in 1982.

Chapter 10

Strategic Intervention: Constructing the Process of Rapid Change

J. Scott Fraser

We ask a man who is highly suicidal, how it is, given his situation, that he has not killed himself yet; and we marvel over the strength it has taken just to be with us and tell his story. We ask another man to see if he can set up the conditions this week to bring on an anxiety attack so we can learn more about it; and we ask a woman to note the times that she resists the temptation to have a panic attack so as to see what she might be doing at those times. We talk with a woman who wants to leave her battering mate about all of the financial, emotional, and social reasons why she might reconsider and decide to stay. We allow that there might just be some reasons for caution and suspicion on the part of another woman who feels that her husband and coworkers are conspiring against her. Then we note that the way she is trying to protect herself might just play into the hands of anyone who might be out to get her.

These cases and many more like them were dealt with just last week in the Crises/Brief Therapy Center. Our stances in each instance grew out of an approach which we have come to call Strategic Rapid Intervention and Brief Therapy. In this approach, our goal is to use a time-limited window of opportunity to help people positively construct the process of rapid change. Throughout all of my work and that of my colleagues in this area, we owe a great debt to the seminal ideas of the Mental Research Institute in Palo Alto, California. It is my honor to be able to pay tribute to the overwhelming influence of MRI on my work on this, the thirtieth anniversary of its founding. This work flows from what I have termed a process-constructive model of social interaction, and proceeds toward the design of rapid and brief intervention at perceived crises points in the lives of our clients.

FOUNDATIONS

As a result of my links with MRI views over the past 17 years, I have come to see social interaction from what I have termed a process-constructive view (cf. Fraser, 1983; 1984a; 1984b; 1986b; Duncan, 1984). This view has evolved in my own work through early readings and clinical work using the MRI concepts (Watzlawick, Beavin, and Jackson, 1967; Watzlawick, Weakland, and Fisch, 1974; Fisch, Weakland, and Segal, 1982; among others), through explorations into the varying definitions of system theory (Ashby, 1956; Weiner, 1948; Bateson, 1972; Buckley, 1967; Maruyama, 1963; von Bertalanffy, 1973), through my early training in constructive alternativism (Kelly, 1955), and, more recently, my contact with constructivism (Segal, 1986; von Foerster, 1984; von Glasersfeld, 1984; Watzlawick, 1976; 1984), through my work on integration and differentiation among family therapy approaches (Fraser, 1982; 1984b; 1986b), through my contact and interest in crises intervention and crises theory (Fraser, 1986a; 1988; 1989; Fraser and Froelich, 1979; Fraser and Spicka, 1981), and through my interest in rapid and discontinuous views on change (Glick, 1987; Gould, 1982; Platt, 1970; Thom, 1975).

My current belief is that, through an evolving process of probable chance and clear thinking, the MRI views represent enough of a distinctly different systems model to be considered an alternate paradigm. I have chosen the term process-constructive to refer to this model simply because I feel that it reflects the combined elements which I see as its basis. These elements are what, following Buckley (1967), I have termed a process model of social systems, combined with the constructivist view of Watzlawick (1984), von Foerster (Segal, 1986; von Foerster, 1984), and others. For me, this model has led me toward a clinical, teaching, and supervisory practice which emphasizes practical integration, flexibility, and creativity in intervention, brief therapy through the life cycle, and a strategic rapid intervention approach.

STABILITY, RANDOMNESS, AND DISCONTINUOUS CHANGE

Simply speaking, the process-constructive model, as I have viewed it, describes social systems as fundamentally open, evolving flow patterns of interaction which thrive on variation and change. As such, these process systems allow much more randomness into the ongoing flow of interaction than anyone would probably care to acknowledge within one's own life. Variation comes both from life cycle changes like childbirth, and incidental changes like car accidents. Through constructive interaction, people attempt to create or find predictable stabilities in an ever-changing world of interaction. Interestingly, our unique and shared concepts on "the way things are" tend to shape things in that direction simply by our engaging with things "as if" they were that way. Against this backdrop of conceived and experienced predictable stability enters inevitable incidental and developmental changes. Consequent action to absorb or adjust to these shifts tends to accelerate change in any case. Curiously, struggles which may look like attempts to regain perceived stability, may actually exacerbate and accelerate change in what often become vicious positive feedback cycles of problem engendering solutions. This description is, of course, greatly oversimplified for purposes of space and ease of discussion.

Given this view of social interaction and problem generation, our tasks as therapists are several. They include noting peoples' definition of a problem, identify those engaged in defining this as a problem and attempting some solution, and identify repeating, escalating processes around its attempted resolution. Through this and subsequent process, our goal is to engage with them to help co-create some dissonance, or alteration in concept and/or action. This is generally achieved by altering premises or constructs; accepting these premises or beliefs and building new action based upon them; or prescribing current action for new reasons. In this format, our goals are to prevent further escalation, and to bump patterns out of vicious cycles and into the initiation of a new process. Most often this is done without disruption (and often by enlisting) the majority of peoples' preexisting constellation of values, motives, constructs, and normal patterns of behavior. The goal is not only to interdict or redirect vicious problem cycles, but to aid people in initiating new and hopefully "virtuous" cycles of their own doing, and to their own credit, and to then quickly step aside. They can always touch base with us again for consultation as needed.

PRACTICALITIES

This view of process-constructing systems moving through varying transitions and perceived crises has evolved through my ongoing engagement with MRI constructs combined with the practical process of directing a large crisis/brief therapy center over the last 13 years. In practical application, what I have chosen to do is to be available to intervene as immediately and intensively as possible at points of identified problems, transitions, or crises. Our work accepts, respects, and utilizes the strengths, ideas, and traditions of those we encounter, and attempts to enlist these in service of change. We attempt to initiate some small shift in concept or pattern around a vicious problem cycle so that those engaged in it move beyond it. The model allows us to deal with solution generated problems, and problem generated systems. By this we mean that our focus is on those engaged in defining and resolving a problem and the pattern of their beliefs and interactions, rather than operating from purely predefined diagnosis, normative expectations, or with normative groups like couples or nuclear families, etc. Through this process, we attempt to remain as consistent as possible with the process-constructive view, and its goal of simply introducing variation around "stuck patterns" and helping those involved to evolve new options. Beyond this consistency, however, we attempt to remain as open as possible to a wide variety of approaches to treatment and problems, and to the acceptance of an exceedingly broad variety of lifestyles and views as being relatively adaptive.

STRATEGIC RAPID INTERVENTION

At the heart of the Strategic Rapid Intervention process (Fraser, 1986a; 1988; 1989) is the idea of understanding and using the common and unique beliefs and interactions around incidental and developmental life shifts in the service of aiding people in moving their life along. As opposed to traditional crisis theory (Caplan, 1964), we do not see our goal as one of restabilizing or moving things back to their pre-crises state. Instead, we see these points as dangerous opportunities wherein things can get worse, yet the goal is to allow people to move beyond their pre-crises patterns. In fact, many of these pre-crises beliefs and interactions may have been the direct contributors of the current escalating difficulty. Perceived crises are seen as prime points for most intervention in that they represent periodic, time-limited windows of opportunity for discontinuous and more rapid change in peoples' lives. Motivation is higher for people to consider outside input due to perceived distress, and growing realizations that usual beliefs and actions are appearing less useful. If people can avoid the process of labeling themselves or others at this time as either "bad or mad" and instead, alter their beliefs or actions to move through this period, not only can considerable future distress be prevented, but also more options for new and possibly more satisfying paths can open.

DEVELOPMENTAL AND INCIDENTAL CHANGES

Thus a Strategic Rapid Intervention approach responds to developmental and incidental life crises or shifts as time-limited windows of opportunity. (It should be noted that other identified problem points are not excluded. They are dealt with in a similar rapid and brief way.) Developmental shifts are generally referred to as life cycle shifts, common to most people in a given culture or subculture. These are shifts such as dating, courtship, marriage, or birth of children, transitions of children to school, adolescence, leaving home, etc., to note just one life cycle domain. Each transition involves learning and testing new roles, beliefs, and patterns and adjusting from previous ones for all involved. In each instance, assimilation or accommodation of these variations may be achieved easily, or those involved may find themselves engaged in vicious cycles of escalating solution generated problems.

Incidental shifts like a rape, break-in, severe illness, premature death of a loved one, job loss, etc., call for a similar process of absorbing or adjusting to these disruptions. This process can mark a time of great change seen as positive by all, or as a time of escalating distress, resulting in responses of confusion, agitation, violence, anxiety, depression, and suicidal thoughts, to name but a few. The nature of the process around the change makes all the difference. Rarely does a seemingly disastrous instance in itself produce disastrous results. Furthermore, even the most malevolent appearing actions and ideas often flow from the best of motives. Our job is to enlist or slightly alter these patterns toward more fruitful paths.

GENERIC AND SPECIFIC RESPONSES

The second and intimately related set of constructs in our approach is the idea of generic and specific response patterns. Whereas the process model suggests that there are no inherently stable patterns invariant across social interactions, the constructive view suggests that commonly shared cultural or subcultural ideas when acted upon in an ongoing process, will tend to co-create that reality. When these common constructs are acted upon in the mists of a developmental or incidental life crises, there tend to emerge typical response patterns. Similarly, there are unique constructs and patterns which have evolved in each separate set of social relationships. These specific patterns may generate their own unique problem cycles around adjusting to crises points or they will add their own unique variation to a generic response cycle.

Generic response patterns may be considered in terms of commonly observed reactions in a number of spheres. For example, they may be patterns around typical cultural or subcultural role prescriptions or "myths" regarding gender or family relationships, such as the ideas that "men don't cry," or that "children should be seen and not heard," and so on. Another sphere is in terms of typical responses to specific problems or emotions, such as both naive and therapeutic attempts to "cheer up" someone showing depression, or urging to "be strong," and that "there is a brighter tomorrow" for the grieving widow, or typical attempts to master anxiety attacks by avoiding anxiety provoking situations, and so on. A third, and related sphere is in terms of typically observed response patterns around various life changes as noted through clinical research, such as the classical patterns referred to as phases of post traumatic stress, typical phases of grief resolution, phases of dealing with one's impending death, or typical phases revolving around developmental phases of children like the "terrible twos," or "adolescent rebellion or identity crises" patterns, and so on. A knowledge of each of these spheres and others can help an intervenor more quickly identify, predict, normalize, interdict, or redirect these patterns as they begin to evolve in problem cycles.

Some simple examples of the use of these generic patterns might be cast under the intervention options of normalizing, predicting, prescribing, and positioning, among others. Generic patterns around developmental life cycle shifts are tremendously useful in normalizing these transitions with parents. Quite often such transitions turn into problem cycles when a parent, for instance, interprets a child's fear and tears at the first day of school as evidence of "badness or madness," and attempts to fix something, rather than accepting the response as a normal variation which most children move through. Similarly, normalizing startle responses and a wish to withdraw as common early phases of a posttraumatic cycle of resolution, allows people to accept these actions as expected aspects of adaptation, rather than indications of pathology to be fixed. Furthermore, a prediction of probable phases to follow, not only inoculates against similar pathological labeling of these future reactions, but often reduces or eliminates the impact of these phases in a "forewarned is forearmed" phenomenon. Prescription in combination with normalization is frequently useful in reversing typical problem cycles around a number of common crises. In acute grief reactions, apparitions of the deceased person can be noted as not only common, but also prescribed as opportunities for resolving "unfinished relationship business," as opposed to indications of instability or frightening events to be avoided or forgotten at all cost. A cognitive behavioral description of the factors usually surrounding panic attacks can be used as the basis of prescribing mild variations of the attacks at convenient times to discover the "typical thoughts and behavioral contingencies" which surround the attacks; thus reversing the avoidance cycle, and adding control, predictability, new information, and redirection. Based upon discovery of the typical "cheer up" patterns around a person complaining of depression, a position of acknowledging the desperateness of the situation, and puzzling over the person's obvious strength in the face of such adversity, can be taken for the purpose of reversing the patterns of frustration, interpersonal distance, and powerlessness. Instead of the conventional tendency of providing reassurance, the therapeutic stance of empathizing with the strength shown by the client in the face of such a difficult situation is used to empower the person. Another variation of the use of generic patterns is when the force of, or phases in the cycle are used themselves in the service of change. One example of this is when the classic honeymoon phase of a battering cycle, which usually draws the parties into a closer relationship to the further exclusion of others, is used to have a man urge his wife to get to an emergency room (Fraser, 1988). Another example is when the so-called delusional suspicions of a person in a paranoid cycle are used to redirect the person's action, and thus alter or reverse the cycle itself (Fraser, 1984a). These are but a few uses of the knowledge of such generic response patterns.

Specific response patterns are those which can be described as uniquely evolving within the specific relationship system involved in the problem. In essence, these patterns add the unique flavor to the generic response pattern encountered, or are at other times at the heart of the unique variation of the problem presented. These typically involve the particular values, motives, concepts of normal or desirable roles or relationships, among other factors which are unique to the parties involved around the problem. I say the parties involved around the problem because (true to process model constructs) these may involve husbands, and wives, or parents and children; but they may also involve emergency room doctors, police, probation officers, teachers, employers, and others. These are seen as problem-determined systems. What is important is to identify those parties specifically involved in identifying a presenting problem and trying to solve it, to note their unique constructs and solution patterns, and to introduce some dissonance or to utilize these in the service of altering the problem cycle. This may include such things as initiating parental withdrawal from attempts to get an adolescent to conform for alternate reasons in alternate relationships. For one set of parents who are angry and seeking revenge, we may note how such a reversal may make the adolescent suffer the consequences of their own actions. Whereas, for another parent who is willing to sacrifice most anything for the sake of a child's well-being, we might point to how the parents themselves will suffer to see their adolescent make mistakes, as the parent allows the child to make his/her own choices. There are innumerable variations in such specific response patterns, their unique contributions to particular problem cycles, and their potential part in its alteration. The combination of the generic and specific patterns in each case gave unique flavor to subsequent interventions.

CHAOS AND CHANGE

One of the major reasons for rapid intervention at points of system change or crisis, is to take advantage of the often more accessible and simply alterable processes at this time. There is an interesting new focus across areas of scientific study which has come to be referred to as the study of chaos (cf. Glick, 1987). In many ways, though not through direct translation, this view adds further light upon the process of change and the evolution of patterns. Much of this view is based upon a positive feedback or morphogenic view similar to that of a process-constructive model.

Without dealing with much of this perspective, there are a few related ideas within it which may have some relevance to our own work. One proposition is that normal processes are much more variable, random, or chaotic than we might expect, and instead, it is the abnormal of often problematic patterns which are typified by greater rigidity or regularity in pattern. A tightrope walker, for instance, makes constant variations in his balance pole during a successful crossing, whereas, a stable pole will often lead to a fall. A second proposition is that during more chaotic phases, slight variations can yield far-reaching progressive evolution in the shape, pattern, or process of what follows. When people's constructs are confused and their usual patterns seem only to feed into further problems as around crisis points, their response patterns often become more rigidly repetitive and predictable. Yet they may also be more open at these times to slight reinterpretations or alterations in construct or process which may thus reshape further patterns.

Slight shifts in idea or action at these times can initiate very large shifts. In a simple example from catastrophe theory (Thom, 1975), the so-called "fight or flight" reaction in dogs has been studied to the extent that slight variations in context or action at a critical point in interaction have been found to precipitate the watershed difference in subsequent reactions between attack and retreat. Similarly, in an analogy to the work on discontinuous change in anthropology (Gould, 1982), already existing alternate repertoires of concept and action may be called forth and engaged full-blown at crisis points given a slight reorientation on the nature of the situation.

SOME EXAMPLES

Some examples of these ideas may be helpful. Recently, I encountered the staff of the Hospital's inpatient mental health unit standing in front of the elevators. They were in a confrontation with a patient who was attempting to leave "against medical orders." He was repeating that they didn't understand his position, and that he was going to leave before more harm was done. They were repeating that he could not leave, and that he must return to the unit. The situation was escalating. In the process of joining with him in his pacing, I agreed with him that they obviously didn't understand his reasons for leaving, and that he needed to sit down and make them understand. After agreeing to sit down, I suggested that the unit would probably be a less distracting place to talk, and the group of them moved to the unit. Although my colleagues referred to this as "the old Jedi mind trick of Obi Wan Kenobi from *Star Wars I,*" I prefer to see it as joining with, accepting, and slightly redirecting the Force toward a direction of mutual interest.

Another similar example occurred when we received a call from the local YWCA where a current client was demanding shelter because of a potential bomb threat in her home. Things had escalated to the point that they were wondering whether we might want to have her hospitalized at the state hospital. After thanking them for their concern, and complimenting them on not disregarding her just because she was "a little eccentric," we asked them if they would mind offering her some temporary shelter while we checked out her home to make sure it would be safe for the evening. Upon checking back with them a little later, they had shifted their repertoire from doubt and rejection to that of support and the provision of free shelter. The next day we helped the woman find new living arrangements.

Often, in vicious cycles around crisis times, the needed responses appear opposite to or contradictory to common logic or current motives that the sheer force of exhaustion or accidental interruption of the ongoing process is a major factor in facilitating the needed change. In another recent case, a grown son was referred to us from a hospital medical unit because of his high state of anxiety, exhaustion, and despondence over the deterioration of his mother who was in the hospital. They had always been close, and she had always been a strength and guide for him during trouble. He had hospitalized her medically during a recent heart attack, and ever since, his caretaking of her not only seemed to result in growing lethargy on her part, but his constant time spent at the hospital was endangering the future of his business. This case was resolved following one session. Following some discussion of honestly honoring the strength of his mother, the son returned to his mother and shared his desperation at potentially losing her and his business. To his amazement, not only were the two of them able to cry together for the first time, but his mother seemed to regain her old energy as she told him that she knew something was wrong. He began to work more, focusing his visits on quality rather than quantity. She regained her old fighting spirit with him and the nursing staff. They remained close through her death. The problem cycle was perpetuated through the son's well-meaning attempts at personal strength and protection. Strength, closeness, and hope were renewed through the seemingly contradictory sharing with his mother of how desperate he found their situation. A slight variation made all the difference.

Other case examples abound in attesting to the utility of a rapid intervention stance. One couple came to us the day after a separation. They had been dealing with the slowly progressing course of the wife's ALS or Lou Gehrig Disease for six years, or since the second month of their marriage. Their caring and supportive relationship was clouded, however, by his wish to protect her from his stress, and her insecurity over whether he was staying out of pity or love. The separation, and our subsequent encouragement of more "brutal honesty," has been the key to a deeper, less stressful, and reassured loving relationship. In another case, a woman came to us complaining of seeing her face melting in a mirror, and seeing her cousin standing beside his casket by her bed at night. It turned out that her mother had forced her cousin to leave town, whereupon he had been decapitated in a car crash. The open casket funeral where they all observed the recreation of his face in wax had been overwhelming for her. Through discussing the range of responses to acute grief (Lindeman, 1944), we normalized her responses, having her use the visions as opportunities to resolve her relationship with her cousin. Within two weeks, with the sharing of her grief with other family members, not only did her visions disappear, but so did similar reactions discovered in her sisters as well.

The above case examples are but a few variations on the wide variety of situations we encounter. From the basic concepts of the process-constructive model, and the value placed upon using natural variation points as opportunities to intervene, all other interventions flow. A knowledge and use of generic response patterns around developmental or incidental life crises and around specific problem reactions is a basic feature of Strategic Rapid Intervention. Attention to, and use of specific relationship patterns unique to each different case encountered, adds the unique flavor to each case. An openness to, and use of multiplicity of varying views and approaches to "personality," human development, and therapy, under the organizing principles of a process-constructive model, adds to the integrative and creative flexibility of the approach. As noted earlier, we attempt to accept the broadest variety of lifestyles as relatively adaptive, and focus mainly on the described problem and the concepts and process around it. In most instances, the forces of current processes and beliefs, even if they may at first seem to be perpetuating the problem, are utilized to move in new directions.

CONTEXT: THE CRISIS/BRIEF THERAPY CENTER

The context of our work opens us to the broadest variety of cases at points very close to perceived crisis. The Center itself has been essentially the "front door" for one of Ohio's largest, hospital-based community mental health centers. As such, it responds with a large staff, 24 hours a day, seven days a week, by telephone, face to face in the Center, in the hospital emergency room, and in the community with police through the Family Crisis Project, and through the Red Cross in disasters (cf. Fraser and Spicka, 1981). We also screen for admission to psychiatric units. In consultation, we work with juvenile court diversion units, and with a home-based intervention program for abusing parents. Across this wide variety of settings and over a broad range of cases, this flexible and adaptive model of Strategic Rapid Intervention and Brief Therapy has proven exceedingly powerful, as we attempt to seize these chaotic opportunities for rapid change.

Overall, our Strategic Rapid Intervention model has evolved through the combination of innumerable MRI concepts with others onto a process-constructive model within the practical setting of the Crisis/Brief Therapy Center. Our current focuses include the elaboration of the rapid intervention approach across a broad variety of generic crises with a recent emphasis on violence (Fraser, 1986a; 1988; 1989); the use of the process-adaptive concepts as a flexible umbrella model for therapy integration (Fraser, 1982; 1984b; 1986b); and the further translation of discontinuous, chaotic, rapid change ideas into the arena of human interaction and clinical intervention. These are our frontiers. Most of these frontiers are based from starting points in MRI ideas. Thank you MRI, and *Happy Birthday!*

SECTION III: CHANGES IN VENUE

The first half of this section consists of three chapters concerned in various ways with utilizing the MRI approach in other cultural settings. Two refer to Argentina–an interesting case because it concerns a culture that largely views itself as essentially European but which certainly involves a unique integration of its own. The other refers to India which certainly should provide a strong test of the generality and applicability of MRI views and practices.

The second group of chapters deals with various forms of a less obvious, but perhaps no less difficult, challenge. This is to transport, probably including to translate, interactional views across not cultural but professional borders–to promote potentially helpful new ways of thinking and acting among physicians, traditionally oriented psychiatrists, even ministers.

Chapter 11

Doing Brief Therapy in India

Prabha Appasamy

This chapter is an account of a clinician's experience with the practice of brief therapy in the city of Madras, South India. It is motivated by the expectation that cross-cultural evaluations of the efficacy of a recently originated form of psychotherapy would be of general interest to fellow practitioners. First the reader, unfamiliar with Indian conditions, is given a quick assessment of the state-of-the-art of psychotherapy in India. Some of the pressures faced by practitioners of this newly emerging discipline are then highlighted. This is followed by a section on the relevance of Brief Therapy in the Indian context. In the final section, a few case studies illustrate the use of some specific and general interventions of Brief Therapy in the environment in Madras.

STATE-OF-THE-ART THERAPY (WITH SPECIFIC REFERENCE TO MADRAS, INDIA)

Psychotherapy as it is conceived and practiced in the West has still not quite made an impression in the Indian context, certainly not to any significant degree, even in the major metropolitan cities of Delhi, Bombay, Calcutta, and Madras. By comparison, psychiatry would appear to have done relatively better, psychiatry being understood to comprise, largely, chemotherapy and electroconvulsive therapy, with some amount of advice-giving and encouragement thrown in (mostly for private patients). There are several practitioners of psychiatry in the larger cities, which also have state-sponsored "Mental Hospitals," often the only source of treatment for large numbers of the poor who are "mentally ill." In recent years, a rash of small "counseling centers" with paraprofessionals, social workers, lay volunteers, feminists, and/or clergy has broken out in the larger metropolitan cities; these centers offer simple counseling services, moral support, practical assistance, and sometimes even legal advice to a population of clients in crises. To complete a description of mental health services in India, one must mention a limited number (perhaps less than ten, countrywide) of addiction treatment centers, which have trained personnel and facilities for detoxification, individual, and group therapy.

Taken together, these facilities are wholly inadequate to meet the mental health needs of a rapidly changing society which is subject to the pressures of coping with emerging socio-economic trends of modernity–but in a milieu of considerable poverty, overpopulation, unemployment, and illiteracy. The gradual erosion of feudal practices, emergence of a free wage-labor force, rising rates of urbanization, and breakdown of the family system are all features of a traditional society in transition, a society with a whole host of problems (which are significantly more palpable at the present time than they were, say, 25 years ago) relating to child-rearing, adolescence, marriage, and old age. If facilities available to cope with the rising requirements of mental health intervention are inadequate in the urban areas, they are virtually nonexistent in the rural areas which account for 75 percent of India's population and where, for the most part, reliance is placed on traditional systems of treatment (among which exorcism features prominently).

Although there is clearly a very great objective need for psychotherapy, practitioners of psychotherapy–i.e., those who deal with human problems of different kinds and who do not depend mainly on drugs or ECT for bringing about change–are very few in number. This includes therapists of varied clinical orientations. Whatever their orientation, practitioners of this form of therapy find themselves operating in a field which has not yet come to maturity, and in an environment in which there is neither large-scale awareness nor acceptance of psychotherapy as a legitimate form of treatment. Psychotherapists have to function as isolates on the fringes of more accepted fields such as psychiatry, medicine, or education. With an unaware public, a largely uninformed and skeptical medical profession, and an indifferent–when not downright hostile–Guild of Psychiatrists, it is hardly surprising that the number of psychotherapy practitioners is very small. Psychotherapy is still at a retarded stage of development where one cannot be a practitioner unless one has a private source of income; in a new field, consultation fees cannot be as high as in the more accepted disciplines. Moreover, when the clients themselves are often pioneers of sorts in volunteering to try out psychotherapy as an alternate mode of treatment, one cannot risk inhibiting them with payment levels they would find difficult to manage.

TYPICAL PRESSURES FACED BY THE PSYCHOTHERAPIST

If one sets aside the pressure to be financially viable through the practice of psychotherapy alone, the single most pressing strain faced by the therapist is the "pressure to perform." Except for a few clients who are either highly educated or otherwise mentally sophisticated, the majority of patients and their families make implicit, and sometimes, explicit, demands for instant change or problem-resolution. (This, in spite of the fact that they might have had the problem in question for a long time, and had it unsuccessfully treated by specialists in other disciplines.) This is partly due to ignorance about what to expect in psychotherapy; and partly due to an expectation generated by psychiatric practice regarding the possibilities of instantaneous cure from the use of wonder drugs. In fact, with many patients, one is obliged to prescribe at least vitamins, general tonics, or mild antidepressants in order to elicit their cooperation for the process of psychotherapy (this does not include the use of placebos, which assumes the form of a specific therapeutic device in a limited number of cases).

Often the referring authority (mostly medical consultants such as pediatricians, surgeons, and physicians) will fail to inform the patient that psychotherapy is not usually a one-shot affair: patients with no notion of why they are being sent to psychotherapy come in with a vague expectation that it will be another medical consultation. When they are informed otherwise, some fail to turn up for subsequent sessions. A case which comes to mind is that of a healthy, educated 40-year-old woman who was convinced she had heart trouble and who insisted on electrocardiograms being taken every time she experienced palpitations. Within a period of two years, she had collected some 50 ECG reports and seen numerous physicians and cardiologists who had all certified that her heart was in perfect condition. This was a patient who was lost because her cardiologist, whom she respected a great deal, failed to prepare her even minimally for psychotherapy although it was he who did the referral; this failure of adequate preparation also rendered intervention with the lady's husband impossible. The pressure on the therapist occurs because of the meagerness of client load–it is hard to lose even a proportion of the few patients one gets in this manner. It should be added here that for the majority of persons seeking professional help for human problems the first choice of treatment is psychiatry. Furthermore, this proportion of individuals is itself very small compared to the many more who need professional help but opt not to seek such services: although the social stigma attached to seeing a psychiatrist has lessened in recent years, it is still very much there.

Language is the medium through which psychotherapy is conducted. That the therapist and client should speak the same language is something which cannot always be taken for granted. In a country where 18 major languages are spoken, the therapist occasionally finds herself with a client who does not know any of the languages she knows. This obviously handicaps the therapist; but given the paucity of clients and the implied pressure from referral sources (who are themselves few in number and who have to be carefully educated and encouraged to consider and recommend to others the option of psychotherapy), there is reluctance to turn the patient away. Attempts are made to conduct therapy through an intermediary–a translator who is usually a member of the patient's family. Under these circumstances, language becomes inevitably stilted, nuances are lost, flexibility in reframing and instruction-giving is curtailed. The situation becomes even more difficult when the patient cannot open up in the presence of the translator–as in the case of a woman for whom it is relevant to discuss her sexual relationship with her husband, but whose son is her translator; or, in cases where the translator himself is, in the client's perception, the source of the problem (as in marital quarrels).

Severe constraints in the objective family circumstances of the client and the limitations in the real world around the client can also impose pressures on the therapist. Poverty–or at least the acutely financially strained circumstance of the patient–limits the number of options open to both the patient and therapist. Opportunities for upward mobility are far more restrictive in India than in the West. With no social security, no medical insurance, and often no realistic prospects of employment for the client, the therapist sometimes has to operate within a bleak framework of constraints. In other cases, there are social pressures which restrict the therapist's freedom to prescribe particular courses of action–to suggest, for example, that an only son move out of his parents' house after marriage, when everyone "knows" that it is the son's duty to look after his elderly parents.

Given the nature of objective constraints in many cases, the therapist's maneuverability is curtailed with regard to timing and pacing. The pressure to achieve at least minimally recognizable results within the shortest possible time dilutes therapeutic effectiveness like nothing else does. The harried therapist often has to walk a tightrope in maintaining a delicate balance between keeping the client from opting out of psychotherapy prematurely, while preserving optimal therapeutic maneuverability. Once the client is half-way committed to change or problem-resolution through psychotherapy, the threat of termination can be (and has been) effectively used to allow the therapist some freedom of movement. But with clients who come in unaware of what to expect from psychotherapy, threat of termination is not very productive. This is all the more so when the therapist recognizes that psychotherapy alone can help the client. For the therapist there is an ethical dilemma as well: in an environment where there are few alternative therapists to choose from, to whom can the patient be referred if one so chooses? Depending on the nature of the problem, in many cases the client has already done a round of medical and psychiatric consultations; and the concerned therapist faces a particularly hard problem when the client in question desperately wants relief or change, and is not obviously playing "window-shopping" games.

Finally, a pressure acutely felt by the practicing therapist in India stems from the professional loneliness and isolation one experiences owing to an absence of professional colleagues with whom one can discuss cases, plan treatment strategies, and from whom one can elicit feedback and seek intellectual stimulation.

THE RELEVANCE OF MRI BRIEF THERAPY IN THE INDIAN CONTEXT

Concern here will not be with an abstract critical appreciation of the theoretical underpinnings of Brief Therapy: its logic and comprehensiveness, clarity and simplicity, elegance and intellectual appeal on the positive side, and the possible over-ambitiousness of its claims, on the negative side. Instead, the discussion will deal with the more immediately pragmatic issue of how and why Brief Therapy is probably the single most relevant form of psychotherapy that can be effectively and widely used in India today.

One obvious reason for its relevance in the Indian context is, precisely, that Brief Therapy *is* brief. In a country like India, only a tiny fraction of the urban elite can afford to indulge in the luxury of long-term insight-oriented psychotherapy. For the rest, people in this country, when they do turn to psychotherapy, do so because they have a problem or a concern which they would like to see solved as quickly as possible. It makes particular sense, in a situation such as this, to "limit therapy to the relief of suffering" rather than to "embark on a lengthy quest for happiness." Long-term psychotherapy (with its slow movement from session to session, and its imprecise linkages between sessions) would scarcely be able to hold a majority of clients whose lives are governed by the sorts of objective conditions that have been outlined in the preceding section. This therapist has lost several clients in the past while relying exclusively on longer, more traditional forms of psychotherapy. In retrospect, if Brief Therapy had been initiated right from the beginning, a clearer understanding of the current problem would have emerged sooner, and problem-resolution strategies could have been devised earlier. This, presumably, would have prevented the client from opting out of psychotherapy altogether. However, there *are* exceptions to the rule: some clients, especially of the class represented by very intelligent and articulate college students, seek and benefit from long-term developmental counseling. But even here, Brief Therapy strategies are the ones this therapist has found most effective in securing relief for the problems with which the clients initially come: panic attacks, the occurrence of facial tics in social situations, and so on.

Brief Therapy–since it involves a smaller number of sessions for problem-resolution (or the setting-up of the process of change, as the case might be)–is clearly more cost-effective than more traditional long-term therapies. This is a matter of acute relevance in the Indian context.

As mentioned earlier, there are very few practitioners of psychotherapy in India today. The profession is dominated by psychiatrists, with their all-but-exclusive reliance on chemotherapy and shock treatment. Such a remarkably narrow range of therapeutic interventions often leads to a wholly misplaced dogmatism: there have been cases in which young teenagers have been given electroconvulsive therapy for truancy from school and other minor acts of misbehavior. The need for a more enlightened view of the potentialities of psychotherapy–of the possibilities it offers for relief of suffering or problems–is only highlighted against this background. When psychotherapy becomes more acceptable in India, therapists who use Brief Therapy will be able to help a relatively larger number of patients than those who use long-term, nondirective, or psychoanalytical therapies.

Brief therapy is directive, and this would seem to suit the average Indian temperament rather better than a nondirective form of therapy. Traditionally, India has had a relatively paternalistic, authoritarian form of society, and people are accustomed to directives. This is not, of course, to say that therapeutic directives are therefore automatically followed; clinical experience suggests that this society has its own share of resistant clients, patients who are not really clients, patients who come in under duress, difficult or restrictive clients, clients who actively resist change, and clients who attempt secret sabotage. But the comforting fact is that Brief Therapy does provide strategies for dealing with all these kinds of "difficult" patients. With there being some universality to human nature, these strategies work as well in Madras as they apparently do in Palo Alto.

One of the major advantages of Brief Therapy for the therapist practicing in India is that the language of the therapy itself–its theoretical precepts, its description of its therapeutic procedures, its tactics and interventions of change–is not "alien" to the Indian situation. Whether it be in setting the stage for treatment, in assessing patient position, in case planning, or in selecting appropriate goals and "selling" the interventions to the clients, the techniques of Brief Therapy seem well-suited to the Indian context. This is not readily discernible in many other forms of therapy, which seem culture-biased in subtle ways, and the use of which could make an Indian patient feel distinctly uncomfortable. The use of techniques peculiar to Gestalt Therapy, for instance, has in this therapist's experience usually resulted in baffled nonparticipation by clients. Conjoint family therapy also tends to fall in this category: Indian family systems seem to be more amenable to change when individual family members are interviewed separately, rather than together; conjoint family therapy often results in embarrassed silence and resistance, leading to quick termination of therapy.

Lastly, Brief Therapy has a limited number of interventions covering a wide range of typical, common problem areas; this makes it easier to identify and formulate therapeutic goals and strategies. Of course, assessing the patient's value-orientation and his particular language, and "selling" the task are the most difficult part of therapy, but for a therapist functioning in isolation, Brief Therapy offers reassurance and support in the fact that while cases differ from one to another in detail, they can also be broadly categorized in ways which make them more familiar to handle.

(1) *The case of "B"–a woman with obsessive-compulsive behavior.* This was a case which was seen only twice, with a gap of six weeks between the two sessions, as the client was from a neighboring state, and being five months pregnant, could not easily travel to Madras. "B" is an orthodox married Muslim woman of 28, educated at the college level, who had developed over the previous eight months a series of obsessive-compulsive behaviors. This was most distressing to her and her husband (a forest range officer). The problem had worsened in recent months to such an extent she was

skipping meals to fit in her rituals, stopped socializing and going for outings, and had difficulty going to sleep.

"B" was able to describe her compulsions in simple behavioral terms. She was bathing seven or eight times a day, washing her hair twice daily, and sprinkling "holy water" (water kept in an earthen pot over which prayers have been recited, an orthodox Muslim custom) all over the house each time she felt something had been contaminated–which was almost all of the time. She would rewash washed clothes hung out on the clothesline if she believed someone had walked past it. She had begun insisting on her husband and young son going through an elaborate body-washing procedure every time they entered the house. She could not tolerate the presence of menstruating women in her house; and her best saris were beginning to get ruined with over-frequent washing. Her husband had tried pleading, reasoning, and losing his temper with her; but all to no avail. She knew she was being irrational and that this was affecting her health, but she felt unable to control herself. She wanted to be able to eat properly, to sleep properly, and to restrict her washing and bathing to "normal" levels. Her motivation to change was high.

"B" had a train to catch later that day, so task instructions were given in the first session. She wanted relief from her distressing symptoms and was aware that she could not be given psychiatric drugs in her present condition. This made it easy for the therapist to give simple, direct instructions, with the remark that "B" would probably find these instructions odd, even silly, but if she wanted relief, she would need to follow them religiously. "B" agreed to do so readily. This has been one of the few cases for this therapist where compliance has been so absolute.

The instructions were basically symptom prescriptions. "B" was asked to keep an accurate alarm clock in her house, and to rigidly follow the schedule given her. Till she came back to Madras for her next visit, six weeks later (her next gynecological assessment was due then), she was to bathe thrice a day at set times. (This was regardless of how many baths she had taken during the rest of the day.) The second instruction was that she was to spend 15 minutes by the clock, after her prescribed baths, sprinkling "holy water" all over the house. She was free to sprinkle it at other times as well.

The third and final instruction was that at 11 o'clock every morning she was to go to the clothesline and drop all the washed clothes to the ground, one by one. She was then to rinse them out again and hang them up to dry. "B" agreed to all this, and was immensely relieved that the therapist had not asked her to stop her obsessive behavior in any way.

"B" turned up for her second appointment six weeks later saying that she had carefully followed the instructions for the first month, but had not done so after that because things were much better. By her own account, she was sleeping and eating well, and not skipping any of her meals. She now bathed only twice a day which, she felt, was normal for the hot weather. Washing her hair was restricted to thrice a week–on Tuesdays and Fridays, which were Hindu auspicious days, and on Thursdays for a Muslim observance. She was able to tolerate menstruating women in her house, and had reduced the holy-water-sprinkling ritual to only those days on which she washed her hair. She had started visiting relatives and friends and had gone to the cinema thrice, something she had not done in over a year's time. "B" 's father, who accompanied her, also stated that his daughter had shown some improvement. She had worn an expensive sari to a wedding recently, and on returning had just folded it and put it back in the closet. Washed clothes were not now washed again, as "B" claimed no one ever touched the clothes hung out to dry.

"B" was not praised in any way for having reduced her obsessive-compulsive behavior, neither was the contrast between her symptoms six weeks ago now highlighted, nor even pointed out. She was told to go back to excessive washing once in a while (in case she should be tempted to go to the other extreme), and to continue the earlier instructions in modified form, for the next four weeks.

When "B" came for her confinement two months later, the gynecologist who had originally referred her, stated that she had not mentioned her obsessive behavior to her even once, which was all she could talk about earlier.

Using symptom prescription in varied forms for the range of human problems which fall into the category of "attempting to force something that can only occur spontaneously"–cases of hyperventilation, stammering, going pale in public, panic attacks, insomnia, excessive sweating, trichotillomania, hiccupping, and vomiting–have all been successfully treated here in Madras. (This is not an exhaustive list.) Selling the task is what is difficult here, not the selection of the intervention itself, as all Brief Therapists know. The following case illustrates features of both initial success and subsequent failure revolving around precisely this issue.

(2) *The case of "V"–a ten-year-old girl with hiccups.* "V" was a small, thin ten-year-old girl, the oldest of four siblings. Her parents belonged to a traditional money-lending community of the state of Rajasthan, and they had little formal education. "V" had had hiccups for the previous 25 days, almost continuously except when asleep or under sedation. She had been taken to numerous doctors, including two psychiatrists, and been admitted in a children's hospital and a private nursing home for two days each, before she was brought to the surgeon who referred her to this therapist. The referral was done as the surgeon was convinced nothing was organically wrong with the patient. He had hospitalized her, put her on Largactil Syrup, and then turned her over to this therapist. (Prior to this, the child had been variously prescribed Melleril, Speedex Syrup, Tryptomer, Nitrosan, Tiniba, Stellabid, Tancodep, Surmontil, Valium, Perinorm, and Phenergan–all in the course of 25 days!)

The first session with "V" was in her hospital room, a day after she had been admitted. She complained bitterly of stomach pain and pain in her chest. Her pretty, young mother hovered around anxiously, endorsing what her daughter had said. A few minutes later when the therapist and the child's mother moved outside the room, "V" started her hiccups. The goal to be achieved was clear enough, so the therapist decided to enlist the aid of the nurses on duty, to carry through the intervention in the shortest possible time. The mother was simply asked to cooperate with the nurses in a new form of treatment. The Largactil Syrup was stopped and the nurses on floor duty were asked to crowd around "V"'s bed every four hours, for five minutes on each occasion (beginning that evening itself), so that they might alternately coax and bully her into bringing on her hiccups as loudly and strongly and rapidly as possible. The nurses agreed to do this with some amusement, but trained as they were to carry out instructions, they simply accepted the explanation that it was a new, experimental form of treatment. As barium meal X-ray studies and other tests had shown that nothing was wrong with "V" 's stomach, the nurses were asked to give her a placebo–a vitamin tablet twice a day, with the information that it was a special, powerful drug from America, and that her stomach pain would definitely disappear as a result. The physician was also asked to follow the same instructions, and to endorse what the nurses said.

After "V" 's session, it was found that "V" had stopped her hiccups. The nurses had faithfully carried out instructions from the previous evening, apparently "V" had fretted and fumed and told them they were mean to make her hiccup. During the morning and early afternoon "hiccupping schedules" when the hiccups had left her, she refused to cooperate, piously claiming that by doing this exercise she was frightened she might bring on an attack again. In response to this, she was told that was exactly what was wanted. The placebo had also worked, and although "V" grudgingly admitted to no stomach pain, she whined a good deal about various other aches all over her body. She also demanded that she be immediately discharged from the hospital as she was all right now. Her parents also pressed for this. As the therapist wanted "V" under observation for one more day, they were promised discharge the next day. An appointment was fixed to see the parents before they left the hospital. The nurses were asked to continue the "hiccup schedule" for the rest of "V" 's stay.

When the parents met this therapist the next day, their daughter had not hiccupped for 48 hours. Flushed with this success, the therapist unfortunately failed to accurately assess the parents' "position" and "language." As they had seen the dramatic results of symptom prescription for two days, it was assumed that they would accept the therapist's instructions. A perfunctory attempt at "selling" was made by pointing out that in order for "V" to learn how to control her hiccups, she needed to learn how to start them at will–it was like learning how to ride a bicycle. In order to gain full control over it, one needed to learn balance, as well as how to start and stop the vehicle. Communication was a bit stilted, as the verbal interaction was in Hindi–a language in which the therapist was not very fluent.

The parents listened politely, and then made anxious inquiries of possible possession by evil spirits. Apparently, "V" had seen a "ghost" in her school bathroom recently. But the therapist enthusiastically steamrolled ahead by pointing out that "V" 's attack was purely psychological in nature and that she probably needed more attention at home, and the basic principles of behavior modification were explained to the parents. Their inquiry about whether *mantra-chanting* would permanently cure their daughter was brushed aside, and symptom prescription was again advised in order to avoid a relapse. The parents listened to everything that was said, and did not come back for the follow-up session.

A couple of weeks later when the therapist called to find out about "V," she was informed by her mother that they had not followed any of the instructions as her poor daughter had started hiccups in the car on the way back home from the hospital. They had taken her next day to a *vaid* (a practitioner of indigenous herbal medicine) who had given her a concoction which had cured "V" of her hiccups on the third day. That same evening she had left with her father, on a two-week holiday, for Bombay. "V" had enjoyed herself immensely with her cousins there, and had not hiccupped even once. Father and daughter had returned only the day before and "V" was quite well, thanks to the *vaid's* treatment.

Postscript: A month later, it was brought to this therapist's knowledge, quite inadvertently, that "V" had been admitted to a leading private hospital in the city for her hiccups. A doctor friend, who worked in both hospitals, had seen the child being wheeled in for yet another barium meal X ray.

This is a clear case of the therapist failing to utilize patient position by ignoring leading position statements by the client. Resistance was never seriously considered because of the therapist's own sense of achievement. Perhaps if the "hiccup schedule" had been redefined as a form of new *mantra*–a kind of newfangled incantation to ward off unwanted spirits, the therapist might have achieved a more lasting cure. A few pediatricians and urban, middle class, educated parents have begun to use the services of the psychotherapist for problems of child rearing, where their attempts to reach accord through opposition or compliance through voluntarism have failed. These parents are usually against medication or sedation for their child, which makes them more amenable to therapy.

The following case illustrates mainly the application of some of the general interventions of Brief Therapy, which are useful in dealing with resistant patients, viz., the dangers of improvement, the go-slow tactic, the U-turn, and so on. This case study is not unique in any way. It has been chosen merely to highlight the point that not only are the specific interventions of Brief Therapy relevant in the Indian context, but also the general interventions or tactics of Brief Therapy, which are often sufficient in and of themselves to set off the process of change in therapy.

(3) *The case of "S"–a patient under duress.* "S" was a big-built, good-looking young man of 23, sullen, unresponsive, and cynical, with a huge grouse against his parents and the relatives who were supporting him and paying for his therapy. He was the only child of an unemployed alcoholic father and an anxious, harassed mother, pathetically keen that her son should complete his engineering course at the premier Institute of Technology in Madras, where he was a final year student. He should have graduated two semesters ago but had four incompletes and a project to work on and finish. He had not made any academic progress in eight months, and had, in fact, failed in the subjects taken the previous semester. He was registered in two courses which he was attending on an intermittent basis, when he was brought to this therapist by the cousin who was supporting him and his parents.

Some weeks prior to this, "S" had attempted suicide by slashing his wrists and waiting for 24 hours to die. His college authorities reacted by expelling him from the dormitory where he resided. This was his second attempt in six months. It was obvious "S" had agreed to therapy under duress. If free board and lodging went with having to see a therapist, his attitude was that he would go along with it. Although he was clearly not the client, it was decided after a session with the chief complainants–his cousin and his mother–that "S" would be seen by the therapist weekly for the next two months. If there was absolutely no change, therapy would be discontinued. As "S" was still suicidal, minimal antidepressant medication was recommended, to be administered by his cousin.

For the first few sessions, "S" was very resistant to change and effort of any kind. He was being dysfunctional at home and college, and although he knew this, he was unwilling to deal with it; instead, he would fantasize about having a rich, beautiful girl to take care of his every need, while he lolled in bed and drank all day. His complainants had said he was a bully at home, demanding money, abusing his parents, and having fits of rage. He was lazy and slothful, and was beginning to get drunk with increasing frequency. In addition, he was not making any visible effort at completing his degree. After a couple of sessions of going around in circles, the threat of termination was used to get him to take the sessions a little more seriously. ("S" knew that his cousin had been advised to not extend indefinite support to him and his parents.) The tactic of "why should you change" was repeatedly used, and the drawbacks of improvement were pointed out to him. He could remain the way he was for the rest of his life, eating and sleeping and listening to music and not working. His relatives might despise him for being a parasite, but since he did not care, why should he change at all? After all, there was not one single thing in his life that needed to be changed, as everything was going his way. "S" demurred, saying there was one aspect of his life he did want to change: he was stricken with self-consciousness in public, he kept his head in rigid positions, his body movements were jerky, he was unable to look people in the eye, and was terrified of what they must think of him. He developed palpitations in social situations, and was unable to smile at or greet casual acquaintances. He wanted therapy for this.

The therapist made the mistake of forgetting Erickson's basic rule of "take what the patient brings you." Instead, a few sessions were wasted in trying to get "S" to examine his bigger and real problems (as perceived by the therapist). When the therapist finally realized her mistake of being argumentative with the client, she made a U-turn, and agreed with him that if his discomfort in public was really bothering him, it was important he should get relief from his symptoms. While it was clear what the task should be, the problem was in selling it to a resistant client like "S," given his natural reluctance to follow any instructions or make any effort at trying something new. Symptom prescription was alluded to but withheld from him for a session, on the grounds that there was no point in telling him as he would not try it anyway; at the same time, frequent references were made to other students from his Institute (their names, naturally, were not given) who had benefitted from such bizarre exercises. It was added that they probably had more guts, or were hurting more from similar symptoms. Finally, when "S" pleaded that he be given the same instructions, the task was outlined. At the end of the session, the therapist accompanied him to the foyer where she has her consulting room, and proceeded to shake her head from side to side, walk up and down with jerky movements, and stare cross-eyed at the receptionists, while "S" watched, in petrified embarrassment. After a few minutes, since no one paid any attention, the therapist terminated the session.

Needless to say, in the following weeks "S" reported feeling much better, although he had only partially attempted some of the tasks. He also unbent enough to say that he was coming for therapy because he wanted it now, and not because his relatives expected it of him. His worries that his old fears were not completely gone, that certain days were still bad, were dealt with by using the tactic of "go slow." The dangers of rapid, sudden improvement were pointed out, and an instruction to bring on a relapse on some days was given.

This case has not yet been terminated. After nine sessions the patient has completed the two courses he had registered for earlier in the semester, and is half-way through his project. Quarrels with his parents have decreased, and he sometimes helps in household chores–something he had never done before. "S" has joined a yoga class which meets every morning, and is now tentatively fantasizing about going abroad for higher studies. He has not had a drink in a long while. "S" has a long way to go, but the impasse he was in earlier has been broken. For the first time in years it is obvious to him that change is possible.

While it has been stated that Brief Therapy is the most relevant form of psychotherapy for a country like India, it is by no means the only form of therapy that can be effectively used here. Not every problem or concern with which the client comes lends itself to the application of Brief Therapy principles. Lithium or other forms of chemotherapy as the predominant mode of treatment is the obvious choice in acutely disturbed patients, at least in the initial stages. A few clients do prefer and benefit from long-term psychotherapy. In certain cases, especially those involving very young children or students with concentration problems, behavior modification therapy has been used with positive results. A combination of Brief Therapy and Behavioral Therapy, or Brief Therapy with Rogerian type client-centered therapy has been used frequently, with substantial therapeutic benefit to the patient. This flexibility often enhances, rather than diminishes, therapeutic effectiveness (no mix of strategies is attempted where Brief Therapy alone suffices or where a combination of other therapeutic techniques will dilute the efficacy of the particular Brief Therapy technique in use).

While this therapist does not endorse doctrinaire monism regarding Brief Therapy, her experience strongly suggests that however eclectic one's orientation, Brief Therapy is an indispensable source of therapeutic change and problem-resolution in India.

Chapter 12

How to Breed "Hippogriffs" That Can Handle Problems

Celia Elzufan
Hugo Hirsch

This heading refers to the breeding of an impossible species, the cross between the different lineages, a way in which we conceive the influence of MRI ideas on our work within Argentine culture: On one hand, an emphasis on pragmatism, problem resolution, and interaction, together with the belief that people are capable of solving their difficulties with brief and limited assistance; on the other hand, a culture fond of a declamatory style that considers "problem solving" as cold and inhuman sounding–where symptoms are looked at from an individual psychoanalytical perspective, where the dominant idea is that individuals are sick, not responsible for their own actions, and require long periods of treatment.

Perhaps this is better explained through a description of the type of patients that constituted our clientele upon our return from training in the United States. A large proportion were the backflow of psychoanalysis, not having been able to resolve their symptoms after five, ten, or 15 years of therapy. Perhaps because "a new broom sweeps well," we were successful in a considerable number of cases. Similar ones are still an important part of our clientele.

These successes caused a renewed debate in our field related to the types of treatment. The practical result is that many of our patients or their "significant others" are in parallel therapies and still many times are referred to us by the therapists themselves, so that we take care of some "undefeatable symptom" while the "deeper" therapy continues to take place. We have learned to work with this type of situation, considering the other therapist as one more part of the problem-system, or in other words, an "uncle with great influence on the family." Sometimes he is even our main client. Influencing him is not easy, and it requires mastering his own language. The skill acquired in these situations allowed us to handle, with similar methods and interventions, a number of educational therapists, social workers, speech therapists, teachers, and other professionals connected with the "psy" culture of Argentina, who form part of children-related difficulties transformed into problems by the parents and the environment.

However, in all cases our interventions are based on a value system that gives priority to action, even though they may be expressed in the language of the people consulting us. When our clients accept these ideas, they are introducing and reinforcing a pragmatic dimension of their thinking. In other words, we have in a way influenced local culture directly by emphasizing results and indirectly when our interventions are accepted.

We believe that not only our trainees but also our clients and their families, and some of our colleagues in the field, have become more concrete in the way of approaching problems. We think that the description of some of our mythical animals can be interesting for a wide group of professionals than only those interested purely in anthropological picturesqueness such as that of "Family Therapy Prescriptions and Rituals in Bali." Perhaps presumptuously we suppose that our readers will be able to extract some procedures useful for their own field from the description of our difficulties and our way of solving them. We are now going to briefly detail two of our favorite "beasts": one, brought to us from the MRI and developed by Celia and colleagues, involves working with organic problems and techniques for handling these clients when they lack motivation, and the other by a team headed by Hugo, that involves converting difficulties into advantages in cases presented as grave.

HIPPOGRIFF I: CELIA'S WORK–LIFE AND MOTIVATION

Among the different areas of thought that sprang from the work done by the MRI, I was inspired by a paper presented by John Weakland (1977) called "Family Somatics–A Neglected Edge."

After carrying out similar work with couples with cardiac patient members as the one described by Fred Hoebel (1975), I developed some procedures which make it possible to bring about or enhance the motivation of clients who traditionally would be described as "window shoppers."

I did this out of a personal conviction that when health and life are at stake, we cannot simply focus on what the person consulting us considers is the problem. It is our responsibility to get that person to really "sweat" about the problem or reason for the consultation. Later, I thought of using this approach in drug addiction cases, based on the same premise: life and health are at stake. The success obtained, not only with organic cases but also in drug addiction cases, resulted in an increasing acceptance by professionals in the health care field, which led them to modify essential aspects of their practice.

Following is a description of some technical aspects of this kind of work with organic patients and drug addicts, and the kind of changes produced in the ideas and health care practices of some services. As mentioned before, these ideas developed from an attempt to duplicate, within a cardiology service of a general hospital, the intervention model mentioned above, with wives of cardiac patients, and, as a rule, without the latter's participation. This work reconfirmed John Weakland's (1977) ideas on the effect of interaction on the development of organic illnesses and the possibility of considering family members of the person who can constitute the leverage for change, as the "best therapists" to achieve changes in behavior.

Realization of the way in which the partners influence each other allowed us to turn the significant person–they always became experts in the illness–into true therapists. What type of cases were referred to us for consultation? As a rule, they included mostly male patients who did not obey doctors' orders and who also resisted any type of psychological therapy. The wives were then asked to come alone and we helped them find an alternative solution to those tried before, to modify the behavior of the husband.

In many cases, we were successful, but in many others two types of difficulties arose: In the first place, some women did not want to come without their husbands, and they dragged them along even against their will. Second, a significant number of wives were not very inclined to do something about the situation. It was as though they said: "I have nothing to do with this, and I can't change anything. He has to make the effort, and your job is to persuade him to make it, so I really don't know why I've been sent here." They had been referred by the cardiologist in charge.

In the first case, I decided to include both spouses in the sessions, making a point of commenting favorably on the concern shown by her in not leaving him alone for even one moment, and on the affection shown by him in the fact that he was coming to a consultation in the effectiveness of which he did not believe. I adapted to their language, moved with flexibility as would a willow in the wind, or, to paraphrase Paul Watzlawick (1978) in *The Language of Change*, I behaved as a chameleon. The wives were fearful that the husbands would take advantage of their absence to disobey doctors' orders. Also, in keeping with the macho attitudes of our culture, the husbands' illness had given them a position of strength from which they could now be the ones to define situations, and therefore they were not very willing to give up this rare opportunity.

Basically, the conversations would take place between the therapist and the wife, with the identified patient hearing comments about himself as if, in a certain sense, he were not there. In some cases, after inquiring about solutions tried by the wife, I would suggest: "Perhaps it would be better if you respected his lack of interest in doing what is necessary and did nothing to take care of him. If he really is not interested, he won't be careful, and that means he will probably die in a short time. On the other hand, if you take care of him, perhaps he'll live for another five years, but he'll leave you a widow at an age in which it will be difficult to make a new start. I'm sure because of his love for you he wouldn't consider it right to leave you alone." As can be appreciated, this conversation affected not only the wife but also her husband.

This leads us to the second problem mentioned: the individuals who come to consultation with a very poor disposition to do something to change the problem. In many cases, the man who came to this kind of interview with his wife changed his attitude because the intervention led him to consider something a problem that up to that moment was not such for him. What is meant by a "problem?" It is behavior that is risky in some sense but also susceptible to change through an action or influence of the therapist. If it is not considered undesirable by the couple, then the therapist knows it will be difficult to modify, and as such no longer a problem.

Many cardiac patients' wives, as well as significant people in the lives of other types of organic patients, feel they are victims of an unfortunate event and can do nothing. They believe only the patient or the doctors can improve the problem. Therefore, the consultation with the therapist is taken as just a preliminary step towards the patient's therapy rather than as an opportunity to find a way they can help the patient make changes in his condition.

It is not only legitimate but even necessary to make the consulting persons aware of the fact that their behavior can influence the outcome of the situation, that they have alternative choices of behavior, and therefore options, and that it is their decision to maintain or modify the patient's behavior. We are not talking here of lecturing the patient. The above example of what can be said to the wife in her husband's presence will have made this point clear. Our aim is to use the consulting person's values for enlisting the patient's cooperation. For example, the therapist might say: "In other similar cases which I had the opportunity to assist, the client changed when the wife behaved differently, but in your case I don't dare suggest it. I can see that you are so disheartened that, although you can help him a lot, I don't think you have what it takes to give it a try. You will possibly need all the time allowed by these sessions to simply unburden yourself and talk about how bad you feel. Not everyone has the necessary fiber to do something at such a difficult time, so even though it won't do much good, perhaps it will be better if he does start therapy anyway."

This type of intervention helps awaken the "will to buy" and then create the necessary conditions to modify the interaction in a way that generally helps the organic patient live whatever time he has left more fully and dignified, perceiving love with respect in the other person, rather than compassion. If we are able to get the consulting person to "buy" what we have to offer, we open the road for improvement in the quality of life of the entire system. Also, the use of such procedures bridges the distance between the MRI brief therapy model premise of working only with what is a problem to the client and our duty as members of the health care services to help preserve or recover the health of those consulting us.

After many years' experience in consultation related to many different organic problems, I thought that a similar conceptual pattern could be useful in handling cases of dug addiction. Here, too, life and health are at stake and the price paid by the body is visible with time. Frequently, the I.P. (identified patient) does not consider his or her own behavior problematic, and those close to the I.P. think that they are victims of an unfortunate event about which there is very little they can do. Many hope that the therapist will "cure" the illness, so that nobody is responsible except the therapist. When drug addiction is treated as a grave somatic problem, the point of view of the consulting person is projected to the very extreme, and this frequently causes enough anxiety in them to make them try to behave in a different way. In some cases, I might say: "From what I hear, you are afraid of frustrating your son, that's why you give him everything he asks for. You think that if he is frustrated he might feel very bad and that that would make his problems worse. I can see that you are ready to do anything for his sake, even to lose him after a short but intense life." If they ask what is meant by that, I can say: "Well, I imagine that you have decided not to frustrate him even though you have informed yourselves about the progressive damage to the nervous system that is suffered as the illness progresses." If they say "no," I briefly list the possible damage and then add: "But this is just for your information. It shouldn't necessarily lead you to change the way you handle him. This reminds me of the case of a diabetic teenager who had to follow a rigorous diet. He hated the limitations and the parents decided to let him follow his own impulses. They chose to give him a short but normal life, rather than an unhappy long one with restrictions. Today, after several diabetic comas, he is blind and deteriorated."

In other cases, I might comment that obviously they consulted me because, in spite of their great understanding and wish that their son "live as he pleases," they no longer seem willing to continue to cooperate with their son's self-destructive habits.

Also, I might work with the disadvantages of a change, stating that although the son's behavior signals his need to be treated as a responsible person, this would imply his becoming mature, which would make the passage of time and their aging evident to them. By showing their behavior in a positive light and pointing out the disadvantages of change, I make it possible for them to realize that they have options. Many times this is enough to interest them in learning more about how to intervene in a different way, and this might be the small change that brings on others and marks the end of a frustrating reiterative behavior. This way of working has attracted the interest of a growing number of health care professionals, therapists, and colleagues of other specializations. Many of them, influential in their respective institutions, attended or are still attending courses at our Center. One essential aspect of my work with these professionals consists of teaching them how to accept the "view of the world" of their patients and others who consult them and how to suggest alternative ideas to help them change some attitudes and behavior. I believe that what is most important is the change operated in the professionals themselves while they learn. They discard an omnipotent and overprotective manner, typical of health care professionals in our culture, and they adopt a position of greater respect for the potentiality of the clients.

In practice, this is translated into offering them more information and making sure they receive it; understanding that the people who surround the patient often have ways of helping them get better which are superior to those of the professional; accepting responsibility for making the patient and the people near him feel co-responsible, and to recognize they have options regarding health.

Many of our trainees have been able to employ this point of view at different institutions such as cardiology, oncology, internal medicine, and psychiatric services. The end result is that today the dominant point of view considers the health care task as a cooperation between subjects rather than an act of a subject-doctor over an object-patient. That this change is owed in part to my contribution is a source of pride and satisfaction to me.

HIPPOGRIFF II: HUGO'S WORK– A PECULIAR PSYCHIATRY

Ten years ago we formed a group that provides mental health care coverage for large groups, something equivalent to a mental health maintenance organization. The consultations for "grave" problems present interesting organizational and technical problems. We have designed a special form of organization and certain conceptual lines along which the technical interventions are carried out. We will refer in particular to one aspect of the latter.

We have deliberately labeled the situations as "grave," rather than pointing to the individual psychopathological characteristics or the family's communicational ones. By "grave" it is meant there is a substantial social risk or a perception of impending catastrophe, and therefore the therapist is asked to take some urgent control and protection measures. Examples of grave cases might be suicide attempts, acute psychotic episodes, or severe anorexia.

A lot of pressure is applied on the therapy team. One family might stress the chance of a new suicide attempt. Another might express its anxiety over the fact that it could be financially ruined because of the head of the family's mental incapacity. The members of the team are made to feel that they have to do something urgently. It occurred to us that the relationship established with these families can be compared to a game between two teams in which each side avails itself of whatever recourse it can to win. In our opinion, the use of this metaphor has an advantage that greatly exceeds its main disadvantage: although it does not describe clearly enough the cooperative aspect that the therapist-consulting individual relationship usually includes, it emphasizes an aspect of resistance to the therapist presented by these families.

When we consider their behavior as moves to prevent, or present as impossible, the attaining of a therapeutic goal, we are encouraging the strategic view of the team. As a result, the therapists plan what discussions must be introduced in each session according to the objectives; which moves were made by the family to avoid being overtaken; in what way these moves were blocked or may be blocked by the team in the future; which would be the family's probable future moves; and how they can be anticipated and blocked. The point is not to win but to organize things in such a way that everybody is benefitted. This is what happens in a good game, but the similarity ends there. In this game it does matter who wins.

I shall now proceed to describe some of the team's usual moves to control the game, and some of the more frequent moves by the families. Our main frame of reference is what we could call a "collective Aikido," in which the strength of the opponent's moves is used to our position's advantage. It starts with the first telephone call, in which an agreement, explicit in appearance, is reached: the therapist is the expert and the family goes to him for help.

In spite of this agreement, the family comes to the consultation with some kind of set ideas about the type of help it needs and what the therapist has to do to produce a change, such as give advice, lock the patient up, medicate him, etc. These ideas agree with their own previous attempts to solve the problem. The family makes two moves: On one hand, they come to us because we are experts. On the other, they place obstacles in the way of our performance when they try to pressure us to act according to their concept of the problem.

This double movement can be described as follows: (1) "This is very grave; (2) We know you are the expert, we recognize you as such, and therefore you will do what we already know must be done; (3) You are going to quickly take this large package; and (4) You are going to take care of it." To which we usually reply: (1) "Thank you very much, you are right, this is truly very grave; (2) I am the expert and therefore when I take charge I am determining that what you say is completely true; (3) Owing to such a grave and urgent situation, you have to first do this little thing; and (4) You have to do it yourselves." We will now describe these moves in detail.

Move 1. The Family Presents the Case as Grave

One of the typical moves of these families is the special use they make of their dramatic situation, as they perceive it. If the therapist accepts this urgency (regardless of whether he considers it real or imagined) by taking over a vacant function at this moment, he will probably be ineffective. His maneuvering ability will be affected, and he will be too involved in an excessive effort to produce a change himself. On the other hand, if he does not accept the definition of the situation as grave, he will lose credibility and the possibility of establishing alliances. Thus, our objective is to have the therapist take and expand the graveness of the case in ways that allow him to remain free while inducing the family to act.

The move consists of defining the situation as even worse, without also making a move to solve the problem. This results in a parenthesis or anxious void that in a way gives back to the family the need to do something that it had delegated to the therapist. Here we seem to verbally take charge when we amplify the problem, but we hand it back when we do not move. We carry out a counter-induction of the induction. For instance, the families might say: "We can't stand it any more" while they stare fixedly at the therapist, who then feels obligated to do something quickly. In this case, the therapist can answer: "This is really unbearable," followed by a silence that puts back in the family's court the need to do something. In other cases, the family might say something like: "Doctor if you don't do something soon, this or that can happen." The therapist might answer: "That and more, but I can't imagine what I can do if you don't change this situation first."

Move 2. The Family Recognizes the Therapist as Expert, Simultaneously Suggesting He Should Handle the Case the Way They Consider He Should

Normally, these maneuvers have a macro and a micro form (what in our jargon we call a "brute" form and an "underhanded" one). The macro or "brute" form consists of pressuring the therapist directly to take a certain stance. For example: "Shouldn't we try it?" or "Shouldn't we increase the medication, doctor?" or "I am sure the doctor agrees with me that it's time for him to leave the clinic."

The micro forms have more to do with the ways of conducting the session, as for example, when one person answers for another. Another side of the same coin is the attempt the family makes to shift from the central axis being worked. Therapist: "And you, George, what were you doing at that moment?" Bertha: (interrupting): "Another important subject is what happened on Tuesday, when . . . "

An interesting variation is not to define the problem and to discuss interminably the reason for the consultation. Each attempt the therapist makes to offer a definition is met with an "It's not exactly so" or "That's so, but . . . ." The therapist is disqualified as an expert in understanding the situation. Now, I will disqualify my own previous classification and offer a brilliant example of an "underhanded-brute" way of disqualifying the therapist. A family that consulted us about their 19-year-old daughter's suicide attempt was an expert at this type of maneuver. The girl said very little and did not answer her parents' repeated questions about the reason she tried to jump off the balcony. The therapist's intervention, aimed at the parents, was the following: "What happened with your daughter is that she's afraid of facing life. That is why we are asking you to temporarily organize her day at home, that you program her activities hour by hour, so that she can count on a safe, not frightening world. It is important that you don't ask her any questions, that you make decisions and find the way for her to obey them." Immediately, the mother said she thought this was completely right and then asked her daughter: "What do you think of it, dear?"

We basically respond to "underhanded" maneuvers with more of the same, being persistent, and to the "brute" maneuvers by making a declaration of retreat and suggesting they find a more appropriate expert. An example of persistence might be to continue asking questions, and to show the suicidal girl's mother that she had just done the opposite of what was indicated, insisting she not do it.

Move 3. The Family Presents the Problem as a Whole, and Expects It to Be Solved All at Once

It might be stated like this: "This started when she began talking to herself four months ago, saying strange things and fighting with everyone. The psychiatrist gave her medication, and saw her four times a week, but she had to quit her job. She doesn't sleep and wants to run away from home, saying she has to go down to the river to commit suicide. Lately, she has become worse. Do you think it will take you long to make her better, Doctor?" The family is asking here that the "picture" be modified very quickly. We do not handle a grave situation in an abstract way, and we do not agree with a global approach. On the contrary, our means are to focus attention, communication, and efforts on achieving one small objective in the direction of our client's wishes. We do not try to cure the psychotic or suicidal patient or drug addict, but to help him or her achieve a small initial change that is concrete, observable by all those involved in the case, and impossible to deny as an improvement.

To continue with the above example, the therapist asked if there was anything that was very important for the patient, that she liked a lot, and that she could not do at present because of her condition. They said that she had studied dancing with great dedication, and that she had to give it up. The therapist stated that although it would be very difficult to modify such a grave problem all of a sudden, it could be done step by step. He then asked the family if they would consider it a definite improvement for the patient to do one small dance step in the course of the following week. The aim changed from modifying the whole situation to "practicing one dance step means she is better," which is certainly much easier to achieve.

Move 4. The Family Expects the Therapist to Produce Change, Giving Him Responsibility for the I.P.'s Behavior, on Which He Can Have Much Less Influence Than They

Going back to the example used before, the family that had disqualified the therapist in an "underhanded-brute" way, asked him to meet with the daughter alone, so that he could persuade her to be more communicative with her mother. The therapist in the case answered: "I am sure that some individual sessions would be very useful, but unfortunately they won't be any good if we don't first calm her down. So I must insist on my request that you contribute to her sense of security, establishing a routine of everyday activities which she has to fulfill, and that you not make it possible for her to have corrosive doubts." The idea is to take advantage of the role of expert, agreeing to take charge of the treatment if they carry out some unavoidable tasks to help achieve the end result.

Another example might be: "You're probably right, your daughter almost definitely is schizophrenic, but what complicates the picture is the lack of discipline. Therefore, while we take care of treating the illness, it will be necessary for you to complete her education, otherwise it will be very difficult to obtain positive results."

In either case, the therapist handles the situation in a way that leads the family to take more charge than the therapist. We believe therapy is a paradoxical game because we get paid to win, but in general the game is played to make us lose. Winning depends on our using all the means at our disposal. It is ethically imperative to do so, because we are hired to dodge obstacles set in our path. The most obvious tool at hand is the therapy team, that functions like analysts of moves in a chess tournament: one person plays, with the backing of several. We have treated 200 cases this way and are satisfied in winning some of the matches.

CONCLUSION

We hope that this brief and perhaps incomplete description of two of our "hippogriffs" will be useful to illustrate our work and the way we develop the ideas of the MRI. We are quite satisfied with the results of our work. On one hand, we have been able to apply a type of treatment which is the result of a pragmatic culture to one that is radically different. An important sector of the population now demands briefer therapies with more concrete objectives, and a growing number of professionals are paying attention to the context and to the interventions that can modify it. On the other hand, we developed some strategies that allow us to work in situations where the effectiveness of psychosocial intervention is generally doubted, such as in organic illnesses, drug addiction, and gravely ill patients. We believe that progress lies in that direction, not so much through development of new ideas that replace the previous ones, but by applying and expanding the present ones to test their results and limitations. This is the road we continue to explore.

Chapter 13

From the Dictatorship of Lacan to the Democracy of Short-Term Therapies

Diana Weyland

From the beginning, my life developed within a system in which dictatorships and military regimes succeeded one another, with only two constitutionally-elected governments, neither of which ended its constitutional period.

Within this context, my life in Argentina was sprinkled by frequent trips to the U.S.A., and I began to notice that the Argentine society reproduced the power relationships of the current government in all its structure and subsystems, schools, clubs, religious congregations, as well as in the practice of different professions. These relationships were based on authoritarianism, arrogance, and lack of respect for the individual, as well as lack of awareness of a person's rights.

This pattern occurs even in those groups which supposedly oppose the system. On the surface, they criticize the system, but in their inner structures, they behave in the same way as the society they reject.

I graduated with a degree in Psychology from the University of Buenos Aires in 1973. At that time, and I understand still today, psychology was synonymous with psychoanalysis or, further still: Lacan.

At some point in my studies, which lasted between five and six years, I accidentally heard that there was something known as Family Therapy, Interactional Therapies, Behavior and Gestalt Therapies. But obviously, they were not considered serious or profound enough to deserve more than mere mention.

To show any inclination or interest toward any of those therapies meant running the risk of being heretic, immoral or, at best, superficial. In such cases, only a good individual psychoanalysis three or four times a week for many years might bring the lamb back to the sheepfold. Of course we all had the moral obligation to begin our own psychoanalysis at least a year before graduating. During such analysis, we were not told how easy and profitable it was to graduate and after acquiring eight, ten, or 25 patients, to just sit behind the couch expecting to receive good enough money at the end of the month. The termination of the therapy was not discussed since it was not good business. The patient who quit the treatment, even if financially broke, was surely being resistant since, undoubtedly, he was about to solve some specially important issue from his unconscious. In such cases one could feel, within the community of colleagues, the accusing finger: "Poor guy, he was very sick."

I should have to add the 2,000 courses psychologists are forced to take all through their lives, for one never stops learning . . . and to fill those free hours with patients so that, mobilizing people, more and more become patients. . . .

At this height, the reader will imagine that in Argentina there is just one group of stubborn professionals determined to repeat a relationship that defines and endlessly redefines whose boot is on top of whom, or how many boots shall I have to climb–with a progressively obscure and esoteric language–to reach the summit of a pyramid of individuals whose boots are on top of as many psychoanalyzed.

No, don't be misled. This pyramid is not limited to a group of professionals of sickness, for one-fourth of the population is under, really under, psychoanalytic treatment. The reader will then rightly think that Argentina is a tremendously rich country, where such a large number of the population can afford fees that are the equivalent, if not to all, at least to half or one-quarter of their monthly income.

Wrong again. Argentina is a very poor country. The reason for so many Argentines repeating this pattern is beyond my comprehension, at least in this chapter. For he repeats it not only with himself, but also with his children whom he evidently was not capable of educating since some psychologist in two to four sessions a week will eventually undo that which he so mistakenly does the rest of the week.

The conclusion is that in Argentina, if one is not for the government, one is either a communist or sold to the Yankee imperialism and he who does not go into psychoanalysis is resistant and therefore profoundly ill. But to be psychoanalyzed, one has to be aware of one's sickness. The deduction is then that all Argentines are sick.

What did I do after graduating? Shyly and inconspicuously I bought books about different ways of shortening and focusing therapies, hidden in dark corners in bookstores, to desperately try to lessen the pains of many people. Most of them wanted to solve their problems and some wanted to play at being analyzed.

I was working in the University Hospital of Buenos Aires surrounded at first by colleagues who somehow opposed the system too, and psychologists who thought that the way to socialize patients was to treat them in groups. It was 1974. The following year, many professionals who had never heard of the Oedipus complex entered the hospital. They ignored some other therapeutical theories too. Some boss liked doing electroencephalograms. He looked for dysfunctional waves. . . .

I worked alone. By that time, psychologists had become terrorists, subversive, and communist for the government in power. Meanwhile, I trained with psychoanalysts that worked with adolescents which luckily gave me some flexibility. During the seven or eight years of this process, I had good and bad results. Since my work was carried out in the privacy and confidence of my office, I could keep my sinful deviations from the psychoanalytic theory secret. Looking over some of the histories I notice I took into account the reality existing outside of the office. I'm relieved to see I didn't consider my patients as delinquents hidden behind their repressions. When I didn't know what to do, I didn't blame the patient's resistance, rather I thought about those corners of my unconscious not yet discovered. I think I loved my patients and this must account for the good results obtained with some of them.

In 1980, a son of mine died. As a docile believer I went back to the couch. How could I go on working with so great a pain and, as my colleagues probably believed, so great a guilt? My treatment lasted three sessions. I must confess my economic situation–I was broke–helped me think like a survivor: "In the rest of the world and for many centuries, all mothers have recovered from these pains without the help of a psychoanalyst. Why shouldn't I now?"

A year later, I was called from my youngest son's kindergarten–another province of the psychoanalytic religion–suggesting a psychological evaluation since he refused to speak English, a necessary condition for him to enter first grade. I did so, and after innumerable tests, I was told that his I.Q. was three years ahead of his age, reason enough for him to undertake treatment. I did not, but I communicated the authorities that Christian was three years above standard and since they were specialists in the subject, they would surely solve the problem effectively. I told Christian the same. The following day my son went to school speaking fluent English and has done so ever since.

I think at that moment I began being systemic without really knowing. Meanwhile, in my office, I interpreted the positive aspect of ambivalence. As to the government, when I stopped interpreting sexual drives, I stopped being a communist. Sometime after that, I met some colleagues whose outlook was close to mine, and from there I went straight to train with psychologists Celia Elzufan and Hugo Hirsch, thanks to whom I managed a revolution similar to Copernicus'.

I became subversive for the majority of psychologists, since believing people, and not their unconscious, are responsible for their behavior is chaotic for the national order. It was now 1983, the year of the first democratic government chosen without the proscription of political parties and the year in which I participated in the creation of the Systemic Association of Buenos Aires. I embraced the systemic cause with passion (one is forever adolescent) and a few months later I was training in a new hospital. My teachers this time were in the line of Minuchin's work–we saw the family together and tried to produce induced structural changes during the session.

The fact of seeing the clients exposed to everyone through the one-way mirror turned me into an artist. If the audience wanted short therapy Palo Alto style, I gave them this; if they wanted change of structure, I changed structures. This led me to a healthy skepticism of all scientific structures which was not too much of an effort since I belong to a family of German-Protestant origin in a

Latin-Catholic country which had given me a rather particular view of the accepted beliefs. In fact, it is difficult for my systemic colleagues to label me in relation to ulterior developments and often they react with suspicion.

Since I love winter, I managed to split Northern Hemisphere winters between vacations and professional contacts in Washington, Philadelphia, and New York. In 1986 I landed at the MRI which offered the idea that people from other latitudes dream of: a month's residence! A month of listening to, discussing, and observing the work of some of the better known professionals. And they, the best in the world, listened to my ideas, answered my questions, and even tried my suggestions with the clients. They taught me I was someone with the freedom to think and spontaneously change the direction of my interventions. I already mentioned a first Copernican revolution. This was my second. I was slow to assimilate it and am thankful for the invitation to write this chapter. It made me ponder on the subject and aware of the importance of the change. It was even therapeutic! I was given the freedom to grow. What MRI did for me is close to what Milton Erickson did for those who were lucky enough to meet him.

As I ended my residence, I started on a road in which I could defend myself well from the pressure of belonging "to them or to us."

Paul Watzlawick held a meeting on an essay in which he concluded that scientific theory was that one which produced the best results. I didn't have much to say, for this epistemological statement was the only one I could accept and feel my own . . . until the next one? Nearing 40, in Argentina, I was still a suspicious rebel without a cause for not belonging to any specific party, and I felt the eternal adolescent with an inborn inability to get involved.

At the MRI I learned that I was a person with *social* permission to think. Except for unusual talents, thinking on one's own or within a context that doesn't facilitate hinders growth and creates insecurity. To do so, surrounded by an atmosphere which promotes it, is good both for the client and the therapist.

It is my belief that thanks to President Alfonsin, during whose government, for the first time in Latin America, the military men responsible for dictatorships and crimes were judged and sentenced, some sectors of the Argentine society started to think and act somewhat more democratically. I also think this context influenced the change in attitude toward new theories in psychology in those remote southern latitudes. The systemic way of thinking has spread and we also hear of Cognitive and Psychoeducational theories. At present, I am head of a group of systemic therapy in a Regional Hospital (Regional Hospital of San Isidro) where there is also a group that works following Lacan's theories. I have been there for two years, they for 20.

At first they looked at me like angry dogs ready to eat me up, through disdain or interpretative aggression. Then they sent me all the mentally deficient patients and their families. It would be interesting to know how many mentally deficient people there are in this area of greater Buenos Aires; I may have met them all. The husbands and wives or parents of their patients were also a problem. They didn't know how to deal with them when they asked for information about the treatment of their children. They were impatient parents; they deserved Family Therapy. After some months, a psychiatrist noticed that chronic patients did not return after having been through systemic therapy. Others discovered that a team who could joke and laugh, though it interrupted the solemnity of rituals, was great fun. As a result they asked if they could observe the sessions.

Part of the time that my team dedicated to deal with the clients, I destined to informal chats in corridors. Some of them presently send us patient-clients, for they believe we can really do something for them. Nationwide, the Systemic Therapies, together with other newly-appreciated therapies, formed a strong and growing opposition front to the undisputed rule of psychoanalysis.

Presently, many Mental Health Services include systemic teams and the coexistence is beginning to be respectful. A week ago, I accidentally met the leader of the country's "Lacanian" movement. When he heard I had "changed sides," he asked me to be a speaker at his institute. I wonder if he is a systemic in disguise? At about this same time, a colleague at the Hospital suggested we work together on some ideas he had heard me develop during our lunches.

All this makes me think about the future. If those of us who received the permission to grow and develop our potentialities–as happened to me at MRI and to others elsewhere, even in Argentina–will spread and multiply this fashion of thinking allowing us to think in a context that is progressively more democratic, I have the hope that my country too will contribute with new developments towards helping growth and change efficiently and economically.

Chapter 14

A Swedish Experience

Klaus Pothoff

In Sweden, roughly 50 percent of hospital beds are to be found in psychiatric institutions. Every second, one of these beds is occupied by a patient diagnosed as schizophrenic. Out of Sweden's approximately 20,000 doctors, some 800 have chosen the task to cater for the psychiatric population. In 1981, I took over a psychiatric rehabilitation clinic with 260 inpatients. According to written communication, the department of health (Socialstyrelsen) did not consider it to be an extraordinary situation that most of the time I was the only doctor for all these patients and staff. The clinic was in a desolate state. Psychologic examination revealed that up to then 43 percent of the examined patients had been misdiagnosed, and, of course, treated according to faulty diagnoses resulting in poor outcome. This state of affairs seemed commonly accepted amongst staff, patients' relatives, administrators, and politicians.

In my desperation, I asked for permission to visit MRI in 1984. I had read several books from the Palo Alto group, participated in seminars held by Paul Watzlawick, and was positively impressed. Arriving at MRI, I was quite doubtful whether all these elegant solutions were applicable to my chronic population. I expressed my doubts–was greeted with warm laughter and invited to look around and make up my own mind.

Participating in seminars and therapy sessions, I was puzzled and still very doubtful; this was not just another way of conducting therapy, but an entirely different approach to central therapeutic issues. It was an amazing and thrilling challenge–but would it work when applied not to a non-selected Californian population, but to a highly selected Swedish chronic inpatient population?

I went back to Sweden and got started. The months-long waiting list to my clinic disappeared. Patient turnover increased from 66 patients a year to 222. In 12 months 80 percent of the chronic patients shown to be misdiagnosed previously were able to leave the clinic. Politicians, administrators, the mental-wardens' trade union, and colleagues *were not* enthusiastic about these changes.

In 1985, I decided to quit hospital psychiatry. I started my private practice. Without any advertising many patients, even from distant parts of the country, came to see me. One year later, the economic result was four times the auditors' forecast. Two years later, I paid off all the money I had borrowed to establish my practice that I was supposed to pay back over a 15-year period. Three years later, I had my own EEG facility. Meanwhile, I conducted supervision in my old home country of Germany, and the group did a marvelous job even with so-called hopeless cases. I still have no waiting list, and so far but one suicide. Now, four years later, I am about to open Scandinavia's first privately owned MRI-scanner (Magnetic Resonance Imaging); it happens to be made in California.

In conclusion, I find the MRI approach to be useful. Perhaps it does not suit you. Perhaps you are just as doubtful as I was in the beginning, or happy with your actual therapeutic instrumentarium and results. In these instances there is no point in giving it a real honest try. Personally, I feel deeply obliged to Paul Watzlawick and his coworkers, and I welcome this opportunity to express my gratitude.

Chapter 15

Teaching Brief Therapy Techniques to Family Practice Residents

Michael Bloom

The "interactional" approach to brief psychotherapeutic treatment that was developed at the Mental Research Institute (Palo Alto Group) is ideal for use in family practice for a number of reasons (Watzlawick and Weakland, 1977). First, it was developed specifically to be a *brief* treatment program. At the Mental Research Institute (MRI), brief treatment program patients were kept to a maximum of ten sessions (Fisch, Weakland, and Segal, 1982; Weakland et al., 1974). In our experience at the Sioux Falls Family Practice Residency, we have seen patients for two to seven sessions with three or four meetings being the mode. The first session is usually an hour in length, while subsequent sessions range from one half-hour to one hour.

Second, although no therapeutic approach is easy to learn, the interactional approach can be adequately mastered in the course of a three-year residency program with sufficient effectiveness to deal with a majority of the common problems seen in family practice (e.g., common psychosomatic disorders which have not yet become long term; situational depression; situational anxiety, common behavioral problems of children; and many acute marital problems). There are many other forms of therapy which are effective, but they require far more training to master, even at a primary care level; they are, therefore, inappropriate for standard residency training.

Third, there is a large margin for error in the interactional model. Even in cases where no improvement occurs, it is unlikely the therapy will make matters worse, unlike many other forms of therapy.

The interactional approach is based on general system theory and therefore relies heavily on family therapy for its effectiveness (Watzlawick, Weakland, and Fisch, 1974). It fits with the emphasis family physicians place on the family being the unit of care. However, it has more flexibility than other family therapy approaches. It can be used effectively with only one member of the family present, as long as the therapeutic solution is seen in the context of the family system. A final advantage of the interactional model is that family practice residents embrace it more easily than most other forms of therapy, especially the so-called "insight" therapies, which seek to "understand" one's past and how it causes one's problems. In "insight"-oriented therapy the physician must remain relatively passive and rather long-term therapy is required. In contrast, the brief therapy model described here is based on the physician being an action-oriented problem solver, a role more consistent with the physician's training.

THE THERAPEUTIC PROCESS

The interactional model primarily focuses on the repeating patterns of family interaction which serve to maintain problems, or at least, do not require them to change. The family's view of the problem, which supports their failure to change is also seen as an area for intervention. The basic strategy of the interactional model is to create a new reality of the problem and the sequence of events which follow from that reality. The ultimate goal is to stop the repetition of old patterns of which the problem is a part and to establish new patterns of behavior which lead to different outcomes (Watzlawick and Weakland, 1977; Fisch, Weakland, and Segal, 1982; Weakland et al., 1974). The therapy process can be broken down into seven stages: (A) joining the family; (B) getting an explicit statement of the problem from each family member; (C) understanding each family member's attempted solutions to the problem; (D) understanding what would be "successful change" according to each family member; (E) reframing the problem; (F) giving directions and homework; (G) getting feedback on the acceptance or nonacceptance of the physician's solution and "closing the deal."

(A) Joining the family: This is done very briefly at the beginning of the meeting. It simply includes making sure the physician makes contact with each family member present, shaking hands, making good eye contact, and having some small talk with each of them. This is followed by a very brief statement by the physician of how a decision was made to have a meeting.

(B) Getting an explicit statement of the problem: Each member of the family is then asked to make an explicit statement of the problem of the identified patient and how it affects them and the family. This must be put in terms of behavioral sequences. For example, it will not do to have a family member say that the man of the household is depressed. A full statement of the problem must entail what behavioral sequences are occurring as a result of the depression. In the above example, we would follow with the questions, "What does he do that makes you think he's depressed?" We would attempt to elicit the following kind of response: "He stays in his room all day; when one goes in and talks to him, he yells and screams at her and tells her to get out of the room; the rest of the family then ignores him for a week." Within reason, it's best to gather as many details about these sequences as possible, given the time available.

(C) Attempted solutions: After the behavioral sequences of the problem are described, the family member is asked about the ways the family tried to solve the problem. Since the solutions the family has tried are not working, the attempted solutions are seen by the physician as part of the problem pattern. Finally, the family members are asked for their present solution. Knowing a family's position on the problem and potential solutions is helpful in tailoring reframes and directives in ways that they will be most easily accepted. Each of the above questions A, B, and C are asked of a family member before the next family member is asked to respond to them. Family members are not allowed to interrupt each other. This demonstrates the respect the physician has for each person's point of view and helps the physician gain a more accurate view of each person's perspective. Each person's turn to talk is based on respecting the hierarchy with the parents going first followed by the children.

(D) Definition of successful change: The physician next asks the family to determine the minimum amount of change which would be required to feel as though there is no longer is a major problem in the

family. It is important to help the family establish realistic goals which are not utopian in nature. For example, a family member suggests that "never arguing" would be the goal of treatment. This would have to be guided into more realistic goals.

(E) Reframing: After the above information has been gathered, the therapeutic intervention begins with the reframing of the problem. Reframing must be distinguished here from insight. Therapies developed around insight are looking for the reason a problem occurred because it is felt this "truth" will lead to resolution of the problem. In the Interactional Approach, the reframed problem may be "truth" or not, but is seen as valuable only in its ability to free the family or individuals from their old pattern of behavior. Reframing means giving people a new explanation for their problem that will lead to new behavior.

For example, a patient is seen for chronic back pain, which has incapacitated him. Medical evaluations have shown no organic pathology which is treatable. The physician notes considerable secondary gain in the form of attention received from the care-giving wife. The doctor believes this is a major contributor to the patient's symptoms, but recognizes that direct confrontation will be met with considerable resistance. The physician, in a meeting with the couple, tells the wife that for successful treatment she will be required to devote herself to her husband's care. The doctor then directs her to distract her husband from his pain by only paying attention to non-pain behaviors, including specific prescribed "distracting" activities (which avoid secondary gain). It is suggested that this will be difficult but that a wife as devoted as she may succeed. The reframe here is changing the meaning of "care giving" from "taking care of" to "distraction." In order to be a devoted wife, then, she must no longer treat her husband like an invalid, thus breaking the cycle of secondary gain.

(F) Giving directions. Within the context of the reframed problem, directions are given for new behaviors to be tried. These new behaviors are aimed at breaking the old patterns, while replacing them with less problematic ones. This is frequently put into the form of homework assignments, which are directives that the family is supposed to do before the next appointment. The main difficulty here is giving directives which will avoid strong resistance.

For example, parents ask for counseling because of a behavior problem in the child. The physician, while inquiring about sequences of events, recognizes that the parents are very distant and the child's "problems" are the one thing that brings the parents together. The physician realizes, however, this couple would deny any problems between them. He, therefore, continues to focus on the problems of the child while attempting to bring the parents closer together. The parents may be told they have to work together to develop rules for the child. They are then helped to get past any difficulties they have in working together on these rules. The child probably does better more in response to the parents working together than the rules themselves. The parents frequently respond to this improved communication regarding their child by transferring this to other areas of their life and being closer.

The major problem most novice therapists have is, although they know what change needs to take place, they take a while to catch on to how to give directives in such a way as to avoid resistance.

(G) Feedback. This consists of listening and watching for verbal and nonverbal cues as to whether they have accepted the reframing and directives. If they have not, a new reframing, new directives, new homework must be tried until an acceptable solution is found.

Follow-up. During subsequent therapeutic meetings, the physician will start out by getting a description from each family member as to how the homework alignments turned out, and whether the hoped-for changes in behavioral patterns have occurred. If they have not, the physician must again alter the reframing and the directives. As soon as change has occurred in the family, leading to the problem resolving, it is time to begin to back out of involvement with the family. This is usually done by scheduling one final follow-up appointment at a significantly distant time, for example a month.

TEACHING RESIDENTS FAMILY THERAPY

Early in the first year of residency, residents are presented with four one-hour didactic presentations on family systems' concepts and therapy. The next teaching opportunity usually occurs when a family presents for family therapy. The family may come out of the resident's own practice, or a referral to me.

Prior to this meeting, the resident and I go over the stages of therapy as I have outlined above. The resident is told he/she is the primary therapist. I will intervene during the course of our session as necessary, but the resident is responsible for leading the discussion. Usually during the first family therapy session, I find myself directing the course of the discussion about half of the time. This is enough direction to ensure things stay on course and that all the pertinent information is gathered, while still allowing the resident to gain experience. Once the necessary information has been attained (A-D as outlined above) the resident and I excuse ourselves and step out of the room for a brief discussion which usually lasts about five to ten minutes. During this time we discuss how we will reframe the problem, give directives, and provide homework assignments. After re-entering the therapy room the resident is again given charge of this discussion with my backup. Often, once the initial reframing and directions have been given, I find myself dealing with any resistances on the part of the family, altering the reframing and prescription as necessary to get the family's compliance. We then set a date for our next meeting. This concludes our first meeting. Following this, the resident and I critique our intervention.

Just prior to our next meeting, we discuss our strategy again. The resident is again put in change of gathering information on how therapy is progressing. After this information has been gathered, the resident and I again step out briefly to discuss any reframing or new directives which may be necessary. After the break the resident again takes the lead. Following the session we have another discussion about how the therapy session went. Subsequently, when we see families the same process is followed, but supervision becomes less active with each therapeutic intervention experience, until the supervisor is no longer in the room. Residents may then get supervision either through use of a one-way mirror, videotape, or consultation, as the situation and the level of ability warrant.

CONCLUSION

We have found Family Practice residents able to develop enough mastery of family therapy techniques during the course of their residency to effectively handle many of the problems they are called upon to treat. As in any other area of medicine, the learning process must include developing the ability to recognize when to treat and when to refer. This is, of course, dictated by individual factors, such as personal interest, ability, and level of training. However, a rule of thumb I teach residents is to diagnose how stable the problem has become in the family system. Problems of relatively short duration (e.g., a few months), and even problems of longer duration such as serious anxiety or reactive depression, frequently respond to brief therapy–often best delivered by the trusted family doctor rather than a more experienced but unknown therapist. In the case of chronic problems, the individual and family have stabilized around the problem and special skill is required to overcome the more pronounced resistance to change common in such instances. Therefore, these cases should be referred.

Chapter 16

A Physician's View: On One-Downsmanship and Treating the Complainant

William Cohen[1]

Some ideas slip quietly through the side doors at dusk, taking up residence in the corners of consciousness, while others use the main entrance in broad daylight, accompanied by music and cheering throngs. For me, the model of the Brief Therapy Center of the Mental Research Institute (the problem-solution interaction) definitely belongs to the brass band/ticker tape variety.

I can date my conscious exposure to the Mental Research Institute to sometime in 1980. The date written in the front of my copy of *Change* (Watzlawick, Weakland, and Fisch, 1974) is "11/80" and I had already read at least parts of the book earlier that year. As a relatively new student of clinical hypnosis, and, therefore, of Milton Erickson's ideas, I was indeed impressed to discover that Dr. Erickson himself had written the foreword to *Change*. My entry into the field of therapy really began at that time, as I included in my education the study of those therapies which utilized the language of change and the conceptual framework Milton Erickson developed through years of clinical work.

My next exposure was the "MRI panel" (Watzlawick, Fisch, and Weakland) at the First Erickson Congress (December, 1980). My copy of *Pragmatics of Human Communication* (Watzlawick, Beavin, and Jackson, 1967) is dated "12/80," and *The Language of Change* (Watzlawick, 1978) appears the following spring. I heard Carlos Sluzki present a workshop in Pittsburgh in February of 1981 on symptom maintenance. *The Tactics of Change* (Fisch, Weakland, and Segal, 1982) is dated 1982, the year of publication.

My reading progressed as I continued the journey from primary care pediatrician to developmental and behavioral pediatrician. As I continued to evolve into the field of family therapy, it was natural for me to pursue my first set of intensive training at the Mental Research Institute. In January, 1984, I attended the Winter Seminar at which time I learned of MRI's diversity. It was at that point that I focused in on the Brief Therapy model, as I recognized there the codification of ideas that has become one of the important frames of reference in my work. I continued my study at the Brief Therapy Workshop in Palo Alto, and at a similar program presented by Dick Fisch in Pittsburgh, PA. In addressing my relationship with the ideas of MRI, I will focus on how the systematic principles of the Brief Therapy model have affected my thinking and clinical work.

The key principle of the Brief Therapy model is that the attempted solution inadvertently maintains the problem. The therapist therefore seeks to block the attempted solution by substituting a behavior which will lead to the desired outcome.

The framework for analyzing any problem was splendidly simple and straightforward. Dick Fisch called it a "parsimonious" theory. (He did warn that it was at times difficult to execute, and Lord knows, I proved him correct on that account many times.) This is how I understood the process:

1. What is the problem?
   (a) How is this a problem?
   (b) For whom is this a problem?
   (c) Why now?
2. What have you tried to do to solve this problem?
   (a) What has been suggested that you did not try?
   (b) Why did you discard those suggestions?
3. What would you like to see happen in the course of treatment? What would be the first sign of change in that direction?
4. What is your explanation for the problem? (This is the first step in defining the client's position: beliefs about the nature of the problem, values, etc.)

The therapist using this model is able to identify the complainant, describe how the problem is acted out, and what the attempted solutions have been. By abstracting the direction of the attempted solutions, the therapist then understands that the "true" solution is 180 degrees in the opposite direction. Using the information about the client's position, the therapist designs an intervention to break the repetitive cycle.

Two particular ideas from the Brief Therapy model stand out as centrally important: the one-down position of the therapist and the principle of treating the complainant. They seem to represent an intersection of the singularities of my personal development and professional training as a physician with the general ideas and theories of MRI's Brief Therapy model.[2]

THE ONE-DOWN POSITION

My personal exploration of the one-down position starts on the airplane, flying back from California. It is August, 1984 and I have spent a week in Palo Alto, attending the Brief Therapy Workshop. I was particularly fascinated by the recommendation to assume a one-down stance. I was quite sure that I had heard it before. After all I had read *The Tactics of Change* in 1982. No matter when the seed was planted, the idea germinated and started to grow in August, 1984.

I remember a sense of joy and playfulness on that last day of the workshop. I remember looking around and wondering why the others seemed so serious. One other participant was also enjoying the lightness of the atmosphere, the gentle good humor of Dick Fisch and John Weakland. I recall feeling smug and satisfied that, like an EST participant of yore, I got it.

On the plane ride home, I pulled out a thick pad of paper, and systemically surveyed my case load with the zeal of the newly converted. As I was musing about this simple, elegant, parsimonious framework, and thinking about my case load, my ongoing struggles with my father flashed into my head.

THE PROBLEM

I live in Pittsburgh, Pennsylvania, my parents live in New York, and we keep in touch by phone. Whenever I hang up the phone, it always feels the same. No matter how I seek to guide the conversations with my parents, I am always left hurt, enraged, or annoyed. Their questions are legitimate, but they stick like a knife. "How are things going? Are you busy? Do you have many patients? Are you getting any new patients? Do people want to come and see you? Are you sure you have enough patients?" This all sounds like, "You don't have what it takes to make it on your own." And no matter how busy I am, and indeed I am busy enough, my stomach churns. My answers are predictable: "Oh, things are going well. They're just fine. I get lots of referrals. Yes, some are even from doctors, but a lot are from satisfied (very slight emphasis here) customers, and you know, Dad, that's even more important."

And so it goes. In each conversation, I hear my father's subtle reproach, and each time I answer the same way. In the interim, between those weekly telephone calls, I find myself thinking up new, more extravagant ways to answer. "How are things going?" had to be a trick question, because it kept getting asked, again and again. How can I assure him that I am competent and financially responsible?

THE ATTEMPTED SOLUTION

In the luxury of my own private "not-good-enough" hell, I dream up statements such as "never been better," or "filling up my hours," and that I feed to my father, along with gross income and net profit figures, truly believing that this will do the trick. No, I somehow know that this will not do the job, but I desperately want to convince him. So I resort to the "Why" questions: "Why can't he recognize my abilities, why is he so negative, why does he cut me down?" On, and so on, *ad nauseam*, year after unsatisfying year.

The Revelation. "If you can do it, you know it."[2]

That week in August, for the third time in my life, I heard stated the premise that the attempted solution inadvertently maintains the problem, and the way out of the circle involves *doing* something 180 degrees in the opposite direction, even though, in fact *especially* though, it makes no sense. (I recall John Weakland's interesting response to those participants who decoded this intervention as a "paradox." He explained that suggesting to a girl with anorexia nervosa that she may be eating "too much for now" could better be described as "counter-intuitive," since it actually does not satisfy the rigid philosophical definition of a paradox.)

Logically, formally, I understood that this was true. It made perfect sense to stop doing more of the same. "What would happen if . . . ?" I will not attempt to convince you that I was testing this scientifically. I really did not doubt this stuff at all. But I was responding to the same thirst for a new kind of knowledge that pulled me to the front of a classroom five years before to have a needle stuck through the back of my hand so I could learn, by doing, what hypnotic anesthesia was all about.

It was quite easy to formulate my plan. All I had to do was predict my ordinary response to my father's questions, and say the opposite. I am aware of the same excitement now as I recall planning what to do and say, anticipating with pleasure the opportunity to put this lovely theory into practice in my personal life. It never occurred to me that the outcome would be anything other than total success, although I had no idea what would happen.

PLANNING THE INTERVENTION

I knew that I would call my parents after I arrived in Pittsburgh and expected that they would ask about the trip. In the past, I would have reported my experience, highlighting the excitement of learning something new, the delight in discovering a fresh approach to my work, pride in achieving my goals, and enthusiasm about the people I worked with. And they would have simply said, "That's nice." Clearly, this was not the toxic situation I dreaded. I recognized that I would not address that specific problem. However, my week in Palo Alto made it easy to see that all of my attempted solutions fell into the category of playing one-up. Consequently, no matter what the situation, I need only take a one-down position. At that precise point, I realized with startling clarity what needed to be done: I had to be uncertain, a bit sad and wistful, disappointed, not with the workshop, but with myself.

EXECUTING THE PLAN

Returning home at 5 o'clock on Saturday, I wait until Sunday morning before I make the call. My mother answers the phone, as usual, but this time I ask for my father to get on the extension: I am playing for keeps.

My mother asks, "So, how was the conference?"

"Oh, it was okay," I offer, tentatively, and then, as an afterthought, ". . . I guess."

In retrospect, that seemed to be the turning point.

"What do you mean?" asks my father, going in for the kill.

"Oh, I don't know if I got everything that I wanted to or could have."

"I know what it was," he said, offering to be helpful. "You are so used to lecturing that you didn't like the fact that other people were in charge. You weren't the big cheese and your ego was hurt."

As my blood pressure starts a slow, silent climb, I get ready to argue. "No" slips out as my mouth begins moving before my brain is fully engaged. Fortunately, my thoughts leap ahead of my tongue and, changing direction, I continue, "Well, maybe you're right. I hadn't thought of it that way. My problem is that I *thought* I understood what was going on, but now I'm not so sure. At the beginning of the week, I was really excited because I believed that I knew what these guys were talking about. After all, I read their books and heard these folks present this material when I was out there in January. But then, by Friday, the last day, I started to notice that everyone was listening seriously and only one other person was smiling and laughing. I thought that I understood what this was all about, but now I wonder if maybe I missed something. I just don't know. . . ."

"Don't worry about it," said my parents, almost in unison.

"I'm just a little disappointed. I guess I'll get over it."

There followed a series of conciliatory statements like, "Are you all right? This is so unlike you. I hope you feel better soon."

The phone call moved along to brush on other relevant family issues and ended on that minor key which I seemed to have struck rather easily. Ringing off, I found that my faith in Dick Fisch and John Weakland allowed me to go through a door which they drew in thin air, passing into a realm where critical parents become loving and caring.

For the next five weeks, I experimented with this new world: my uncertainty eliciting my parents' clear explicit expressions of caring: "Are you any better? We're concerned; we love you." It seems I found the Holy Grail, and it has always been close at hand. Being able to hear that they are concerned about me seems to require that I shift my position from "nothing could be better" to "things aren't the way I'd like them to be."

In addition to this powerful validation of the ideas and principles of the Brief Therapy model, I discovered how comfortable it can be to get lost in "helplessness," even of so minor a sort as mine. I recall with nostalgia the comfort of hearing these caring words and the simultaneous intellectual awareness of how they related to my new position of uncertainty. I understood how it was possible to get lost in that caring–a strong seductive pull toward symptomatic behavior. I also discovered that it took some effort to change my position, to move in the direction of "I'm okay" but with a difference.

I suspect that the difference is twofold. Now I can be mostly all right, but at times be down in the dumps, and now my parents can accept my statements of being okay, because they know that I am human enough to feel depressed. Things are no longer *always* fine. The edge is off. And having done it, I know it.

COMMENTS

Fisch, Weakland, and Segal suggest the routine adoption of the one-down stance in the context of therapist maneuverability in order to enhance compliance, increase the release of information, and reduce the possibility that the client will feel blamed for having failed to resolve the problem by himself (p. 34).

At the same time, the shift to a one-down stance most often involves a 180-degree shift ("U-turn") in that the majority of professionals of any sort, by nature, take a one-up or expert stance. Indeed, this seems to be implied in the concept of "professional," leading to reciprocal expectations on the part of the provider and the client.

Medical education encourages overresponsibility. Early in training, professors and practicing clinicians begin to model the process of constructing a differential diagnosis. (The differential diagnosis can be understood as a list of "might be's," starting with the most likely, but continuing to the most obscure. Any individual with an illness can appreciate the process of systemically considering the probable cause/explanation for his/her symptoms.) However, that sense of responsibility, coupled with the process of differential diagnosis which is based on uncertainty ("what if") seems to lead to enormous pressure on the physician to come up with the one correct answer. The physician lives under the uncomfortable expectation of having all the answers and solving all the problems while knowing that she may be missing the "real" answer. The physician can resolve the inherent tension between the desire to know and the awareness of the inability to truly know in at least two ways: by acknowledging uncertainty or by attempting to deny the uncertainty by taking a position of great certainty. The physician using the latter approach adopts a one-up position in an attempt to solve the problem of uncertainty. Since the attempted solution maintains the problem, the cycle continues, with greater pressure to know the ultimately unknowable.

Fourteen years of medical education had inculcated me in the one-up position: almost everywhere I went, I saw it modeled. My fellow classmates were most skilled at using it at the beginning of our clinical rotations. They talked about their exploits with great bravado while I quivered in fear of the potential consequences of my limited expertise. Although I remember quite well those physicians who seemed more at ease, but I am not sure I fully understood how they differed from the masses until I discovered how exquisitely comfortable I felt shifting to the one-down position. The relief I experienced is akin to the feeling one gets when one leaves a stuffy, underventilated, overheated house and walks out into the bright sunshine of a clear winter's day.

My love affair with one-downsmanship grew as I examined the dynamics of helping. Clients/patients come for help in distress, feeling one-down, at the mercy of their problems. I presume that adults feel uncomfortable in this position, even though some individuals adapt and blame themselves repeatedly for their dilemmas, dwelling in the eternal house of "poor me." A one-down therapist levels the uncomfortable distance, and moves toward greater flexibility in the relationship, with each partner having some responsibility for change. The locked-in complementarity of a patient's statement "I'm broken" matched by a physician's reply, "I'll fix you" is fraught with peril.

Adopting a one-down position automatically releases me from my pre-existing expectations, and those of the patient and client. My personal values include the importance of empowering the client, so that they emerge from treatment with a sense of ownership of the outcome, sharing Jacobson's notion that "the strategic approach (can) be used most humanely, benevolently, in a way that contributes not only solution of the presenting problem, but also to the client's autonomy and sense of mastery of his own life" (Jackson, 1983, p. 77).

TREATING THE COMPLAINANT

Over the last five years in both practicing MRI brief therapy and in teaching this problem-solving approach, one of the central components has continued to be the importance of defining the complainant and focusing treatment solely or predominantly on him/her. In reviewing *The Tactics of Change*, the handbook of Brief Therapy Center, I was surprised to see just how little space was given to developing the concept of treating the complainant (pp. 42-43).

My experiences as a consultant were particularly helpful in clarifying the issues. By way of the example, an internist requested that I make an urgent trip to the hospital to see a 26-year-old man who was just diagnosed with diabetes mellitus. This man was having a great deal of difficulty accepting the ramifications of the diagnosis: i.e., the need to test his blood and inject himself with insulin several times a day, the dietary changes, etc. He was on the verge of leaving the hospital against medical advice. The internist hoped I could persuade him to change his mind by convincing him that staying was most important to his health, although this was what the physician had already attempted in the first place. I replied that I could see this man, but I doubted I would have much success, because I did not believe I could tell him anything that would change his mind. However, I did believe that I might be able to be of some assistance to the physician directly in dealing with this young man.

As a member of a Health Maintenance Organization, this patient would continue to receive care by the same physician or a colleague and I wondered aloud if it might be worth analyzing the situation to discover some way that the physician himself could address the issues directly with the patient. The physician eagerly agreed.

I suggested that this young man was overwhelmed by the diagnosis and feeling out of control of his life. His threats to leave the hospital struck me as an excellent way to assert his control, with the possible unfortunate consequence of angering the physician and the hospital staff. Since this young man had appropriate intellectual abilities, I supposed that he in fact knew very well how serious this disease was, and he was not information-deficient. This made sense to the physician, who was willing to consider what he could do. I suggested that he communicate his respect for the young man's position, commenting on how upsetting all this information must be. The physician was able to understand that by giving this man his freedom, he no longer needed to struggle to attain it. After some further discussion, the physician felt comfortable talking to this patient. I asked him to call me after he spoke with his patient. Several hours later, the physician reported back. He had told the patient that he had been thinking about the problem, had spoken with a colleague, and realized that the information was quite upsetting. Indeed, it seemed that the patient needed some time to consider the matter. He then offered to discharge the patient and told him he was available to discuss the illness and its treatment at the patient's convenience. The patient then decided against discharge and began to learn about how to care for his illness.

My discussion with the physician hinged on one central issue: how could he maintain (or, in this case, restore) a cooperative relationship with the patient? If they fought, I did not believe that they would be able to work together, because the patient would have a most difficult time coming back for treatment: he would have to admit he had been wrong. When the physician was able to understand the legitimacy of the man's reaction to the diagnosis and shift from seeing him as a bad patient to a scared person, the intervention flew on its own.

I learned to work with the complainant rather than the patient when the intended recipient of my services was less than cordial in welcoming me to her room: "Who are you and why are you here?" I would reply: "Dr. X asked me to talk to you about the problem you are having with your leg/back/etc." The dilemma seemed to reside in the fact that the patient was expecting the treatment to come from his/her physician. Although this was not always the situation, most of the referrals I received seemed to be requests to deal with complaints which the physician had determined was either not of physiological origin, or, if they were, did not respond to standard medical treatment.

These psychosomatic complaints were particularly difficult to deal with since it was extremely difficult to contract with the patient on any mutually agreeable goals. The concept of the "complainant" defined the dilemma. It was the physician who was the complainant, and, in the best of all possible worlds, I would be able to be most helpful to the symptomatic individual if I focused my intervention on the physician.

Frequently, the physician would want to be rid of the patient. When the patient was not a co-complainant and when the complainant was uninterested in exploring what he could do differently, I respectfully bowed out. In those instances regarding patient management or compliance issues, such as the one described above, physicians were more wiling to accept the role of the complainant by accepting consultation from me and dealing directly with the patient.

The following case from a medical teaching setting also demonstrates the usefulness of the notion of treating the complainant. As the behavioral pediatric consultant to a family medicine residency training program, I have the opportunity to participate in teaching systemic thinking to third-year residents by means of a case consultation. Residents bring a family from their practice and present the case for discussion. After two interviews (with observation and feedback), residents present the case.

Family medicine teaches an ecosystems approach, seeking to integrate information from a wide variety of sources to develop a comprehensive understanding of the issues which impact on the health of the various family members. During the course of a well-child visit, Dr. M. learns that the nine-year-old boy was having some problems in school. Dr. M.'s ears perk up, and he wants to learn more about the situation. There were behavior problems in the classroom which led to a change in school placement. This change had occurred at the beginning of the current school year. In addition, the boy was seeing a counselor. Mother reports that the situation is improving. When Dr. M. needs a case for his behavioral pediatrics rotation, he remembers this family and calls them to come for a special consultation about the school problem.

When the family fails to show for the consultation, the resident is visibly agitated. We use the block of time fruitfully, leading the resident to the conclusion that the mother seems to have little reason to come in to discuss with an expert a "problem" which may no longer trouble the family. Dr. M. discovers that his curiosity in learning about school problems is distracting him from paying attention to the needs and requests of this family. He has become the complainant. Discovering that the identified patient (in this case, the whole family) is frequently not the complainant proves to be a fascinating lesson. (For instance, it explains problems of noncompliance with medication: the doctor is the complainant and the patient doesn't care. The physician has much more energy and interest in the patient's compliance than the patient himself.)

The resident in question is delighted with this new frame of reference, and we proceed to the Behavioral Pediatrics conference. Our teaching agenda is to develop this notion for his colleagues. As the case is presented, we discover how well these young physicians have been indoctrinated: in hearing that the family failed to keep the appointment, one resident becomes indignant. By trying to investigate the problem, she says, Dr. M. has been faithfully discharging his responsibility as a family physician, and this family obviously does not care. She suggests that we involve the county child protective services to investigate for possible child neglect if they do not keep the next appointment! It takes a bit of effort and patience to highlight the previously-noted fact that the child is already in treatment and the problem had significantly improved without any intervention from Dr. M. or the health center. The major teaching point of the conference is the importance of asking, "For whom is this a problem?" (At each subsequent conference in the series, the resident dutifully identifies complainants in each case.)

CLOSING REMARKS

The simplicity of the Brief Therapy model becomes its greatest strength. The four questions outlined provide a beginning course in systems thinking for all the stuck helpers I encounter in my educational activities. And the great clarity of the model explains its utility. These days, I walk on many paths as Developmental Pediatrician, Behavioral Medicine Consultant, educator, and therapist. Nevertheless, at times of confusion, I find myself moving back to these questions, and like the string in the labyrinth, they lead me back home.

NOTES

1. This paper is dedicated with love and gratitude to my parents, Joseph and Ethel Cohen. I wish to express acknowledgement to V. Bonnie King for editorial assistance in the preparation of this manuscript.

2. I am indebted to Mony Elkaim for his stimulating discussion of singularities, and Paul Watzlawick's description of moire patterns at the Eighth Biennial MRI Conference, San Francisco, 1987.

3. Heinz von Foerster, speaking at the Plenary Session entitled "The Processes of Reality Construction" at the Sixth Biennial MRI Conference, *Maps of the Mind, Maps of the World.* offered a variant of this notion in the following: "If you desire to see, learn how to act" (p. 27).

Chapter 17

Influence of MRI Brief Therapy on Research Within Psychiatric Settings

Stefan Priebe

In the 1970s, most students of psychology in West Germany were excited by the ideas of MRI, and Paul Watzlawick was a prominent exponent. Out of a nonconformist rejection of fashion, I did not read his books at that time. So it was only after some years of practice in psychiatry that I approached the publications of authors from MRI. At that time, I was looking for an approach beyond my training in client-centered and behavior therapy, and beyond psychiatrist's mere common sense. My search was mainly for an effective and concise method of bringing about change in psychotic and nonpsychotic in-patients, and to deal successfully with everyday problems in their treatment. I felt immediately attracted by the systemic views and the concept of brief therapy as developed at MRI and decided that I had to have some personal contact with MRI. In 1983, I spent five enjoyable and inspiring weeks at MRI under the monthly residency program. Afterwards, I felt more competent in manipulating even severely disturbed patients into doing what was thought to be positive, such as taking their medication, resuming a job, or giving up some of their symptoms. I had adopted new ways of doing therapy with individuals and with families. Principles of brief therapy seemed to be adjustable to conventional psychiatric settings and to work within them very well.

However, working at a psychiatric department of a university, my job and my ambition were not only to treat patients, but also to do research. As far as research was concerned, the situation was more difficult as research and publications in conventional psychiatry are based upon empirical quantitative data. Measurement may not be the heart of science, but statistically significant results are definitely what counts in the world of psychiatric research of today. One may complain about this, but if one wants to promote new ideas in psychiatry, one should respect this rule and utilize it. The question was how to apply principles of MRI Brief Therapy and produce convincing statistical data.

A first step was to shift away from the family as the system research and therapies mainly focus on. Family therapy seems to be the most popular offspring of MRI all over the world. Yet, in ordinary psychiatry, limitations of family therapy are obvious. Maybe unlike in the United States or in Italy, in Berlin, very few psychiatric patients–at least the severely disturbed ones–live within a family. Parents, siblings, or children of the patients may live in different parts of Germany and at least in psychotic patients, consistent partnerships are rare. Additionally, many family members and partners reject any idea of family or couple therapy. A survey recently carried out in different treatment settings (in-patients, partially hospitalized patients, and out-patients) in Berlin (West) shows that the majority of even those patients who have relatives or partners available and are prepared to take part in therapy, do not want their relatives to be involved in treatment. And as we belong to a community health system, we are not in a position to refuse treatment for those patients who refuse family therapy. Psychiatrists take some responsibility for their patients and cannot merely just send them away.

Regardless of its feasibility, there is another problem of family therapy in conventional psychiatric settings. Most current concepts of family therapy seem to be set up as if phenomena and treatment approaches on a biological level would be irrelevant. Often drug treatment which dominates conventional psychiatry and family therapy can be applied by the same psychiatrist only with great difficulty. For example, a psychiatrist who tells a family that the patient should for some reason, persist with his symptoms and who at the same time, prescribes the patient drugs against those symptoms, would hardly be credible. As a consequence, within those settings, family therapy does not determine a general approach to psychiatric problems. It rather tends to be viewed as an additional method, which is administered by different therapists only in special cases and independently of medication. That exclusion of a biological perspective might be necessary in order to develop a consistent approach in theory. However, it sometimes enhances opposition between biological and psychological views of illness and treatment, which seems to be unhelpful in research within those conventional settings. Now, how can research be done based upon MRI brief therapy in settings in which drugs are often given and family therapy is rarely feasible?

Instead of focusing on families, we began to study therapeutic systems. A therapeutic system–as we understand it–necessarily consists of at least two persons: the patient with his symptoms or complaints and a psychiatrist/therapist, who defines the symptoms or the problem as psychiatrically relevant and whose definition is widely accepted because of his expertise and social position. One may also include the patient's family, a larger social system or parts of it on the patient's side, and nurses, social workers, occupational therapists and so on up to a comprehensive health service system on the therapist's side. Who is and is not included depends on the given therapeutic setting and on what the research is aiming at.

Brief therapy as based upon systems theory, and Ericksonian hypnotherapy is certainly more than a cookbook method, yet it follows some basic principles. An essential principle is that in therapy, the patient should experience an approach to his problem which is different from what he has been used to. When the difference is in terms of quality and not just quantity, the new experiences can induce change in the patient's views and behavior. Our research is to demonstrate that this principle may also account for changes occurring in conventional psychiatry, regardless of whether the different experiences have been intended by the psychiatrists or not.

Using the concept of a therapeutic system, we take into account that interactions and relationships within a system are very complex and difficult to assess. There seemed no point in looking for a method which could comprehensively reflect all such complexity. So we applied fairly simple methods in order to assess just a few possibly temporary attributes of a therapeutic system which might be relevant for treatment outcome and lead to successful interventions.

Two examples–a field study and an intervention study–may illustrate this approach, although methods and results will not be explained in detail here. In the first study, we examined therapeutic systems in a psychiatric hospital without being involved in treatment ourselves. The hospital was part of a biologically oriented university department, and treatments were of the usual kind in such a setting. Therapeutic systems were considered to consist only of the patient, his/her significant others, and the psychiatrist.

Forty-one unselected depressive in-patients were asked how they viewed psychiatrists' and significant other's attitudes toward the severity of their illness. Along the principles of brief therapy, those patients who viewed attitudes in psychiatrist and significant others as dissimilar were hypothesized to benefit more from treatment. Length of stay in hospital and treatment methods applied during this time varied greatly among the patients. Patients received different psychotropic drugs and different other therapies such as group therapy or occupational therapy, but no family therapy. Both groups, those patients who viewed attitudes in psychiatrists and significant others as similar, and those who viewed them as dissimilar, showed equal and significant improvement by the time of discharge. However, after a follow-up period of three to four months after discharge, those 15 patients who viewed the attitudes as dissimilar reported a significantly better outcome. The difference was not related to single treatment components–as far as they were recorded–during the time in hospital or within the follow-up period. In a modified way, the result has since been replicated in a larger sample. We are aware that empirical results such as this do by no means provide a systemic view of how change occurs in psychiatric treatment settings. But they may be helpful to achieve small steps toward such a view.

In another study, we looked at the treatment of hospitalized patients with chronic neurotic or personality disorders, who had been suffering continuously from their symptoms for at least nine months and had undergone at least one failed therapy within this time (the criteria was so strict that among colleagues, the study was known as the "desperate cases" study). Usually, these patients have a poor prognosis and cause much distress in the therapeutic team. According to brief therapy, we analyzed the approaches which had been tried in the treatment of those patients so far. Then we set up three to five guidelines for the therapeutic team (psychiatrists, nurses, occupational therapists, etc.) opposed to these attempted solutions. The guidelines were illustrated by statements which could have been made to the patients by the personnel, and aimed at a general interactional approach. They did not determine specific single therapeutic interventions. Intervention in the therapeutic system was only through the therapeutic team. We were outside the hierarchy of the wards and had no direct contact with the patients themselves.

The teams on the wards rated our interventions as very helpful for themselves and for the patients. The patients' outcome was quite encouraging in comparison with that of a matched pair control group. We now try to apply similar methods for the examination and for intervention in therapeutic systems with long-term treated out-patients. We concentrate on systems which have been unsuccessful in the view of the therapists and patients concerned, use tape recorded sessions for our assessment and have no restrictions in terms of patient's history, current problems, or psychiatric diagnosis. Again, we look for interventions which may not be easy to find, but which are simple enough to be adopted by psychiatrists without any special training, and which are effective.

As has been shown, ideas of MRI brief therapy have led to an approach for research within traditional psychiatry. The quality of data gained through this approach matches the rules of psychiatric research. Within this approach, the concept of a therapeutic system has shown to be helpful. In doing that research, MRI has been regarded as a source of inspiration and encouragement. Our research does not aim only at enhancing the reputation of brief therapy among psychiatrists. It should also contribute to better explanations of psychiatric disorders and treatments and thus to a psychiatry with more adequate theories and more effective treatments.

Chapter 18

Persuasive Public Speaking: How MRI Changed the Way I Preach

Douglas J. Green

"You want me to study grief therapy?" "No, no, no," he said, sounding like a man who had been through this exchange before, "Not grief therapy, brief therapy!" "Oh," I thought, that makes more sense." After all, for the last 30 minutes I had been explaining to this family therapist and professor that I was searching for a new model to do parish counseling. My complaint was that most pastoral counseling was based on long-term intrapsychic models which I had found highly ineffective and inappropriate for a busy parish minister faced with numerous tasks, problems, and crises. Studying something called brief therapy made sense. "Gee, I hate to admit this," I said, "but I've never heard of brief therapy." The professor smiled and said, "That's not surprising. Most clergy have never heard about it. Go over to the library and take out a book entitled, *Change* by Watzlawick, Weakland, and Fisch (1974). I think you'll find it interesting." And you know, I did.

Back in 1983, I began an independent study on brief therapy at Colgate Rochester Divinity School in Rochester, New York under the guidance of Professor J. C. Wynn. Over the next six years, with much help from Bruce Hartung, former President of the American Association of Pastoral Counselors and Executive Director of the Onondaga Pastoral Counseling Center in Syracuse, New York, I attended numerous symposiums, conferences, and workshops at the Mental Research Institute (MRI) in Palo Alto, California. With support from Paul Watzlawick, Jim Moran, Phyllis Erwin, Joyce Emamjomeh, Richard Fisch, and, especially John Weakland, I wrote a doctoral dissertation in which I applied brief therapy to a wide range of counseling, administrative, and preaching problems.

Although this chapter examines problems preachers face, any teacher or public speaker encounters the same difficulties. Speaking before a group of people can be an intimidating and frightening experience. Attempting to persuade an audience of one's point of view is a challenge and sometimes a problem.

As a Pastoral brief therapist, preacher, and community leader, I've been asked to speak at numerous educational, religious, and secular functions. Whether trying (emphasis on the word trying) to explain brief therapy to a group of clergy, teaching a special high school class on religion, or even delivering a sermon, I have found the techniques used in MRI's brief therapy helpful in becoming a persuasive public speaker.

Every weekend, millions of Americans attend synagogues and churches where they hear sermons which attempt to persuade, change, influence, and even convert them. Nothing else a religious leader does has the power to affect people so profoundly and immediately as his or her sermon. No other role offers clergy such opportunities to influence and persuade or conversely, to create problems.

The theories and tactics of change developed at the MRI's Brief Therapy Center grew in large part out of MRI's research and work in communication. It is surprising no one has tried to translate these insights into the practice of preaching, not to mention public speaking. In 1985 I asked Paul Watzlawick if anyone had ever applied MRI's ideas to the field of preaching. He paused, looked simultaneously puzzled, and said, "Not to my knowledge." Then he waved his hand in the air and smiled saying, "It's yours." During the last five years I have translated some of MRI's principles into what I have said and the way I have said it from the pulpit. The following example demonstrates the way a pastor can use these principles to handle preaching problems effectively, efficiently, and even faithfully. Using the brief therapy model let me begin by presenting a common preaching problem and its attempted solution.

CASE: THE PREACHING PROBLEM AND CLIENT'S (OR CONGREGATION'S) POSITION

When I was interviewing with my present church, which is located on the edge of Cornell University, members of the church

Search Committee warned me about the dangers of preaching in this community. I was reminded that this was a church full of professors and experts who would not only listen to every word, but judge, correct, and grade it. I was told some members of this church were top authorities in their field and not at all afraid to express opinions and disagree passionately with their pastor. Before I accepted the call to this church, the Search Committee went through a soulful litany of past preachers and their failings which, regrettably or not depending upon one's view, resulted in their early departure from the parish. As the committee beat its collective breast over this perceived problem, I was asked if I would be intimidated preaching to such a congregation.

During my first month this myth was embellished by other members of the congregation. On my first Sunday, two appealingly sweet old ladies came up after the service, sadly shook their heads, and said, "We do hope they warned you that we eat preachers alive in this church. If you preach on politics they'll cut your ears off." Welcome to the parish ministry. Yet for all the talk about how unique and problematic preaching was in this particular church, the situation here did not strike me as different from public speaking problems in other contexts or churches. Speaking persuasively, effectively, and yet faithfully on difficult and problematic subjects to informed people who are well read, well bred, and well educated is always a problem. Preaching to successful people who do not suffer from a lack of self-confidence is a challenge. In the free church tradition of main-line Protestant America, where independence, freedom of thought, diversity of opinion, and a healthy dose of simple human stubbornness and arrogance exist, I have found that directly telling people what to believe or how to act seldom works.

THE ATTEMPTED SOLUTION

Over the years I have tried different ways of handling this dilemma, usually by trying to be more persuasive by being more passionate, sincere, honest, blunt, and direct. Yet to stand in the pulpit and shout at, threaten, beg, or command my congregation to believe or behave in a certain way usually had meager results.

The presenting problem for me and for many preachers and speakers is finding the best way to be heard. As they say at MRI, to influence you first have to be heard. When communicating with and hopefully influencing people whose position or frame of reference is that they are bright, informed, intelligent, independent, and already have strong opinions on certain controversial issues, one needs first to be heard. The position of many Protestant churches today seems best captured by a local cliche. "You can always tell a Cornellian, but you can't tell him much." Rephrasing it to our situation we might say, "You can always tell a Congregationalist (or a Presbyterian, Episcopalian, Unitarian, or Methodist), but you can't tell him or her much." Since my attempted solution to this presenting problem was not always effective, I turned to brief therapy for ideas to help me be heard by others and persuade them.

PRINCIPLES AND STRATEGIES

Within the narrow confines of this chapter, any attempt to present those MRI ideas and insights that might apply to preaching is bound to be somewhat limiting. Although such a presentation is necessarily oversimplified, certain basic principles need to be highlighted.

The MRI has developed a theory called the Interactional View which, in essence, states that all behavior is communication and all communication is behavior, and communication or behavior of one person affects, influences, or interacts with the communication and behavior of another within a system of feedback loop (Watzlawick, Beavin, and Jackson, 1967). In a relationship between people, MRI proposes the following two maxims: one cannot not communicate and one cannot not influence.

In short the concept being advanced here is that words will have an effect upon other people, effecting or influencing their behavior. In MRI's view, the power of words, what people say and do not say to each other, is taken very seriously. As Watzlawick (1978) writes, "Language is a powerful determinant of moods, views, behaviors and especially decisions . . . ." For the preacher who tries to influence his or her flock by the power of the spoken word, this is good news. All those Sunday morning words may not be in vain. The challenge, however, is to harness the power of communication effectively.

MRI's research has demonstrated that through communication, human problems are both created and resolved. Using a medical model, we could state that communication can make us sick or well. Words can hurt or heal us. From this theoretical view, MRI has developed practical tactics to communicate more effectively which may help pastors preach more persuasively. Using the brief therapy model, we have already determined a common presenting problem for preachers. The dilemma is to preach effectively and persuasively to independent people who already hold strong opinions of right and wrong on certain controversial subjects. How can a preacher best influence or persuade people to move more toward his or her position?

In a significant way, this is one of our great challenges as brief therapists. We face this problem in counseling sessions, how to influence a client to try new behavior which is often radically different or even opposed to that which he or she has known. Persuading clients or, in this case parishioners, to see and act upon a problem in a new way lies at the heart of brief therapy and much of preaching. The challenge is finding the way to change people.

At MRI, I learned that a most efficient and effective way to change behavior is to adopt and reframe the client's position. This is most easily done by taking a one-down position. Instead of claiming to be the expert or authority, a brief therapist will play down his or her authority. Such a move diminishes the possibility that the therapist will become a target for the client's fantasies, frustrations, anger, or dependence and allows the therapist to avoid the temptation of coming on strong with the so-called right answer. To do this, a brief therapist uses different approaches or tactics. Every brief therapist adopts some strategy to help him or her relate to a client in an indirect, nonthreatening way.

Richard Fisch often approaches clients like Detective Columbo from the popular television series. He acts confused, fumbling, inefficient, and incompetent. In this almost amusing way, he elicits cooperation from uncooperative people. This method has proved especially effective with stubborn teenagers. It is carried out with utmost seriousness, deliberation, intention, and planning. Columbo is one of Fisch's favorite shows.

Similarly, John Weakland is an avid mystery reader. Indeed, Weakland has remarked that the lack of quality in therapy today could be directly related to the fact that therapists do not read enough mysteries. Since brief therapy is problem-solving, a therapist, like a detective, needs to ask many specific questions. We need concrete, detailed information from the client. MRI teaches us to avoid being pushy, arrogant, direct, and blunt which is quite a challenge for a preacher! Coming from a one-down position brings those results.

John Weakland plays down his authority and position by using what I refer to as the Sam Ervin method. Weakland often refers to himself as just a little old brief therapist from West Virginia. This is, of course, very similar to what Senator Sam Ervin used to say at the Watergate Hearings, "I'm just a little old country lawyer," right before he drilled and questioned those big-time, slick city lawyers. By putting himself down, Weakland disarms highly critical, suspicious, and opinionated people and puts them more at ease by simply giving them the feeling of the upper position.

Taking a one-down position is also a creative and effective way for a public speaker or preacher to approach a highly educated, professional, and often strongly opinionated congregation or audience especially, when speaking on controversial subjects. Being able to say in the beginning of a sermon on abortion, "I am just a simple Christian pastor, and not an expert on medical technology and ethics," is somewhat useful in disarming one's critics. To say in the beginning of a political sermon, "I'm just a parish minister concerned with the gospel of Jesus Christ and not a professional politician who understands geopolitical strategies and realities," will free a pastor from having to have all the answers, allowing people to disagree, even vehemently, because the pastor has not claimed to be the authority and has not painted himself or his critics into a corner.

When presenting a difficult new idea in brief therapy, I've watched brief therapists appear very hesitant and reluctant to make any suggestion. He will often voice indecision about whether or not to even offer the idea. Acting in this way massages the client and prepares him or her to accept the radical idea about to be proposed.

Sometimes such an approach even makes the patient impatient to hear the suggestion, which is highly desirable. In MRI's experience, direct orders and commands usually backfire. In the world according to MRI, nothing would be worse than "preaching," especially, when preaching a difficult, radical, or new idea.

Consider that the word "preaching" carries some negative connotation. Such expressions as "Don't preach to me," "You are preaching to me," and "You sound like a preacher," all strongly suggest how ineffective it usually is to preach to people in a forceful, direct, and authoritative way. Such preaching, for all its good intentions, often brings about the exact opposite results one wishes or intends. It can make people more resistant and defensive to the very idea being proposed. The irony of this would not be lost on the people at MRI. John Weakland once remarked to me that a good debate between therapists today would be on what is more important, good results or good intentions. Without the right strategies, the best intentions in communication can bring about the worst results.

To avoid this, a preacher can easily adopt a one-down position. From one already in a supreme, almost divine, one-up position, standing high over a congregation in the pulpit wearing official robes and vestments, such a move might be deeply appreciated. It might be compared to a generous, gracious, and loving parent stooping down to look into a child's eye when talking. It makes communication much easier. It puts the child at ease, and in a church sanctuary is likely to put parishioners at ease and make them more receptive. Instead of playing up his already one-up position, a preacher's persuasive powers may be enhanced if he or she acts a little more gracious and generous and makes a move toward the listener.

To accomplish this, I have often introduced controversial issues and ideas with many qualifications and reservations. Trying to be one-down, I may begin very slowly and hesitantly, sometimes wondering aloud whether what I am about to suggest is a good idea or if I should even preach on the subject. Sounding reluctant and almost apologetic for even bringing up an idea in the first place, I might say, "Gee, I don't know if this is a good idea or this sermon will probably ruin your Sunday," in an effort to soften any opposition. Even voicing and articulating some of the criticisms that I assume will emerge from the congregation makes people more receptive to what

I am about to say. Naming resistances and defenses has a way of taking away some of their strength and poison. Mentioning possible concerns about a controversial subject before one preaches on that subject places the minister on the parishioner's side and allows parishioners to approach the subject with the preacher and not against him or her.

To do this, the preacher must know his or her people. A knowledge of one's audience is something all good speakers and preachers have always been taught. Similarly, a vital step in our practice of brief therapy is learning our client's position.

Knowing where our clients stand on any problem or issue is essential to bringing about change. Once we understand the client's position, how the client sees the problem, then we can adopt that position, redefine and reframe it before presenting it back to the client. In brief therapy, we try to take a stand on the problem similar to the client's stand and then, and only then, give the problem a slightly new and different twist. To accomplish this, we need to be highly flexible. In *Tactics of Change*, an entire chapter is devoted to "therapist maneuverability." Watzlawick talks about our need to see ourselves not as a firm rock in a sea of trouble, but as a chameleon. To learn the client's position, the therapist needs to be able to listen very carefully to the client. To fully utilize the client's position, one even needs to use the client's very words and phrases. Adopting the client's position means adopting his or her language. Watzlawick (1978) writes the therapist:

> not only does his utmost to arrive at an understanding of the client's values, expectations, hopes, fears, prejudices–in short, his world image–as quickly and as completely as possible, but also pays attention to the actual language of his client and utilizes it in his own verbalizations. (p. 140)

Through a variety of ways including committee meetings, counseling sessions, fellowship events, and worship, a pastor has an opportunity to get to know the fullness of his or her parishioners' positions. Even more, pastors are in a unique profession in being able to call on people in their homes and places of employment. Pastoral visitation gives a pastor a marvelous opportunity to get to know a parishioner's language and world view. The way people feel about controversial issues is something a pastor can discover before ever opening his or her mouth in the pulpit. Finding out about the positions of my parishioners, discovering their language, and even using some of their phrases and words has connected me with them. Couching a sermon subject in their terms and thoughts helps me reintroduce the subject in a new way. For example, I sometimes use the word "naive," a favorite word of some conservative men in my congregation to describe a position with which they disagree. At other times I've used the phrase "to feel strongly." This is another common phrase, used by liberal women in the congregation who often say they feel strongly about an issue. Using my parishioners' own words and phrases builds bridges between the pulpit and the pews.

In offering a client a new solution to a problem, brief therapists often see that the best solution is exactly opposite of, or at least different from, what the client has been trying to do. Our paradigm is that the attempted solution is the problem. Helping people to try another solution often means helping them to adopt a course of action which is quite different, if not the exact reversal of what they have been doing. Such suggestions sometimes strike people as crazy and paradoxical. MRI has taught me a deep appreciation for the power of paradoxical thinking.

Of particular relevance here is that a minister preaching on a problem may discover that a more creative and constructive approach to that problem may be to reverse the way people are trying to solve it and to offer that in a sermon. Such an approach for Christians should not be surprising. After all, much of the gospel message is paradoxical. The first shall be last, the last shall be first, to gain your life you must lose it, he who exalts himself will be humbled, he who humbles himself will be exalted, the meek shall inherit the earth. Paradoxical suggestions may not be only creative, clever and effective, but also biblical and faithful.

Finally, when problems and complaints arise after a difficult sermon has been preached (and the good Lord knows plenty do), MRI has some helpful suggestions. The first is to never argue with the customer or in this case parishioner. Arguing seldom works, and usually it only strengthens the opponent's position making people more defensive and resistant. When attacked by a parishioner because of a sermon, I have found it far more useful to simply listen, or even agree, until a more thoughtful and careful response can be made. At MRI, I learned that arguing with clients should be done deliberately and only when I want to light a fire under a client or motivate a client to take a new step or try a new solution. Trying to convince or persuade anyone to move to a new position or solution by arguing is avoided. Certainly telling a client (or worse "preaching" to a client) that he or she is wrong and the therapist is right, is taboo. Such attempts inevitably backfire. It is also painful and long experience that such attempts, to say the least, do not work well when confronted with an angry response to a sermon.

In this Thanksgiving sermon I tried to persuade people to give thanks. The presenting problem was that people do not give thanks, even though they know they should. The common attempted solution is to remind people to count their blessings and present all kinds of reasons why they should give thanks. I decided to reverse this idea.

THE SERMON: "A NATIONAL DAY OF COMPLAINING"

Did you get it? Did you notice in our scripture lessons that the Scribes and Pharisees are always complaining and criticizing? If you read the Gospel of Luke from the beginning to the end, you'll notice that the Scribes and Pharisees are always like that. They're never grateful, they're never appreciative, and they never give thanks. And this is very troublesome and puzzling, because quite frankly, the Scribes and Pharisees were very nice people. They were very good people. They were the guardians of the law, and the pillars of the community. They were well respected, well regarded, well-heeled; they were the educated elite, the professional class of their day, well read, well bred . . . sound like anyone you know?

Now this lack of thanksgiving should bother and puzzle us, because they knew they should give thanks. They knew they were called and commanded to give thanks. Thanksgiving was a major part of their religion. King David appointed special priests just to thank and praise the Lord, to enter into His gates with thanksgiving and into His courts with praise. Again and again in Psalms we hear the line, "O give thanks to the Lord. Give thanks to the Lord for He is good." Yet we never see the Scribes and Pharisees giving thanks in the scriptures. Indeed, we see them in a very different light.

The little lines we heard this morning from Luke, these snapshots of scripture were taken from larger scenes where Jesus is healing and preaching and helping people. And the Scribes and Pharisees are criticizing and complaining. In one place, He forgives a man for his sins, He frees this man from his burdensome past and all the Pharisees can say is: "Who's this guy to forgive sins? Who does He think He is?" Or in another place, He heals a man with a withered hand. He brings wholeness to this broken man, and the Pharisees simply criticize when He did it and how He did it. Or in another place, Jesus' disciples sit with the sinners and the tax collectors, and they share food and fellowship with those who need acceptance and approval and love the most, and all the Pharisees can ask is: "Why are you sitting with them? Why are you wasting your time with those people?" No matter what Jesus did, no matter what Jesus said, the Pharisees found fault. No matter how hard he tried to love, and to care, and to preach, and to minister, they were always standing there criticizing and complaining.

Even as He entered into Jerusalem, even in the joy of the moment on Palm Sunday, even on the high of that Hallelujah, the good old Pharisees maintained their consistency to the end and snapped and snarled and said: "Why don't you tell your disciples to be quiet?" And all Jesus can say is that their remarks are so off-the-wall, all He can say is, "If the people are silent, the stones will cry out." And all this is, as I said, very puzzling because these were really good people. And they knew in their heads, they knew intellectually that they should give thanks, they should count their blessings, they should see the positive things in life. But, the problem was that they never seemed to practice it. With all they had, with all their blessings, and gifts, they seldom practiced it.

And I guess with the advent of Thanksgiving, with our celebration of communion, communion which is also called the Eucharist, which means thanksgiving, in such a service where Jesus breaks the bread and gives thanks and shares the cup and gives thanks, in such a time it occurs to me that the question is not should we give thanks. We all know we should give thanks. The question is: How can we give thanks? Especially, when there is a Pharisee alive within us?

You see, it's not just that sometimes we act like the Pharisees. It's not just that sometimes we play the role of the Pharisees. It's more that part of us, inside of us, is just like the Pharisees. You know that part! Call it the superego. Call it the parental part. Call it the preaching part, the pulpit part, the perfectionist part, the purist part, the supercritical, successful part, call it the Pharisee within you. It's there. It's in all of us. It's the resident critic that resides within. The resident complainer who sees the negative first, who expects the worst, and who loves to point to the flaws, the cracks, the imperfections in others as if somehow people were supposed to be perfect and pure. And so it seems to me that maybe, maybe we need to take that inner Pharisee a little bit more seriously. Maybe we need to pay a little bit more attention to that part of us that complains and criticizes no matter what the situation. Maybe we need to give that inner Pharisee his due respect–give him the time, attention, and energy he demands.

You know, the other day I was reading an article in the most recent issue of *Psychology Today* about a fellow who has been working with people who are chronic worriers. And he says that people who find themselves worrying off and on during the day and worrying all the time need to structure their worrying. They need to take time out each day to worry, to really wallow in their worries, to really get into it. And he's done some research on it. It sounds crazy, but he has done some research on it, and he found when people who worry put aside a half an hour or an hour a day and really get into the business of worrying that the rest of the day is free from worry.

You know, I know it sounds crazy, but it's one of the techniques we use in brief therapy. We often find that people have these disturbing feelings that keep popping up all during the day: anger, grief, guilt, anxiety, and no matter how hard they work to beat them down, the feelings keep coming back stronger and stronger. Sometimes what we need to do is give those feelings more time, more attention, to structure the time, to give those feelings some concentrated time, to really deal with what we are avoiding so much. Sometimes to get out of a problem you really have to get into the problem first.

And so, it's occurred to me that maybe part of the problem we have with that Pharisee is we're always beating the Pharisee down, ignoring the Pharisee, pretending he's not there, and then we just go around complaining all the time. It just pops up here and there. You know, instead of ruining part of the day, it ruins the whole day, and everyone else's day. So maybe, maybe what we need to do is take a little time and really complain. You know, half an hour a day, an hour a day. Maybe, maybe what we need instead of a national day of Thanksgiving, maybe what we really need, (because we don't need a national day of Thanksgiving, every day should be a day of thanksgiving), what we really need is a national day of complaining.

You know, one day a year when we can put aside 24 hours and just complain about everything and everyone. Get it all out, get it all over . . . one day a year when we can be totally, completely, and absolutely negative. One day a year when we can feel free to express the worst, to see the worst, to point to the worst in those we love and care about. One day a year. A day to gripe and growl, to disagree, to denounce, to beef and bellyache and make a fuss, to kick up a fuss, to raise a howl, and to do it without any lingering feelings of guilt, remorse, or regret. Now this really sounds good to me. I think we should get into it. I think we should do it and really be negative. I mean, what do we have to be thankful for anyway? Just because we live in the richest, most powerful, and freest country in the world, what have we got to be thankful for? There are plenty of other places to live on this planet . . . beautiful downtown Beirut–there's a nice chunk of real estate if you own a tank. You know, a lot of choice places in the world where one can follow one's dreams and raise one's family–Họ Chi Minh City, Northern Ireland, Colombia; places like Iran, South Korea, Afghanistan, the Soviet Union, the list goes on. Take your pick.

Let's get negative. What do we have to be thankful for living in Ithaca, New York? Just because we have this beautiful lake that extends 40 miles out where you can go sailing and fishing and boating, just because we have all these natural resources and gorges and waterfalls. That doesn't stop the Pharisees within you because, you know, it's not perfect. It's not Paradise. It's not Palm Springs.

And there's always the weather, right? I mean, expert complainers everywhere know that the weather offers boundless creative opportunities to complain. After all, nothing beats complaining about something you can't do anything about. It's a gem. It's a jewel. And hey, if we're going to be here in Ithaca and we're going to have our national day of complaining, let's put aside some time each day and do it, and let's make sure we get all the gripes out that keep popping up all the time about you-know-who . . . the big boy on the block, high above Cayuga's waters, you know, old Cornell.

I mean, you know, heck, a seasoned complainer will not be intimidated by the fact that Cornell University is one of the greatest education research institutions in the world. You know how those professors are. You can just complain about the fact that they live in ivory towers and not in the real world. Just because Cornell writes half the checks in this county, and supports most of us, and pays the bills, a good critic and a good Pharisee knows how to turn that good news into bad news. He knows the charge and thrill that comes from kicking Daddy in the shins. When it comes to complaining, nothing beats the thrill of biting the hand that feeds you.

And while we're at it, let's not forget Ithaca College sitting up there smugly on South Hill. Why, just because they have one of the best music schools, health schools, and physical education programs, the Pharisee can overlook all that positive stuff in a second. We'll just talk about the kids up there. Maybe they're a little spoiled, right? And while we're talking about spoiled kids, let's beef and complain about the students, right? Forget the joy and richness they bring into our lives, a subtle Pharisee, a sophisticated Pharisee who has been there for sometime will tell you how much nicer it is here in Ithaca in the summer. And they're not talking about the weather. When you really think about it, there's so much to complain about. There is so much to criticize. I don't know if we can get it all in one day. We haven't even begun with that gold mine of complaints called the family.

Every good critic knows that nothing looks as good close up as it does far away, right? Good complaining, like good charity, begins at home. The grass can always look greener in the other fellow's yard. Just think of that juicy long list of little gripes and resentments you can put together about your spouse, your parents, your kids, your in-laws. It boggles the supercritical soul's mind to imagine that list. And that list just goes on and on. From public school teachers to your family doctor. From the guy who lives next door and doesn't cut his lawn, to the person sitting next to you in the pew who can't carry a tune.

And for those of you who are just beginning on the road of complaining, novice complainers, you know, inexperienced Pharisees or for those of you who have been at it for a long time, don't forget the wonderful opportunities to complain that exist within the Christian church. I mean nothing is easier to criticize than Christianity and the church. It's the easiest mark in the world. No matter what happens or does not happen, there's always something to complain about. I've never been disappointed in the creativity people have when it comes to complaining about the church. If your church isn't dying, if it's not struggling to maintain itself like most churches in the United Church of Christ and you can't complain about that, I bet you can complain about the fact that it's growing too much, you know? And I'll bet you'll say, "Gee, I can't find a parking place, and I don't know anyone, and there aren't enough seats, and gosh, there are no more coat hangers." The good Pharisee within you can see the negative in the most positive situations.

I think you've got the point. I don't want to push it anymore. The problem is we're all laughing because we're all good at this, and I'm good at this. It's a lot easier to do that than to give thanks. Sometimes I think our situation is like Murphy's Law. Murphy once said: "If anything can go wrong, it will, and if anything can't go wrong, it will. And no matter what does go wrong, there's always someone there who'll tell you they knew it would go wrong in the first place." It's much easier to criticize than to correct. It's much easier to point a finger of blame than to get your hands dirty trying to make something. Anyone can criticize; few can create.

This is the way it is–the way we are. It seems to me, though, what we need to do is to take those criticisms, those complaints, and to use them in one moment, get them over, have a national day of complaining, then maybe we can begin to free up our days, so we can be free to give thanks, so we can have days of thanksgiving, days where we can be free like our Lord who sat at a table and looked at the end of His life, in a bittersweet moment of joy and pain, a time of love and betrayal, life and death, seeing the imperfections and flaws of those people He's worked with and loved, He could still speak of thanksgiving. He could still pray to God and give thanks. As He approached His end, He could still speak of new beginnings. He could still give thanks and break the bread. He could still give thanks and share the cup. And He could still tell us to do the same, to give thanks for all we have, to be grateful, to find better and more creative ways to express our appreciation for one another. This is our chance–our one lifetime. This is our season, our communion, our Eucharist. This is our thanksgiving. Amen.

RESULTS

Throughout the sermon, people laughed heartily. After the service most people made remarks indicating they appreciated it. During the following week, usually quiet and restrained staff members said that it was a great sermon. The secretary said some people had called and asked for copies. Even one of my most severe Unitarian critics said she was impressed with my recent creativity and wondered where I had been getting these ideas. I had to tell her that I had been getting them from MRI. On the other side of the aisle, one of the most fundamental members of our church asked a staff member, "Is it just me or have the sermons been getting much better in the last few weeks?" The staff person responded by saying the sermons had been getting better. Out of all the comments from this sermon, that most intriguing response came from a woman who told me, "After your Thanksgiving Sunday Sermon, I wanted to punch you in the nose." When I related this comment to John Weakland, he laughed and said, "That's the most complimentary thing I've ever heard about any sermon."

As part of a requirement for MRI's symposium on brief therapy held at Stanford University in August 1986, I sent a tape of this sermon to Weakland. His comments to a group of therapists at that symposium follow: "Doug has tried to apply this (brief therapy) in other areas besides counseling, something I've always been interested in. Here is a brief therapy sermon. Boy, this guy is far gone. He's trying to influence and persuade people in preaching. Here's someone infected with brief therapy. I'm afraid his case is terminal."

SECTION IV: THE OUTER REACHES

It seems appropriate that this final section consists of three chapters each of which, in its own way, looks well beyond the specifics of psychotherapy. The first, concerned with cancer, seeks to move beyond viewing the disease in terms of individual psychology–about which much has been written–toward viewing it in an interactional context–which has largely been neglected, despite a hopeful call 15 years ago for more exploration of somatic disease from this viewpoint (Weakland, 1977). The second proposes that brief therapy represents not just a specialization of development within psychotherapy or family therapy, but a "separate psychotherapeutic tradition," based on a new conceptualization of what our field is about. It suggests that MRI has not said the last word on the matter–with which we might agree, since we believe that for any living enterprise there is never a last word. For its point of departure, the final chapter returns to a major source of all our subsequent work, the original "Toward a Theory of Schizophrenia" paper from the Bateson projects. By reexamining first some of the basic early concepts–schizophrenia, the double bind, and paradox–and then some later ones–second order change and reframing–not in the usual framework of classical logic but in terms of a "quantum logic" related to modern quantum physics, this chapter proposes that even on such fundamental matters the last word has not been said. Let us close with the hope that all of the chapters in this volume will help lead on to further useful words and related useful actions.

Chapter 19

Interactional Thoughts on Cancer

Helen Haughton

Some time after being a monthly intern at MRI, I heard Helm Stierlin speak on psychosomatic families in Munich at an MRI Conference. I became interested in cancer families–partly because I belong to one. My elder sister, still alive and well has had two major operations for primaries-colostomy and thyroidectomy. Reading the literature I could obtain, I found patterns replicated in my own family. Including recent bereavement before the diagnosis of cancer, in a centrifugal, independent, and extremely altruistic system.

I persuaded the MD of a cancer unit to allow me to explore these dynamics in a research module, and so started a joint endeavor with the social worker of this unit, Tony Walsh. Our objectives were twofold. We aimed at exploring family dynamics, but also the constructions of reality that underpinned personal meanings. Our sample was random in the sense that our time was limited, and we took on the next patient available when we were free, regardless of cancer type. It was selected in the sense that we confined ourselves to those living close enough to Dublin to make home visiting possible, if required. We decided against controls on three counts. First, we could not see what this would achieve for an initial descriptive study. Second, time and logistics were serious factors. Third, the Brief Therapy Center does not use controls. Using Wirsching's questionnaire (for breast cancer patients), we conducted interviews with 30 patients and their families when feasible.

An initial interview was with the patient in the hospital, at which time we explained that we were doing some research, etc. None of those approached were averse to participating, although a couple were protective about the involvement of their children. Tony and I met weekly to review our information, share idea,s and develop hypotheses. Ultimately, we wrote down four hypotheses, as follows:

Hypothesis 1: In the families of those who are likely to include cancer patients, there is a basic construct that the problems and difficulties of life must be accepted stoically, independently, and altruistically. Sharing doubts, fears, anger, etc., even with family members, is perceived as a weakness. Thus, these families can be seen as centrifugal, placing heavy emphasis on individualism.

Hypothesis 2: A sense of unresolved meaning to life permits the development of a cancerous condition. This may be due to: (1) The ending of an important career/role, whether as a spouse or parent or in an outside occupation. The meaning given to this is life's task is completed, and there is permission to die. (2) An awareness of a gulf between the ideal of self, in the world, and in relationships, and the reality of actual life experience of the self, which leads to a diminution of courage and commitment to life.

Hypothesis 3: Unresolved power struggles within significant family relationships can lead to long-term stress levels, which permit/encourage the development of terminal cancer. Outcome falls into two categories: (1) Altruism and self-sacrifice are perceived as high ideals, and thus, death may be an acceptable resolution. (2) Death may be chosen as a final triumphant statement, as it is a victorious and heroic conclusion to the power struggle.

Hypothesis 4: When the experience of serious illness is used to make positive changes in restructuring relationships and reconstructing the meaning of life so that a wider range of options for personal development are available, prognosis is more likely to be favorable.

HOW DID MRI INFLUENCE ANY OF THIS?

My initial contact with the ideas of brief therapy came as a result of reading *Change* by Paul Watzlawick, John Weakland, and Richard Fisch (1974). I then spent a month at Palo Alto listening, asking questions, absorbing, examining tapes, joining the brief therapy sessions, various workshops, etc.–under a supervisor. It was a marathon flooding, from which it was impossible to go back. Moving from an established clinical psychologist post to being a founder of the Marriage & Family Institute (Clanwilliam Institute) gave me the freedom to think differently without hindrance, not to mention time to enjoy myself, as John Weakland had suggested. Five years later, I have added some more pieces, some reading, a lot of experience, and a move toward telling stories and having daydreams with all. Perhaps it's a symptom of age (57), being a grandmother, feeling too relaxed, or maybe learning something from the fourth hypothesis which endorses a spiritual pattern to life's possible rich meanings. Nevertheless I must blame MRI for doing something to me, a second order change, I presume. My thanks to everyone concerned.

Chapter 20

The Brief Therapy Tradition

Steve de Shazer
Insoo Kim Berg

Although this is the thirtieth anniversary of the Mental Research Institute, it is near enough to the twentieth anniversary of MRI's Brief Therapy Center and near enough to the twelfth anniversary of the Brief Family Therapy Center (BFTC) and thus the focus of this brief chapter.

MRI

The development of brief therapy over the past 20 years owes a lot to the work done by MRI and people associated with MRI during MRI's first 30 years. Without the development of the interactional view (at MRI) and the other work of Weakland, Haley, Jackson (of MRI) and the work of Bateson and Erickson during the first decade, this tradition of brief therapy (and all of family therapy) would certainly have a different form.

MRI as a whole needs to be thanked for initiating the systemic view, i.e., demonstrating that a family or any interactional situation can be seen as if it were a system and thus it can be mapped following the "laws" of general system theory. This construction is, after all, the foundation of family therapy as well as of brief therapy.

BRIEF THERAPY

As we see it, this tradition of brief therapy is not psychotherapy (a therapy organized around the individual-as-a-monad), nor is it

(Ericksonian) hypnotherapy (a therapy organized around the individual in a context) nor is it family therapy (a therapy organized around the family-as-a-context) but it is rather a separate therapeutic tradition (a therapy organized around the context which people built for themselves and/or in which they find themselves) with a distinct philosophy. (Neither of us being philosophers by trade, we have had to put the following premises in plain english rather than in more esoteric, philosophical jargon. We are also aware that calling what follows "a philosophy" may be rather grandiose.)

CENTRAL PHILOSOPHY OF BRIEF THERAPY[1]

1. If it ain't broke, don't fix it.
2. If it doesn't work, don't do it again: Do something different.
3. Once you know what works, do more of it.

Premise 1: If It Ain't Broke, Don't Fix It.

This premise is so central to life that it seems self-evident. There, in fact, should be no need at all for this premise which, among other things, we take to mean the following: If something is not a problem for the client and, therefore, the client does not complain about it, then–no matter how obviously problematic that something might be in the eyes of the therapist or "society"–it is none of the therapist's business. Unlike many other types of therapy, brief therapy (within this tradition) is non-normative and thus the need for explicitly stating this premise. Although it should go without saying, this premise is actually broader in its implications and applies to doing therapy as well. For brief therapists it means that if you know a solution that works, do not unnecessarily look for another way. Never forget what works.

Premise 2: If It Doesn't Work, Don't Do It Again: Do Something Different.

It also seems as if this premise should be self-evident, but given the folklore idea: "If at first you don't succeed, try, try again," this premise cannot be overstated because it seems to run counter to common sense.

In the brief therapy tradition the focus is on resolving the problem through interrupting the stability and redundancy of the problem. The problematic situation has been simply and clearly described as "the same damn thing over and over again." Clearly, problems have self-maintaining properties including repeats of the same old failed attempts at solution. Obviously, things are not working and Premise Two the Central Philosophy suggests that–in such a problematic situation, someone needs to do something different in order to disorganize the problematic pattern(s). In fact, when anyone in the problematic situation does something different, anything that cannot be seen as "the same damn thing over again," then the problem is on the way to resolution, i.e., what was problematic becomes just another of the damn things that make up life. Simply, the problem is resolved by stopping the failed attempts at resolution.

Premise 3: Once You Know What Works, Do More of It.

On the surface, this premise should be so self-evident that stating it seems stupid. Once the problematic pattern is broken–by the clients' doing something different–then Premise 3 comes into play: the client needs to continue doing what works.

As we see it, the program known as brief therapy has long been involved in a major research project: Constructing a general view of (1) the nature of human problems and how they develop, and (2) solutions and how they work. As a result of this research, related specific procedures have been developed for both problem solving and solution development. In brief therapy the focus is on "the problem to be solved" and, in a certain sense, these "problems" are the clients rather than the people that therapists work with and for. Brief therapy can be defined as a way of solving human problems and there is an (perhaps implicit) assumption that any individual in the same situation as the one the client describes would have the same problem. That is, problems are seen as situational, i.e., problems are more a result of the definition of the situation than they are a result of any causative underlying maladjustments or psychopathology or systemic dysfunctions.

Obviously, a tradition based on such simple premises is frequently going to be seen as deeply flawed. Surely the resolution of chronic human problems cannot be so simple. In fact, it is easy to see these central premises as simpleminded rather than just simple. It came as a shock, as brief therapists, to discover there is a serious flaw in the MRI version of the Central Philosophy.

At BFTC, we serendipitously found out that, when asked in the right way and/or at the right time, many, perhaps most, clients will report that there are times when the complaint/problem does not happen, even though they had every reason to expect it to happen! This means that Premise 3 should take precedence over Premise 2 and thus we have been forced to revive the Central Philosophy:

1. If it ain't broke, don't fix it.
2. Once you know what works, do more of it.
3. If it doesn't work, don't do it again: Do something different.

(Is this a difference that makes a difference?) Of course, on a different level, deliberately replicating an exception–doing what works instead of what does not work–is a way of doing something different. But that particular something different is already part of the clients' repertoire and therefore promoting clients' cooperation (and task compliance) is greatly enhanced. Simply, a solution is developed by doing more of what is already working.

Thus the flaw we see in the MRI version of Brief Therapy is that they actually take their philosophy seriously and, therefore, since their model ain't broke they do not try to fix it. Weakland, Watzlawick, and Fisch stubbornly continue to do more of the same since it works. We owe our development to this "flaw" and pushed beyond it; the ultimate tribute disciples can pay to their masters.

NOTE

1. This is the MRI version of the Central Philosophy. See below for the BFTC version.

Chapter 21

Quantum Psychology and the Metalogic of Second Order Change

Eddie Oshins

The 1950s was a time of radical reformulation within psychology regarding the definitions and nature of psychological problems and interventions. Within a representationalist context (Oshins, 1987a), Eriksonian approaches to hypnosis (Haley, 1972, 1973) attracted attention to subtle and often puzzling strategies of therapeutic intervention. The systems approach toward communication and feedback (Ruesch aand Bateson, 1968; Watzlawick, Beavin, and Jackson, 1967; Bateson, 1972) focused interest on various contexts of individuals in interaction within entire systems, including the observer or therapist.

No longer could the therapist justifiably claim to be out there, just looking in, while enlightening their patients with insights in order to help these patients resolve their personal limitations toward accepting a presumed fixed, external reality. Instead, the therapist was conceived as part of a dynamic system which was continually changing and transforming within a pragmatic image of experience. In some sense, the new therapeutic role was to help the patients develop more effective participation in their ongoing life, often through the strategic redefinition of the situation or system (Haley, 1961, 1963, 1973; Ruesch and Bateson, 1968; Watzlawick et al., 1974; Weakland et al., 1974).

The double-bind theory of schizophrenia (Bateson et al., 1956) both pioneered and exemplified this new approach to therapy and to more general psychological systems. It also focused attention on the metalogical structure of communications. In contrast to the prevalent view of schizophrenia as a disease, or impairment in functioning, of an individual's mind, double-bind theory proposed that schizophrenia was an understandable, systemic reaction to a certain type of absurd, inviable, and self-reifying communication context. In particular (Bateson et al., 1956; Oshins, 1988; 1989 and references therein; 1994), the six "necessary ingredients for a double-bind situation," as specified by the authors, underscores that the circumstances involved are *not* merely "conflictual," but include disconfirmation ("negative injunction") on *at least two* logical levels, in a manner such that any selection from among the entire, perceived range of possible reactions will perpetuate the untenable circumstances.

In so doing, the authors based their problem conceptualization upon the Whitehead-Russell theory of logical types, which in part sought to avoid certain so-called "self-referential paradoxes," such as Russell's antinomy ("Does the class whose members are precisely those classes which are not members of themselves contain itself?" It would contain itself if and only if it did not.) or the well-known variant of Epidmenides' "liar's paradox" (Is "This statement is false," true or false? If it is true, then it is false; if it is false, it is true, etc.). From this perspective, double binds involve metacommunications (at a higher level), any response to which reinforces and sustains the untenable situation. The proposed remedy for avoiding corresponding predicaments was to adopt such a rule as: whatever involves *all* of a collection/class must *not* be a *member* of this collection/class. This recognition of the importance of maintaining proper logical levels in communications and of the consequent pathologies which can develop from mixing logical levels was a major contribution to psychology and to philosophy.

As is often the case with epistemic reformation, the initial, pioneering ideas spawn new questions, the answers to which provide new information and new conceptualizations, which can be tested and which in turn generate new questions. "Propositional thinking" such as this provides a bedrock enabling psychology to grow as a science (Cromwell, 1984; Kelly, 1968; Oshins, 1988). As is the case with *good* such reinvigorization, as it grows, it increases our understanding and our ability to anticipate and influence, and thereby to chose how we participate within our personal and mutual experience.

Regarding my own work, I believe it appropriate to acknowledge the creative inspiration which I received from insights of the "MRI school." Although my specific conceptions are somewhat variant to the ones developed by people at the MRI, particularly as regards formal representations–anticipatable, since my training is in foundations of theoretical physics–I find it extraordinary how close some are. In cases where they differ, my own representations have often been an extension or rigorization of concepts which I came to recognize first through reading MRI publications, or through insights and understandings from numerous discussions over the years with John Weakland, Lynn Segal, and other members of MRI. As such, their conceptualizations provide fertile ground for me to plant my own roots and to develop my own model of experience which I refer to as "quantum psychology." This chapter represents a gesture of appreciation on the thirtieth anniversary of the MRI.

The structure of the chapter follows: First, I will present the background of my involvement with MRI and what I mean by quantum psychology. Then, I will discuss some examples of metalogic structure and focus on the structure of the metalogic involved in second order change, as described in *Change: Principles of Problem Formations and Problem Resolution* (Watzlawick, Weakland, and Fisch, 1974). I will next show how simple polarizers can be used to model the logic and metalogic of experience. They will be used to describe the difference between classical logic and quantum logic. Some examples from psychology will be given to illustrate the usage of a "filter logic" approach. I will also discuss what appears to be common parallel structures between the brief/strategic therapy approach and a quantum psychology model. In particular, I will show how the violation of the distributive law of classical logic allows for a complementary metalogic to the filter which I will associate with the logical structure of second order change. In an appendix, the Stern-Gerlack experiment will be discussed as an example of the fracture of classical logic in physics.

At certain points, I will use specific technical language. For readers familiar with some of these terms, I hope that this usage will add clarity and depth of understanding to my overview. After all, the economy of expression of mathematics, when correctly applied, seems peerless. Nevertheless, this chapter is *not* meant to convince the reader that quantum psychology is true or right, only to indicate that it might be possible. Thus, I recommend that others just skim the technicalness. Rather, try to focus on the limited number of basically simple principles involved, try to play a bit with the examples given, and try to come up with some of your own. Enjoying is often an easier and better, complementary road to understanding than is trying to understand!

BACKGROUND

My own direct involvement with the MRI began in 1976. I had been interested in various controversies in the psychological literature concerning the nature of schizophrenia as a logical phenomenon (Oshins and McGoveran, 1980; Oshins, 1989, 1991, ft. nt. 2; Hilgard, 1989). In particular, I was interested in the formal arguments (Oshins, 1991, ft. nt. 2) between Arieti (1974) and Bateson et al. (1956), concerning what are referred to as von Domarus' principle of "identification by predicates" and "double-bind theory." According to von Domarus' principle, subjects are identified on the basis of having a common predicate, called the "identifying link," believed to govern certain unconscious, associative, "primary process" reasoning. The prototype is the paleological syllogism (Arieti, *op. cit.*) "I am a virgin. The Virgin Mary was a virgin. I am the Virgin Mary."

My impression was that the arguments were mostly interpretive and representational, and were not in essential empirical contradiction. I felt that the disagreements were due largely to an insufficient symbolic representation for defining and comparing the differing points of view. As these issues were considered important in psychiatry, I thought that I would try to construct a more adequate symbolic language for representing the logical structures concerned. My purpose was to produce an intellectual tool for clarifying the matter as I understood it, in order to accommodate both sides of the controversy within a single, unified framework.

During the spring and summer of 1976, while "playing" with "fuzzy logic" (Oshins, Adelson, and McGoveran, 1984; Oshins et al., 1989) and "the laws of form"–generalized classical logics being developed by computer scientists in an attempt to model thought–I came up with the idea to construct *matrix representations* for them, similar to what Heisenberg had done in quantum physics. I had been thinking about the suggestion to apply the mathematics of group theory to linguistic interaction, by Watzlawick, Weakland, and Fisch (1974) in *Change*, because of their *misdefinition* (pp. 4, 7) of mathematical "groups" as *being "commutative"* (order independent), since *all* quantum interactions take place through the property of *not being commutative.* I had come to the MRI from New York to discuss this issue with Paul Watzlawick.

Paul directed me to Bateson to whom I proposed my formal ideas about double binds that summer. Bateson said that although he thought they were interesting, he no longer believed that schizophrenia was about double binds, but instead about something called von Domarus' principle–thus, indepently, proposing von Domarus' principle to me. We went on talking about my ideas about the possible relation between the two, among other things.

I believed that if I could properly integrate some of my reinterpretations of notions from the computer logics–such as measure, orthogonality (negation), and transformation–then, I could possibly "quantize" the structure. Using an approach akin to "recombinant psychology," I had started to examine the psychological issues concerning schizophrenia. By attempting to develop matrix representations of the variant logics, while simultaneously constraining my formalism by requiring empirical validity, I hoped to induce a *physical logic of psychological processes* that could clarify the psychological disputes, embody features from the computer logics, and at the same time be identifiable with actual physical events (Oshins, 1984a, 1987b, 1989, 1994; Oshins, and McGoveran, 1980, Oshins, Adelson, and McGoveran, 1984; Oshins, et. al., 1992).

At this point, although I had previously heard the term "quantum logic," I was not aware of the almost 50 years of rich mathematical structures given birth to by von Neumann (Birkhoff and von Neumann, 1936) and expanded by Birkhoff, Gleason, Mackey, Piron, Mittelstaedt, Finkelstein, etc.; nor was I familiar with the more interpretive structures, extending the Bohr/Heisenberg physical perspectives, by von Weizsacker, Stueckelberg, Finkelstein, Jauch, Watanabe, etc. I was also not then informed about some of the more immediate psychophilosophical precursors of the quantum epistemology such as can be found within William James, Kierkegaard, and Hoffding, etc. (Holton, 1973). My interest focused upon examining and contrasting intrapsychic processes and "artificial intelligence."

As an illustration of my "perspective," I retranslated Arieti's above example as "I ≡ Virgin Mary (modulo virginity)." As such, "I" becomes equivalent to and nondistinguishable from "Virgin Mary." This *intertwining* of constructs, based upon the common predicate or "attribute 'virginity,' in principle, would be a more primitive type of association" (Vigotsky, 1934, pp. 1064-1065; von Domarus, 1944; Arieti, 1974; Oshins, 1989 and references therein)–possibly due to functional, brain impairment; to stress induced, hormonal elevation; etc., which could change neuronal firing patterns or thresholds, or could degrade such functions as lateral inhibition.

In a quantum formalism, one considers a type of encoding of patterns and of regularities in physical experience which is at fundamental variance with classical, parallel process modeling, such as either the generic, McCulloch-Pitts-type, neural nets, or Pribram's classical "hologram hypothesis" (Oshins 1984a,b, 1989 and references therein, 1991; Oshins, et. al., 1990, p. 43; Hilgard, 1989). Quantum parallel processing occurs when two empirical processes are possible but there is no empirical procedure that is capable of distinguishing which one has actually occurred. It is then *empirically meaningless* to speak about there being individual events (in the classical sense of having a fully defined and fixed sample space). The reader is referred to the discussion of the empirical logic of the Stern-Gerlach experiment in the appendix.

In quantum theory, this type of fundamental, "operational ambiguity" (Oshins, 1984a, 1988, 1989, 1991, 1994; Oshins et al., 1992, p. 54) is effected in terms of symmetries on irreducible equivalence classes of alternative, competing possibilities, realized as a (nondistributive, orthomodular, atomic) lattice (Oshins, Adelson, and McGoveran, 1984; Oshins, et. al., 1992). The quantum process is described as a "non-discriminating measurement" (Schwinger, 1970) of "interfering alternatives" (Feynman and Hibbs, 1965) realized by an irreducible or "coherent" (Jauch, 1968) lattice of propositions. This equivocation process provides a type of irreducible, representational *ambiguity* which dos not exist in classical representations, such as in computers. Rather than trying to avoid ambiguity, I elevated this specific type of ambiguity into a *fundamental principle* which I believe governs primary processes, describable according to von Domarus' principle (Oshins, 1989, 1991; Oshins et al., 1992, p. 54-55; Hilgard, 1989).

Operationally, quantum physics has shown that there is an empirical difference in coding between (Schwinger, 1970, esp. p. 27-28; Oshins, 1984a, 1991; Oshins et al., 1992, p. 54-55): (1) forming a class (virtual ensemble) of possible states (subensembles) which *are distinguished* by some specific attribute (e.g., subensembles having either predicate-A or incompatible/complementary predicate-B and (2) forming a class (virtual ensemble) of possible states (subensembles) which are *not empirically distinguishable* according to such a predicate–i.e., there is no empirical procedure that discriminates between the alternative, possibly incompatible / complementary predicates. This is true *even if no member of the class is distinguished or separated out*, as long as, operationally, one could be.

A psychological example which I thought might carry the same type of representational alternatives is the difference between saying a person (= a "male or female," if distinguished) came into the room and saying that a "male" or a "female" came into the room (distinguishing gender as opposed to a different, competing context). Of course, the existence of such complementarity, competing construct attributes is an empirical issue. Other possible examples of complementarity alternatives might involve a metachoice between, say, the good/bad-attribute-dichotomy and the love/hate-attribute-dichotomy. See also, Bohr (1987a, p. 81) regarding "justice and charity," Heisenberg (1958, p. 179) regarding "enjoying music and analyzing its structure," Orlov (1982), and Oshins (1987b, 1988). That there are empirically discriminable consequences to these two operational ways to code "nonselecting measurements" became (Oshins, 1987a, 1988, 1989) a foundation for my "quantum psychology" approach.

A related type of equivocation exists in children. Using an example pointed out to me by Gordon Bower, a young child might identify dogs, cats, and horses as if the same (e.g., a "bow-wow") because they all have the common characteristic of four-leggedness. I have applied formal theorems from the mathematics of "lattice theory" to show how classical logic would result from the development of a capacity for serialization such as is claimed in Piaget to take place in operational stages of child development (Oshins, 1987a, 1989).

Similarly Oshins, 1984a,b), I have proposed possible experiments using a "superconducting quantum interference device" (SQUID) to try to determine neurophysiological prerequisites for the developmental and evolutionary capacity to form negation in terms of signal synchronization. Along with Freud, I have suggested the capacity to form negation to be a precondition for consciousness. Thus, the beginning of my project.

I should try to be clear in this regard about my use of the term *quantum psychology*, so as not to confuse the reader into thinking that I am applying quantum physics to psychology. As I have tried to sketch above, this would invert the actual development of the model.

To the contrary, I believe that I have *found* quantum physics in psychology. Still, as described above, there is *no basis* here, as yet, for asserting this work to be quantum. Although I have indicated reasons for claiming to find mathematics in psychology in common with that in quantum physics, mathematics by itself is still not physics.

In order to claim a physical model, I am obliged to provide a "semantically consistent," physical interpretation having empirical validation. In addition, in order to claim a quantum representation, I am obliged to provide a role for Planck's constant (quantum of action). I shall *not* do this here. I merely stress that my current interest is in posing "separating alternatives" which can distinguish in principle between competing theories and in determining the answers which nature provides. Where Planck's constant comes from in my formalism has been discussed in Oshins (1984b, ft. nt. 9, 1989, ft. nt. 3, 1991, ft. nt. 16). The role that I envision for Planck's constant in quantum psychology is as a "contraction parameter" allowing for the *classicalization* of psychological experience, as it does for physical experience. That quantum physics does indeed violate classical logic will be discussed in the appendix on the Stern-Gerlach experiment.

METALOGIC, SCHIZOPHRENIA, AND SECOND ORDER CHANGE

This section uses examples to illustrate the metalogic structure involved in double binds and in second order change. The difference between first order and second order change is delineated.

Schizophrenia as Metalogical Communications (Oshins, 1984a, 1987b, pp. 15, 22-25, 1989 and References Therein)

The "double-bind theory of schizophrenia" (Bateson et al., 1956) describes errors in logical typing that develop in individuals raised in environments: (1) which negate in a "paradoxical way" at both level and metalevel; (2) which forbid commenting upon this; and (3) in which one's "choice" is experienced as being survival related. Let us consider an example suggested by Paul Watzlawick during my 1978 talk at Stanford's psychology department (Laing, 1965):

Mother: "I don't blame you for talking that way, I know you don't really mean it."
Daughter: "But I do mean it."
Mother: "Now, dear, I know you don't. You can't help yourself."
Daughter: "I can help myself."
Mother: "No, dear, I know you can't because you're ill. If I thought for a moment you weren't ill, I would be furious with you."

Metalogic representation: The mother is *not* telling the daughter that she (mom) disagrees with what the daughter is saying, e.g., she (mom) does not say, "I disagree with what you (daughter) say (or mean)." Instead, she (mom) effectively says "You (daughter) do not *mean* what you say (or think) you (daughter) *mean.*" The mother is *not* commenting on what is being said by the daughter but making a *metacomment* on the truth value of what the daughter is saying, i.e., the mother essentially decrees that the construct frame which the daughter is asserting is wrong (not-true), not whichever answer may be chosen *within* a particular construct frame is wrong (not-true).

The daughter is being forced to label her behavior as "bad" or [as] "mad." Thereby, the mother invalidates the daughter's framing mechanisms. Alternative evaluations, such as perhaps due to inquisitiveness or hunger, are excluded. The daughter can neither avoid the "choice," nor comment on it, and must "chose" or distinguish one (the power involved being obvious and significant).

Boundary formation: (Orlov, 1982; Oshins 1984b, 1987a,b, 1988, 1991, ft. nt. 6, 1994). From his imprisonment in the Soviet gulag, Yuri Orlov independently described a type of intrinsic ambiguity to information which is similar to my quantum psychology approach. He envisioned a type of "doubt state," similar to my concept of operational ambiguity, when there is "inadequate resolution to resolve" a situation. An example given by Orlov (1982, p. 43) is Hamlet's "To be or not to be?" He provides (Orlov, 1982, pp. 46-47; Oshins, 1987b, pp. 19-23, 1988) a list of "the necessary ingredients for a doubt state" which is remarkably similar to the Bateson et al. (1956, pp. 253-254) list of "the necessary ingredients for a double bind situation." I have suggested that the difference may lie in the locus of control of the decision (Rotter, 1966; Oshins, 1987b, 1988, 1994).

In this regard, Kubie comments (1953 p. 77) about the differences between boundary forming processes in neurosis and in psychosis is interesting:

> The conflict, however, is not the illness. Psychopathological illness begins as the conflict engenders a repressive-dissociative process which obscures the links between symbolic constructs and the percepts and conceptualizations which represent the body and its needs and conflicts: i.e., the 'I' pole of reference. *This is the primary point of rupture in any psychopathological process.* [Emphasis in the original.] Alone, however, this produces only the neurosis. In the psychotic there is an additional specific distortion in the relationship between the symbol and its pole of reference to the outer world: i.e., to the 'Non-I'."

This boundary forming distinction is particularly interesting because of the arbitrariness and yet the necessity of drawing a boundary in the act of knowledge/measurement. Consider Bohr's example (1961, p. 99) of the changeableness of boundaries.

> when attempting to orient himself in the dark room by feeling with a stick. When the stick is held loosely, it appears to the sense of touch to be an object. When, however, it is held firmly, we lose the sensation that it is a foreign body, and the impression of touch becomes immediately localized at the point where the stick is touching the body under investigation.

This is particularly provocative in light of De Witt's depiction (1971, p. 220) of an inadequate coupling between an observed system and a physical measuring apparatus as "a kind of schizophrenic state in which it is unable to decide what value it has found . . . ."

The Metalogic of Problem Framing

A prototype of MRI's technique of "problem reframing" is Tom Sawyer's restructuring of his chore to whitewash a huge fence, not as a burden, but as a desirable opportunity worth paying for (Watzlawick, Weakland, and Fisch, 1974, pp. 90-91): "Like it? Well, I don't see why I oughtn't to like it. Does a boy get a chance to whitewash a fence every day?" This resulted in his friends paying him for the "privilege" of painting the fence. We can depict this *metalevel reframing*, thus:

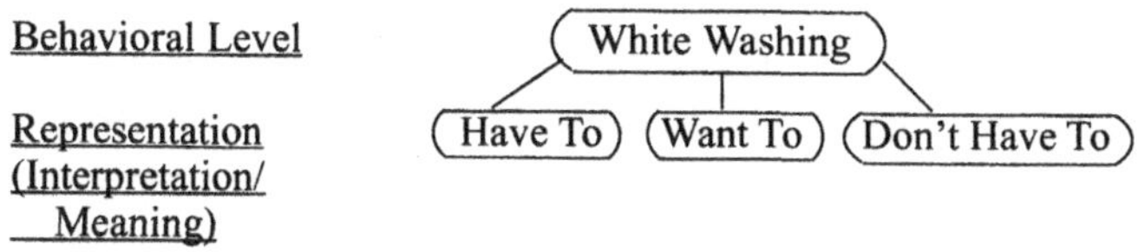

To affirm on the lower level, by necessity, affirms on the higher level.

Similarly, from hypnosis we might consider: "Do you want to go into a trance, now, while sitting there, or later, when you get up?" To affirm any of "now," "while sitting there," "later," or "when getting up" is to affirm the trance induction. Or, from new wave therapies: "Do you want to sign up for the training now or mail in a check?"

Or, consider the example of a "hostile" woman's "frigidity" towards her husband. Successful intervention consisted in supporting the wife's "overprotectiveness" towards her husband, framed as: clearly "he would not know how to cope with the impact of her uninhibited sexuality" (Watzlawick, Weakland, and Fisch, 1974, pp. 102-103). This redefinition of the *same* circumstances led to her sexual acting out her hostility, thereby "defeating" the "problem."

First Order and Second Order Change

In their book *Change*, Watzlawick, Weakland, and Fisch (1974, pp. 10-11) distinguish two types of change: "one that occurs within a given system which itself remains unchanged, and one whose occurrence changes the system itself." They use the example of a nightmare to differentiate between the two:

> a person having a nightmare can do many things *in* his dream–run, hide, fight, scream, jump off a cliff, etc.–but no change from any one of these behaviors to another would ever terminate the nightmare. *We shall henceforth refer to this kind of change as first-order change.* The one way *out* of a dream involves a change from dreaming to waking. Waking, obviously, is no longer a part of the dream, but a change to an altogether different state. *This kind of change will from now on be referred*

> *to as second-order change* . . . Second-order change is *change of change.*

Regarding second order change, I draw particular attention to the following formal features of such "metachange": (1) metalogic, (2) reframing, and (3) second order change. (See Table 5, "Formal Features in Common between Second Order Change and Quantum Psychology" pp. 270-271).

In the next section, I shall use an analogy with polarizing filters to explain how quantum psychology provides a structure which accommodates the metalogic of incompatible frames. In particular, we shall formulate a notion of complementarity which accommodates the metalogic of second order change.

FILTER LOGIC

This section describes some commonality between formal features of second order change and those of quantum psychology. Polarizing filters are used to characterize certain rules of the logic of experience. These "representational tools" are then used to explain a fundamental difference between classical and quantum representations of experience–whether or not the distributive law of logic is universally valid, respectively. Although we shall be using the polarization of light in order to exhibit certain aspects of interference, the reader is cautioned that the type of wave interference that is relevant to a quantum context has *nothing to do with* the interference of physical fields such as light (e.g., as in holograms) (Oshins, 1989, 1991). A corresponding metalogic of complementary constructs, as found in quantum logic, is proposed as the proper formal structure of MRI's second order change (Oshins, 1987a,b; Oshins and McGoveran, 1980). Quantum psychology's metalogic basis for double binds and for second order change is discussed.

FORMAL FEATURES OF SECOND ORDER CHANGE AND OF QUANTUM PSYCHOLOGY

As in the case with MRI's strategic therapy approach, quantum psychology presents a model of *"entire systems" in interaction.* The classical image of an external, objective reality, independent of the observing system, is rejected. In asserting an *operational meaning to knowledge about experience* (Oshins, 1989) quantum psychology maintains that the existence of *complementary constructs*–i.e., that are mutually exclusive, but equally necessary in a different context to give an entire description of the phenomena–gives rise to a metalogic. These common formal features are compared in the following table:

TABLE 1

Formal Features in Common between Second Order Change and Quantum Psychology	
Second Order Change Features	**Features of Quantum Psychology**
(1) Interactive Whole Systems: " . . . problems that people bring to psychotherapists . . . [usually are] situational difficulties between people–problems of interaction" (Weakland et al., 1974, p. 147); thus, they shifted "from the observation of the individual to the observation of a system and to . . . the needs of a system rather than the needs of a person" (Haley, 1961, p. 78);	" . . . the fundamental difference with respect to the analysis of phenomena in classical and in quantum physics is that in the former the interaction between the objects and the measuring instruments may be neglected or compensated for, while in the latter this interaction forms an integral part of the phenomena. The essential wholeness of a proper quantum phenomenon finds indeed logical expression in the circumstance that any attempt at its well-defined subdivision would require a change in the experimental arrangement incompatible with the appearance of the phenomenon itself. . . . it is indeed more appropriate to use the word phenomenon to refer only to observations obtained under circumstances whose description includes an account of the whole experimental arrangement" (Bohr, 1987a, pp. 72-73). " . . . the unavoidable interaction between the objects and the measuring instruments sets an absolute limit to the possibility of speaking of a behavior of atomic objects which is independent of the means of observation" (Bohr, 1987a, p. 25).

TABLE 1 (continued)

(2) Metalevel Problem Reframing: " . . . there are two different types of change: . . . [first-order change] occurs within a given system and . . . itself remains unchanged, and . . . [second order change] whose occurrence changes the system itself . . . thus *change of change*" (Watzlawick, Weakland, and Fisch, 1974, pp. 10-11); and	*Complementarity—the basis for meta-change:* Quantum theory "forces us to adopt a new mode of description designated as *complementary* in the sense that any given application of classical concepts precludes the simultaneous use of other classical concepts which in a different connection are equally necessary for the elucidation of the phenomena" (Bohr, Weakland, and Fisch, 1961, p. 10). As noted by Bohr: "the nature of our consciousness brings about a complementary relationship, in all domains of knowledge, between the analysis of a concept and its immediate application" (Bohr, 1961, p. 20).
(3) Pragmatism and Avoidance of Insight About Causes: Problem conceptions and interventions are based upon "what is going on in the systems of human interaction . . . . Correspondingly, we avoid the question "Why?' . . . [since it] tends to promote an individualistic, voluntaristic, and rationalistic conception of human behavior, rather than one focused on systems of interaction and influence" (Weakland et al., 1974, pp. 150-151, 155; Also, Watzlawick, Weakland, and Fisch, 1974, pp. 83,86) in the present.	To Bohr, perhaps the most fundamental of all instances of complementarity involved "the space-time coordination and the claim of causality" (Bohr, 1961, p. 54). Oshins has likened this complementarity between the locational or situational degrees of freedom and the causal degrees of freedom to a complementarity between a "What?" and a "Why?" He has suggested this underlies the distinction between the MRI approach and the traditional psychoanalytic search for "the cause." This reflects the *modal* structure of quantum logic. There is only a virtual future with no facts, only possibilities. Facts are attributes of the past and are fixed through the thermodynamically irreversible act of obtaining knowledge.

	Because of its modal structure, quantum physics rejects the notion of *determinism* from classical physics and, likewise, from classical logic. Although there is still a *causal structure* to the precedence-antecedence relation of events, instead of a deterministic meaning, such as event-A caused event-B, one has a quantal causal relation—event-A can cause or influence event-B. (This can be true iff B lies "within the future light cone" of A, which places a bound on the speed by which material information can travel).

The Logic of Propositions and the Logic of Filter

As in a game such as bridge, chess, etc., logic also has elements, actions, and rules. The elements usually represent propositions about various predicates. These actions include ways to order (such as a "containment" relation), ways to aggregate (the adjunction "or"), ways to disaggregate (the conjunction "and"), etc. The rules tell us what happens when we make a logical action with various elements.

We shall illustrate three rules using the logic of propositions as filters. The first two rules (law of the excluded middle and law of contradiction) are usually assumed to be true both classically and quantally. Although, classically, the distributive law for elementary, unit propositions is universally valid; quantally, it is violated for unit propositions about *complementary* properties.

The filter logic correspondent to the law of the excluded middle (see Table 2) is that *all* light will go through either the vertical filter or the horizontal filter, as parallel alternatives.

The filter logic correspondent to the law of contradiction (see Table 3) is that *no* light will go through both the vertical filter and the horizontal filter (as serial alternatives).

The filter logic correspondent to violation of the distributive law (see Table 4) is that although no light will go through both the

TABLE 2

Law of the Excluded Middle	
For propositions A and not-A and for vertical and horizontal filters.	
Logic of Propositions	**Logic of Filters**
A or not-A = True	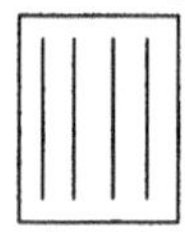 Or 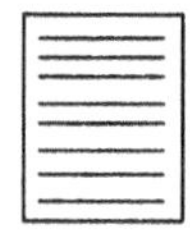 = All

TABLE 3

Law of Contradiction	
For propositions A and not-A and for vertical and horizontal filters.	
Logic of Propositions	**Logic of Filters**
A or not-A = False	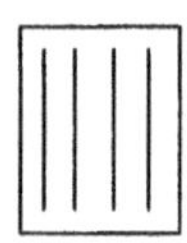 And 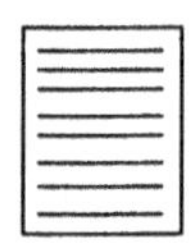 =None

vertical filter and horizontal filter (as serial alternatives), an intermediary diagonal filter B exists which can effect such a transition.

I point out that if B ⊊ A, then light going through not-A would not go through B. Likewise, if B ⊊ not-A, then light going through A would not go through B. As such, even though all light that goes through A or not-A will go through B, B is a "thing in itself" with its own irreducible integrity. As an example, consider that a mulatto

TABLE 4

Violation of Distributive Law

For propositions A, not-A, and B, & for vertical, horizontal, and diagonal filters

Logic of Propositions	**Logic of Filters**
(A or not-A) and B = True ≠> (A and B) or (not-A and B) = True Alternatively, A or not-A = True ≠> (A = True) or (not-A = True), i.e., There exists a complementary B/not-B system	There exists a complementary B/not-B filter system such that: 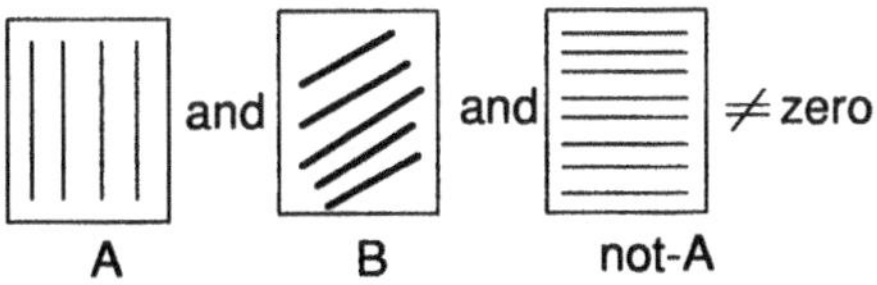

does not have a black arm and white leg but its own *coherent integrity*, which is *not* part black and part white.

Classical Logic and the Quantum Logic of Complementarity

Classical logic asserts that there is a unique, fixed set of compatible filters, or compatible propositions (i.e., simultaneously can be made either to line up or to be orthogonal to each other). This is known as the Frege principle.

Quantum logic asserts that there is *not* a unique set of compatible constructs but that there exists *complementary constructs* "in the sense that any given application of classical concepts precludes the simultaneous use of other classical concepts which in a different connection [sic. context] are equally necessary for the elucidation of phenomena" (Bohr, 1961, p. 10). As such, complementary constructs provide competing, alternative frames of reference.

From this point of view, the double bind is seen as *fragmenting the integrity of the individual's representation* (Oshins, 1987b, pp. 19-23, 1988; Kubie, 1953, p. 77; Rotter, 1966). Due to the "tertiary negative injunction prohibiting the victim from escaping from the field" (Bateson et al., 1956), the individual *cannot* comment upon the circumstances. Consider the example (Oshins and McGoveran, 1980) of my *friend* Jane who asks me "Do you love me?" Although I might be able to "choose" "yes" or "no" to label any example, if I were *forced* to do so, the true integrity of my experience is that "I *like* you (Jane)." In such context, "love" and "like" are being considered as complementary and competing for my experience. Although to my friend Jane, I might be able to express: "Your construct is incompatible with my experience. They don't line up with mine," often one, such as a double-bound child, cannot assert his/her construct frame. Table 5 delineates quantum psychology's representation of three formal features of second order change:

TABLE 5

Metacomments on the Principles of Second Order Change from the Perspective of Quantum Psychology

Principles of Second Order Change	**Metacomments from the Perspective of Quantum Psychology**
(1) metalogic: ". . . to express or explain something requires a shift to one logical level above what is to be expressed or explained. No explaining can be accomplished on the same level, a metalanguage has to be used" (Watzlawick, Weakland, and Fisch, 1974, p. 79);	• The metalogic question is not "Is it a_1 or is it a_2 from the A frame of reference?" but "Is it a_1 from the A frame or is it b_2 from the B frame?" It is not "Is it up or down from the vertical/horizontal frame of reference?" but "Is it up/down from the vertical/horizontal frame or is it diagonal (upward/right) from the diagonal right/diagonal left frames of reference?" • Likewise, it is not "Is the person black or white?" from the racial frame of reference, but "Is the person black or female?" thereby defining a racial or a gender metaframe of specification. • Or, "Do you think I am innocent or guilty?" "No, I love you."

(2) reframing: "Reframing means changing the emphasis from one class membership . . . to another, equally valid class membership, or, especially, introducing . . . a new class membership into the conceptualization of all concerned" Watzlawick, Weakland, and Fisch, 1974, p. 98); and	• As is the case with polarizing filters, operational ambiguity allows one to reframe the "A/not-A" system into a "B/not-B" system and then reframe this intermediate "B/not-B" system back into the "A/not-A" system in a manner that induces a transition from "A" into "not-A." • The popular lingo goes: to get/knock someone "off of it." A more spontaneous example is when "surprise" induces a transition from being "angry" into "disappointment." Or, when "like" takes one from "not-love" to "love."
(3) second order change: "As long as the solution is sought within this dichotomy of a and not-a, the seeker is caught in an illusion of alternatives . . . The formula of second order change . . . is 'not a but also not not-a" (Watzlawick, Weakland, and Fisch, 1974, pp. 90-91). I add that although it is, say "b", it still is "a or not-a."	• Instead of asserting an objective reality, quantum psychology is interested in operational reality. It replaces the distributive law of classical logic (not the laws of contradiction or of the excluded middle) with a *Principle of Operational Ambiguity*: • If one cannot (operationally) distinguish between two unit predicates A & B, there will always exist a third possible contrary (unit) predicate C such that (A or B) = (B or C) = (C or A)," ie. they are equivalent perspectives–there is no operational way to distinguish between A, B, & C. • In the earlier cases, we considered "B" to be "not-A" and "C" to be either "B" or "not-B". The principle then reads that the metalogic of quantum psychology will apply if there is no (operational) way to distinguish whether "A or not-A" is the case then there will be an equivalently valid "B/not-B" system which could be the case.

APPENDIX: STERN-GERLACH EXPERIMENT AND FRACTURE OF CLASSICAL LOGIC

In the early part of the century, an experiment was performed by Stern and Gerlach in which a beam of silver atoms carrying the spin of a single electron is passed through an inhomogeneous magnetic field with gradient (See Figure A). This experiment is sufficient to derive the transformation properties of 1/2-integral spin matter, such as electrons and nucleons. The beam is split into precisely two separate beams which are either in the direction of the gradient of the magnetic field or opposed to it. (This is *not* a statistical effect and can be done one atom at a time.)

If the initial magnetic field's gradient was aligned, say, vertically we could call the emerging beams *Up* and *Down*. This is a dicotomic event. As discussed in Oshins and McGoveran (1980), we can define an *operational logic* for the Stern-Gerlach experiment. What we mean by *empirical truth* is quite specific: (1) we agree upon a collection of questions; (2) we agree upon criteria by which observations pass the test of the questions; and (3) we ask the questions of the observation set. Empirical truth is distinguished by whether or not the answers satisfy the agreed upon criteria. In this sense, empirical truth is identified with the occurrence of an event

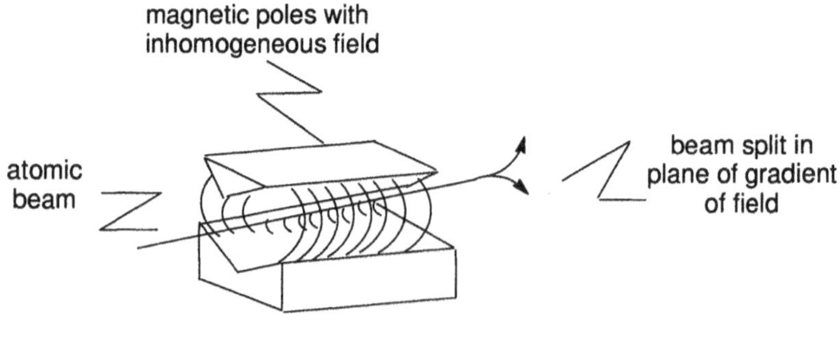

FIGURE A: Stern-Gerlach magnet separating the beam into two beams.

having the properties under consideration–*determined* by some measuring apparatus, possibly a human.

The operational meaning to the logic is (1) that if the single electron atom is "prepared" such that its magnetic moment is pointing *Up*, as is depicted in Figure B, then it will *pass* any attempt to "determine" whether it is indeed pointing *Up*; (2) that it is *true* that the single electron atom is determined to have gone *Up means* that it is always *false* that it had been "prepared" *Down*; but (3) that it is *false* that the single electron atom went *Up* does *not mean* that it is *true* that it was originally *Down*. It may have been "prepared" with its magnetic moment pointing *Right*, which means that it would be *false* that it could be determined *Left*!

Figure B: Up is true, and Up is true. This means that if a single electron, silver atom is "prepared" such that its "state" has orientation *Up*, and it is tested to "determine" what its orientation is, one will always determine the single electron atom is oriented *Up*. The empirical logic can be represented: (*Up* and *Up*) = *Up*.

If we should select out *Up* and subject this known beam to a second Stern-Gerlach apparatus which has its gradient aligned horizontally, thereby allowing only a *Right* or *Left* determination, it is *empirical truth* (always the observed case) that if there is no empirical procedure which could operationally determine whether it was *Right* or was *Left*, then it is as if *no measurement had taken place*, as depicted in Figure C:

Figure C: Up is true, and (Right or Left) is true. That (*Right* or *Left*) is true means that *all* preparations will either go *Right* or will go *Left* if determined by a horizontal (i.e., right/left) apparatus. That there does not exist an operational procedure which could deter-

FIGURE B

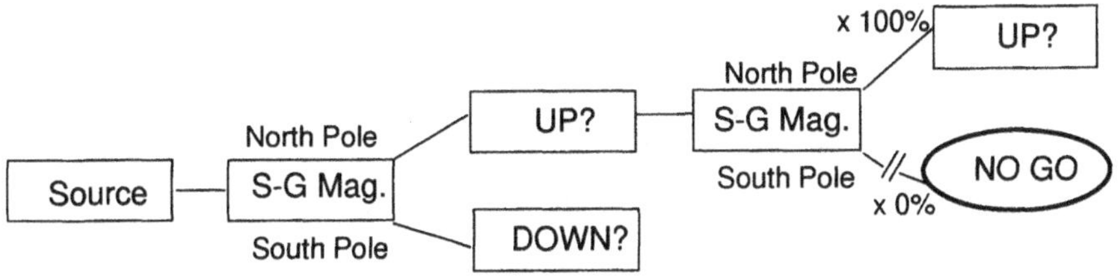

FIGURE C

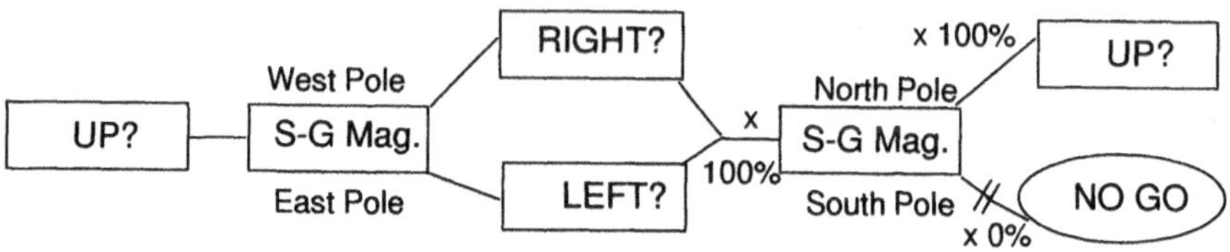

mine if *Right* had occurred or if *Left* had occurred is the same as no empirical distinction having taken place. E.g., "I need a person" not "I need a 'boy or girl'."

It is empirically false that:

FIGURE D

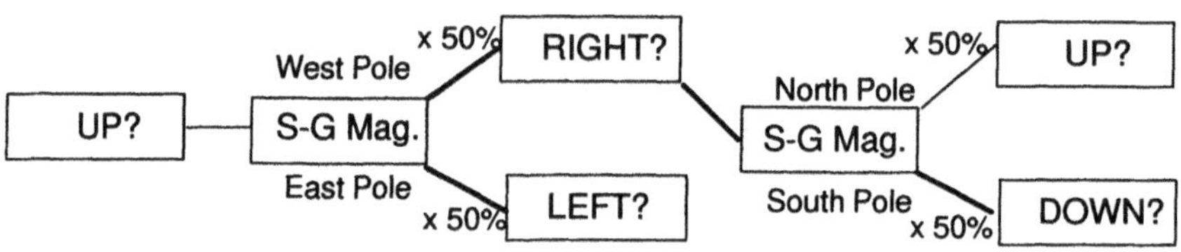

Figure D: Up is true and Right is true. This is so because if *Right* were true, then *Left* would be false. The analogy here is that I might be looking for a "boy or a girl," i.e., a person, yet the context is not one of gender but of race. Specifically, *a* "black" is a "boy or [a] girl" but *a black* (as an abstractia) is neither *a boy* nor *a girl* (cf. also, Oshins, 1989, ft. nt. 8, since if a black were a boy then a black could not be a girl. Thereby, it is claimed that introducing the context of race (e.g., "black") would presumably allow for transitions between boy-labeling and girl-labeling which would not take place given a strictly gender context. This might occur for our example with a contextual issue dealing with empathy and discrimination.

FIGURE E

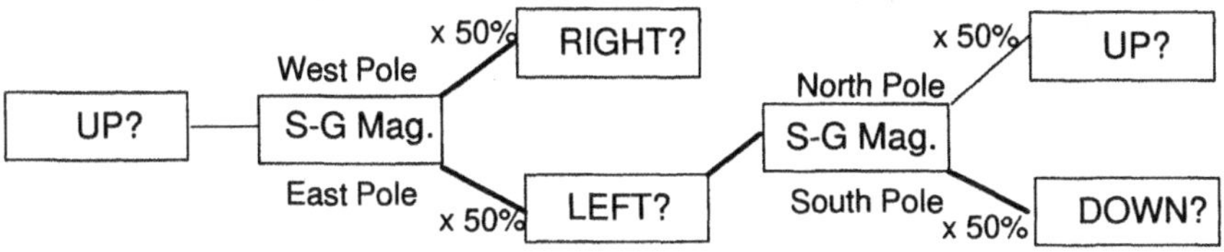

Figure E: Up is true and Left is true. Likewise, if *Left* were true, then *Right* would have to be false.

The distributive law of classical logic asserts that it is always true that: [A and (B or C)] = [(A and B) or (A and C)]. Upon substituting the empirical data we, find for a state with *Up* being true, (with obvious abbreviations):

$$\text{U and (R or L)} \stackrel{?}{=} \text{(U and R) or (U and L)}$$
$$\text{T and T} \stackrel{?}{=} \text{F or F}$$
$$\text{True} \neq \text{False}$$
$$\text{False}$$

We are forced to conclude from this "non-classical two-valuedness" that the *distributive law* of classical logic is empirically violated. It is replaced by the *principle of complementarity*: If two constructs are not-distinguished, there will always be a third within the span (or plane generated by the two) such that non-distinguished aggregates of any pair will equal the span.

POSTSCRIPT

The chapter is based upon my March 21, 1989 talk of the same name at the MRI, and in turn is based upon my earlier unpublished paper (Oshins, 1988). Joyce Emamjomeh suggested not only the talk but also that I write it up as a chapter for this volume. Her friendship and encouragement over many years have helped to make this work possible. The present chapter is an edited revision of my original paper. An extended version, having substantial technical elaboration, was presented at the February 1994 meeting of the Alternative Natural Philosophy Association and published in their proceedings (Oshins, 1994).

Bibliography

Ackerman, N. (1970). Don D. Jackson memorial conference, A eulogy. *Family Process*, [special edition], 9 (2), 117-121.

Arieti, S. (1974). *Interpretation of Schizophrenia*. New York: Basic Books.

Ashby, W. (1960). *Design for a brain*. London: Chapman & Hall, Science Pb.

Ashby, R. (1956). *Introduction to Cybernetics*. London: Chapman & Hall, Science Pb.

Bandler, R., Grinder, J. (1975). *The Structure of Magic*. Palo Alto, CA: Science & Behavior Books.

Bandler R., Grinder J. (1975). *Patterns of the Hypnotic Techniques of Milton H. Erickson*. Cupertino, CA: Meta Publications.

Bateson, G. (1951). Information & codification: A philosophical approach. In J. Ruesch & G. Bateson, *Communication: The Social Matrix of Psychiatry*, New York: W.W. Norton, pp. 168-211.

Bateson, G. (1954). A theory of play & fantasy. *Psychiatric Research Reports*, 2, 39-51.

Bateson, G. (1958) *Naven*. Stanford, CA: Stanford University Press.

Bateson, G., (1972). *Steps to an Ecology of Mind*. San Francisco: Chandler.

Bateson, G. (1976). Foreword. In *Double Bind: The Foundation of the Communicational Approach to the Family,* C. Sluzki and D. Ransom, (Eds). New York: Grune & Stratton, pp. XI-XVI.

Bateson, G., (1979). *Mind and Nature*. New York: Dutton.

Bateson, G., Jackson, D., Haley, J., & Weakland, J. (1956). Toward a theory of schizophrenia. *Behavior Science*, 1, 251-264.

Bateson, G. & Jackson, D. (1964). Some varieties of pathogenic organization. *Disorders of Communication*, 42, ARNMD, 270-283.

Berger, M., (Ed.) (1978). *Beyond the Double Bind*. New York: Brunner/Mazel.

Bertalanffy, L. von (1973). *General System Theory.* New York: Braziller.

Birdwhistell, R. (Producer). (1964). *Hillcrest Family Series* [film]. Philadelphia: Pennsylvania Psychiatric Institute.

Birkhoff, G. & von Neumann, J. (1936). The logic of quantum mechanics. *Annals of Mathematics*, 37, 823-843.

Bodin A. (1980). The interactional view. In *Handbook of Family Therapy.* A. Gurman & D. Kniskern, (Ed). New York: Brunner/Mazel, pp. 267-309.

Bodin, A. (1988, July 15). Interview with Art Bodin, PhD, conducted by Wendel Ray. Palo Alto, CA.

Bohr, N. (1961). *Atomic Theory & the Description of Nature*. Cambridge, MA: Cambridge University Press.

Bohr, N. (1987a). *The Philosophical Writings of Niels Bohr, Vol. II.* Woodbridge, CT: Ox Bow Press.

Bohr, N. (1987b). *The Philosophical Writings of Niels Bohr, Vol. III.* Woodbridge, CT: Ox Bow Press.

Boscolo, L., Cecchin, G., Hoffman, L., & Penn, P. (1987). *Milan Systemic Therapy: Conversations in Practice*. New York: Basic.

Bowers, J. W., & Sanders, R. E., (1974). Paradox as a rhetorical strategy. In *Rhetoric: A Tradition in Transition*, W. Fisher (Ed.). East Lansing, MI: Michigan State University Press, pp. 300-315.

Buckley, W. (1967). *Sociology & Modern Systems Theory.* Englewood Cliffs, NJ: Prentice-Hall.

Caplan, G. (1964). *Principles of Preventive Psychiatry.* New York: Basic.

Cecchin, G., Lane, G. & Ray, W. (1992). *Irreverence: A Strategy for Therapists' Survival*. London, U.K.: Karnac Books.

Chubb, H. & Evans, E. L. (1990). Therapist efficiency & clinic accessibility with the Mental Research Institute Brief Therapy model. *Community Mental Health Journal*, 26 (2), pp. 139-149.

Chubb, H., Nauts, P. L., & Evans, E. L. (1984). The practice of change: A working MRI/Brief Therapy clinic. *Australian Journal of Family Therapy*, 5, pp. 181-184.

Cromwell, R. (1984). Preemptive thinking and schizophrenia research. In *Nebraska Symposium on Motivation,* W. D. Spaulding (Ed). Lincoln, NE: University of Nebraska Press.

Dell, P. & Goolishian, H. (1981). Order through fluctuation: An evolutionary epistemology for human systems. *Australian Journal of Family Therapy.* 2, pp. 175-184.

De Witt, B. S. (1971). The many-universes interpretation of quantum mechanics. In *Foundations of Quantum Mechanics: Proceedings of the International School of Physics "Enrico-Fermi", Course IL.* B. d'Espagnat (Ed.) (1971) New York: Academic Press.

Domarus, E. von (1944). Specific laws of logic in schizophrenia. In *Language & Thought in Schizophrenia: Collected Papers,* J. Kasanin (Ed.). Berkeley: University of California Press, pp. 104-114.

Duncan, B. (1984). Adopting the construct of functionality when it facilitates system change. *Journal of Strategic & Systemic Therapies,* 3, pp. 60-65.

Duncan, B., & Fraser, J. (1987). Buckley's scheme of schemes: A foundation for teaching family theory. *Journal of Marital & Family Therapy,* 13, (3), pp. 229-305.

Elkaim, Mony, (1985). From general laws to singularities, *Family Process,* 24: pp. 151-164.

Ellis, A. (1972). Rational and irrational jealousy. In *The Civilized Couples Guide to Extramarital Adventure,* A. Ellis, (Ed.). New York: Wyden.

Erickson, M. (1982). *The Collected Papers of Milton H. Erickson.* Volumes I, II, III, IV. New York: Irvington.

Erikson, E. (1953). Growth and crisis in the healthy personality. In *Personality in Nature, Society & Culture,* C. Kluckholn & H. Murray, (Eds.). New York: Knopf.

Ferber, A., M. Mendelsohn, & A. Napier (Eds.), *The Book of Family Therapy.* New York: Science House.

Feynman, R. & A. Hibbs. (1965). *Quantum Mechanics and Path Integrals.* New York: McGraw-Hill.

Fisch, R., Weakland, J., & Segal, L. (1982). *The Tactics of Change: Doing Therapy Briefly.* San Francisco: Jossey-Bass.

Fisch, R., Weakland J., Watzlawick, P., Segal, L., Hoebel, F., Deardoff, M. (1975). *Learning Brief Therapy.* Mental Research Institute: Palo Alto, CA.

Fisch, R., Watzlawick, P., Weakland, J., Bodin, A. (1972). On unbecoming a family therapist. In *The Book of Family Therapy,* A.

Ferber, M. Mendelson, A. Napier (Eds.). New York: Science House, pp. 597-617.
Foerster, H. von, (1978a, June). Self-fulfilling prophecies. Presented at the 3rd Annual Don Jackson Memorial Conference.
Foerster, H. von, (1978b, December). Paradoxes. Lecture presented at the Mental Research Institute, Palo Alto, CA.
Foerster, H. von, (1981). *Observing Systems.* Seaside, CA: Intersystem.
Foerster, H. von, (1984). On contrasting a reality. In *The Invented Reality,* P. Watzlawick (Ed.., New York: W.W. Norton, pp. 41-63.
Framo, J. (1982). Husbands' reactions to wives infidelity. In *Explorations in Marital and Family Therapy: Selected Papers of J.L. Framo* New York: Springer, pp. 152-160.
Fraser, J. (1982). Structural and strategic family therapy: A basis for marriage or grounds for divorce? *Journal of Marital & Family Therapy,* 8, (2), pp. 13-22.
Fraser, J. (1983). Paranoia: Interactional bases of evolution and intervention. *Journal of Marital & Family Therapy,* 9, (4), pp. 383-391.
Fraser, J. (1984a). Paradox and orthodox: Folie a deux? *Journal of Marital & Family Therapy,* 10, (4), pp. 361-372.
Fraser, J. (1984b). Process level integration: Corrective vision for a binocular view. *Journal of Strategic & Systemic Therapies,* 3, (3), pp. 43-57.
Fraser, J. (1986a) The crisis interview: Strategic rapid intervention. *Journal of Strategic & Systemic Therapies,* 5, (3 & 4), pp. 71-87.
Fraser, J. (1986b). Integrating system based therapies. In *Journeys,* D. Efron (Ed.). New York: Brunner/Mazel, pp. 125-149.
Fraser, J. (1988). Strategic rapid intervention in wife beating. In *Troubled Relationships: Families in Trouble Series.* E. Nunnally, C. Chilman, & F. Cox (Eds.), Volume 3. Newbury Park, CA: Sage, pp. 163-191.
Fraser, J. (1989). The strategic rapid intervention approach. In *Treating Stress in the Family,* C. Figley (Ed.). New York: Brunner/Mazel, pp. 122-157.
Fraser, J., Froelich, J. (1979). Crisis intervention in the courtroom. *Community Mental Health Journal,* 15, (3), pp. 237-247.
Fraser, J., Spicka, D. (1981). Handling the emotional response to

disaster: The case of the American Red Cross/community mental health collaboration. *Community Mental Health Journal*, 17, (4), pp. 255-284.

Fromm, E. (1973). *The Art of Loving*. New York: Harper-Row.

Gergen, K. (1985a). The social constructionist movement in modern psychology. *American Psychologist*, 40, pp. 266-275.

Gergen, K. (1985b). Social constructionist theory: Context and implications. In *The Social Construction of the Person,* K. Gergen & K. Davis (Eds.), New York: Springer-Verlag.

Giannatassio, E., & Nencini, R. (1983). Conoscenza e modellizzazione. In *la Goliardica A. Psicologia*. Roma, Italy: Ventaglio.

Glasersfeld, E. von (1984). Introduction to radical constructivism. In *The Invented Reality,* P. Watzlawick (Ed.). New York: W.W. Norton, pp. 17-40.

Glick, J. (1987). *Chaos: Making a New Science*. New York: Viking Penguin.

Gould, S. (1982). *The Panda's Thumb*. New York: W.W. Norton.

Greenberg, G. (1977). The family interactional perspective: Study and examination of the work of Don D. Jackson. *Family Process,* 16 (4), pp. 385-412.

Greenberg, G. (1980). Problem-focused brief family interactional psychotherapy. In *Group & Family Therapy,* L. Wolberg & M. Aronson (Eds.). New York: Brunner/Mazel, pp. 307-322.

Haley, J. (1958). An interpersonal explanation of hypnosis. *American Journal of Clinical Hypnosis,* 1, pp. 41-57.

Haley, J., (1959). The family of the schizophrenic: A model system. *Journal of Nervous & Mental Diseases,* 129, pp. 357-374.

Haley, J. (1961). Development of a theory. In *Double Bind,* C. Sluzki & D. Ransom (Eds.), (1976), New York: Grune & Stratton, pp. 59-104.

Haley, J. (1963). *Strategies of Psychotherapy.* New York: Grune & Stratton.

Haley, J. (1967). *Advanced Techniques of Hypnosis and Therapy, Selected Papers of Milton H. Erickson.* New York: Grune & Stratton.

Haley, J. (1973). *Uncommon Therapy.* New York: W.W. Norton.

Haley, J. (1976). *Problem-Solving Therapy.* San Francisco: Jossey-Bass.

Haley, J., (Ed.). (1985). *Conversation with Milton Erickson, MD., Volume I, II, & III.* Washington, DC: Triangle Press.

Haley, J., Hoffman, L., Jackson, D. (1967). The eternal triangle. In *Techniques of Family Therapy,* J. Haley & L. Hoffman (Eds.). New York: Basic, pp. 174-264.

Harris, L. (In press). The maintenance of a social reality: A case study of a paradoxical logic. *Family Process.*

Hilgard, E. (1989). Reflections on the future of scientific psychology. Paper to panel on "The future of scientific psychology." 1989 AAAS Annual Meeting, San Francisco, CA.

Hoebel, F. (1975). *Coronary Artery Disease and Family Interaction: A Study of Risk Factor Modification.* A doctoral dissertation. San Francisco, CA: California School of Professional Psychology.

Hoffman, L. (1974). Deviation amplifying processes in natural groups. In *Change Families,* J. Haley (Ed.). New York: Grune & Stratton, pp. 285-311.

Hoffman, L. (1981). *Foundations of Family Therapy: A Conceptual Framework for Systems Theory.* New York: Basic.

Hoffman, L. & Long, L. (1969). A systems dilemma. *Family Process.* 8, pp. 211-234.

Holton, G. (1973). The roots of complementarity. In *Thematic Origins of Scientific Thought: Kepler to Einstein.* Cambridge: Harvard University Press.

Jackson, D. (1944). The therapeutic uses of hypnosis. *Stanford Medical Bulletin,* 2 (4), pp. 193-196.

Jackson, D. (1949, January 28). Unpublished transcript of a research discussion, Chestnut Lodge, Rockville, Maryland, involving Don Jackson and led by Harry Stack Sullivan. MRI, Palo Alto, CA.

Jackson, D. (1952). The relationship of the referring physician and the psychiatrist. *California Medicine,* 76 (6), June, pp. 391-394.

Jackson, D. (1953). Psychotherapy for schizophrenia. *Scientific American,* 188, pp. 58-63.

Jackson, D. (1954a). Office treatment of ambulatory schizophrenics. *California Medicine,* 81 (4), October, pp. 263-266.

Jackson, D. (1954b). Some factors influencing the Oedipus Complex. *Psychoanalytic Quarterly*, 23, pp. 566-581.

Jackson, D. (1957a). The question of family homeostasis. *The Psychiatric Quarterly Supplement*, 31 (part 1), pp. 79-90. Presented May 7, 1954 at the APA Meeting, St. Louis, MO.

Jackson, D. (1957b). A note on the importance of trauma in the genesis of schizophrenia. *Psychiatry*, 20 (2) pp. 181-184.

Jackson, D. (1958). Guilt and the control of pleasure in schizoid personalities. *British Journal Medical Psychology*, 31, (2), pp. 124-133.

Jackson, D. (1959). Family interaction, family homeostasis and some implications or conjoint family therapy. In *Individual and Familial Dynamics*, J. Masserman (Ed.). New York: Grune & Stratton, pp. 122-141.

Jackson D. (1960). *The Etiology of Schizophrenia*. New York: Basic.

Jackson, D. (1961). Interactional psychotherapy. In *Contemporary Psychotherapies*, M. Stein (Ed.). New York: Free Press, pp. 256-271.

Jackson, D. (1962). The question of insight. A recording of a presentation by Jackson, March 8, 1962. Palo Alto, CA: MRI.

Jackson, D. (1963). A suggestion for the technical handling of paranoid patients. *Psychiatry*, 26, pp. 306-307.

Jackson, D. (1964). The sick, the sad, the savage, and the sane. The annual academic lecture to the Society of Medical Psychoanalysts and Department of Psychiatry, New York Medical College, New York.

Jackson, D. (1965a). The study of the family. *Family Process*, 4 (1), pp. 1-20.

Jackson, D. (1965b). Family rules: Marital quid pro quo. *Archives of General Psychiatry*, 12, pp. 589-594.

Jackson, D. (1967a). The individual and the larger context. *Family Process*, 6 (2), pp. 139-154.

Jackson, D. (1967b). Schizophrenia: The nosological nexus. In *Excerpta Medica International Congress, The Origins of Schizophrenia*, 151, pp. 111-120 (Proceedings of the First Rochester International Conference, March 29-31). Rochester, NY.

Jackson, D. (1967c). Aspects of conjoint family therapy. In *Family Therapy and Disturbed Families*, G. Zuk & I. Boszormenyi-Nagy (Eds.). Palo Alto, CA: Science & Behavior Books, pp. 28-40.

Jackson, D. (Ed.) (1968a). *Human Communication, Volume 1: Communication, Family, & Marriage*. Palo Alto, CA: Science & Behavior Books.

Jackson, D. (Ed.) (1968b). *Human Communication, Volume 2: Therapy Communication, & Change*. Palo Alto, CA: Science & Behavior Books.

Jackson, D., Bodin, A. (1968). Paradoxical communication and the marital paradox. In *The Marriage Relationship*, S. Rosenbaum & I. Alger (Eds.). New York: Basic, pp. 3-20.

Jackson, D. & Haley, J. (1963). Transference revisited. *Journal of Nervous & Mental Disease*, 137 (4), pp. 363-371.

Jackson, D., Riskin, J., & Satir, V. (1961). A method of analysis of a family interview. *Archives of General Psychiatry*, 5, pp. 321-339.

Jackson, D., Watzlawick, P. (1963). Acute psychosis as manifestation of growth experience. *Psychiatric Research Reports*, 16, pp. 83-94.

Jackson, D., Weakland, J. (1959). Schizophrenic symptoms and family interaction. *Archives of General Psychiatry*, 1, pp. 618-621.

Jackson, D., Weakland, J. (1961). Conjoint family therapy: Some considerations on theory, technique, and results. *Psychiatry*, 24 (2), pp. 30-45.

Jackson, D., Yalom, I. (1964). Family homeostasis and patient change. In *Current Psychiatric Therapies*, J. Masserman (Ed), pp. 155-165.

Jacobson, A. (1983). Empowering the client in strategic therapy. *Journal of Strategic & Systemic Therapies*, 2, pp. 77-87.

Jakobson, R. (1956). The twofold character of language. In *Fundamentals of Language*, R. Jakobson & M. Halle. New York: Hague & Mouton, pp. 58-62.

Jauch, J. M. (1968). *Foundations of Quantum Mechanics*. Reading, MA: Addison-Wesley.

Kaplan, A. (1973). *Love and Death*. Ann Arbor: University Michigan Press.

Kelly, G. (1955). *The psychology of Personal Constructs*. New York: W.W. Norton.

Kelly, G. (1963). *A Theory of Personality*. New York: W.W. Norton.

Kelly, G. (1968). The role of classification in personality theory. In *Clinical Psychology & Personality,* B. Maher (Ed.). (1969). New York: Wiley.

Kopp, B. (1972). *If You Meet the Buddha on the Road, Kill Him*. New York: Bantam Books.

Kubie, L. (1953). The distortion of the symbolic process, *Journal American Psychoanalytic Association*, 1, pp. 59-86.

Kuhn, T. (1970). *The Structure of Scientific Revolution*. Chicago: University Press.

Lederer, W. & Jackson, D. (1968). *Mirages of Marriage*. New York: W.W. Norton.

Laing, R. (1965). Mystification, confusion, and conflict. In *Double Bind*, C. Sluzki, & D. Ransom (Eds.). (1976). New York: Grune & Stratton.

Lindeman, E. (1944). Symptomatology and management of acute grief. *American Journal of Psychiatry*, 101, pp. 141-148.

MacGregor, R., Ritchie, A., Serrano, A., Schuster, R., McDanald, E., & Goolishian, H. (1964). *Multiple Impact Therapy with Families*. New York: McGraw Hill.

Maruyama, M. (1963). The second cybernetics: Deviation amplifying mutual causal processes. *American Scientist*, 51, pp. 164-179.

Masters, W., & Johnson, V. (1975). *The Pleasure Bond*. New York: Bantam Books.

Maturana, H. (1975). The organization of the living: A theory of the living organization. *International Journal Man-Machine Studies*. 7, pp. 313-332.

Maturana, H. (1978). Biology of language: The epistemology of reality. In *Psychology and Biology of Language and Thought,* G. Miller & E. Lenneberg (Eds.). New York: Academic Press.

Maturana, H. & Varela, F. (1987). *The Tree of Knowledge: The Biological Roots of Understanding*. Boston: Science Library, Shambhala Publications.

McGoveran, D. (Ed.) (1984). *Discrete Approaches to Natural Philosophy.* Boulder Creek, CA: Alternative Natural Philosophy Association. Information about copies from T. Etter, ANPA West, 112 Blackburn Ave., Menlo Park, CA 94025.

Minuchin, S. (1974). *Families and Family Therapy.* Cambridge, MA: Harvard University Press.

Morris, C. (1938). Foundations of the theory of signs. In *International Encyclopedia of Unified Science*, O. Neurath, R. Carnap, & C. Morris (Eds.), 1: 2. Chicago, IL: University of Chicago Press, pp. 77-137.

Morris, G. & Wynne, L. (1965). Schizophrenic offspring and parental styles of communication. *Psychiatry,* 28, pp. 19-44.

Nardone, G. (Ed.) (1988). *Modelli di psicoterapia a confronto*, Roma, Italy: Ventaglio.

Orlov, Y. (1982). The wave logic of consciousness: A hypothesis. *International Journal of Theoretical Physics*, 21(1): pp. 37-53.

Orwell, G. (1967). Revenge is sour. In *Collected Essays of George Orwell,* S. Orwell & I. Angus (Eds.), New York: Harcourt, Vol. 4, pp. 3-6.

Oshins, E. (1984a). A quantum approach to psychology: Spinors, rotations, and non-selecting ambiguity. "In *Discrete Approaches to Natural Philosophy,* D. McGoveran (Ed.). (1984). Boulder Creek, CA: Alternative Natural Philosophy Association."

Oshins, E. (1984b). "Anecdoted 'quantum psychology excerpt'" from 4/27/84 letter from Oshins to Orlov. Note #10 of Oshins, 1987b, pp. 72-79.

Oshins, E. (1987a). Quantum psychology looks at Kelly's constructs. 7th International Congress on Personal Construct Psychology, August 5-9, 1987, Memphis State University, Memphis, Tennessee. *Stanford Physics Technical Report* # Tecp-5831, 9-1-87.

Oshins, E. (1987b). *Quantum Psychology Notes, Vol. 1: A Personal Construct Notebook.* Menlo Park, CA: Eddie Oshins.

Oshins, E. (1988). Complementarity constructs in psychology from the perspective of quantum physics. Unpublished manuscript.

Oshins, E. (1989). Quantum psychology & future directions. Paper to panel on "The future of scientific psychology," 1989 AAAS Annual Meeting, SF, CA. Published as "Quantum Psychology of Nots." In *Divertissements in Natural Philosophy,* E. Jones, (Ed.). Carmel Valley, CA: Alternative Natural Philosophy Association.

Oshins, E. (1991) About models and muddles, part I: Why Brown's *Laws of Form* and Pribram's 'hologram hypothesis' are NOT relevant to quantum physics and quantum psychology. In *Alternatives in Physics and Biology*, M. Manthey (Ed.). Cambridge, UK: Alternative Natural Philosophy Association.

Oshins, E. (1994). Technical comments on quantum psychology and the metalogic of second order change. Paper presented at the 10th Western Regional Meeting of the Alternative Natural Philosophy Association, Feb. 19-21, Cordura Hall, Stanford. In *Mind-Body Problem and the Quantum*, F. Young (Ed.). (1994). Menlo Park, CA: Alternative Natural Philosophy Association.

Oshins, E., Adelson, D., & McGoveran, D. (1984). Clarifying fuzzy logic: A spectral decomposition and iconic realization. In McGoveran (Ed.) (1984).

Oshins, E. & McGoveran, D. (1980). Thoughts about logic about thoughts . . . the question 'schizophrenia?' In *Systems Science & Science*, B. Banathy, (Ed.). Louisville: SGSR, pp. 505-514.

Oshins, E., Ford, K., Rodriguez, R., Anger, F. (1990). Classical, fuzzy, and quantum logics: Relations & implications. In *Advances in Artificial Intelligence Research*, M. Fishman (Ed.), Greenwich, CT: JAI.

Pekarik, G. (1985) The effects of employing different termination classification criteria in dropout research. *Psychotherapy*, 22, pp. 86-91.

Platt, J. (1970). Hierarchical growth. *Bulletin of the Atomic Scientists*, 2-4, pp. 46-48.

Potter, S. (1971). *The Complete Upmanship: Including Gamesmanship, Lifemanship, One Upmanship, Supermanship*. New York: Holt, Rinehart, & Winston.

Protinsky, H. (1977). Marriage and family therapy. *Family Therapy*, 4.

Prigogine, I. (1976). Order through fluctuation: Self-organization & social system. In *Evolution and Consciousness: Human Systems in Transition,* E. Jantsch & C. Waddington (Eds.). Reading, MA: Addison.

Ray, W. (1991). Our future in the past: Lessons from Don Jackson for the practice of family therapy with hospitalized adolescents. *Family Therapy*, 19 (1), pp. 61-72.

______ . (1991). Die interaktionale Therapie von Don D. Jackson. Eine Einfuhrung. *Zeit Schrift Fur Systemiche Therapie*, 14, pp. 5-30.

______ . (1993). John H. Weakland–An Appreciation. *AAMFT News*, 24(1), pp. 27-28.

Ray, W. & Keeney, B. (1993). *Resource Focused Therapy.* London, U.K.: Karnac Books (U.S. distribution–New York: Brunner/Mazel).

Ruesch, J., & Bateson, G. (1968). *Communication: The Social Matrix of Psychiatry.* New York: W.W. Norton.

Russell, B., & Whitehead, A. (1961). Principia mathematica. In *The Basic Writings of Bertrand Russell,* R. Egner, & L. Denonn (Eds.). New York: Touchtone Books, pp. 145-207.

Salmon, W. (1970). *Zeno's Paradoxes*. Indianapolis: Bobbs-Merrill.

Salzman, L. (1968). Reply to critics. *International Journal of Psychiatry*, 6, pp. 473-476.

Scheflen, A. (1965a). Quasi-Courtship behavior in psychotherapy. *Psychiatry*, 28: pp. 245-267.

Scheflen, A. (1965b). *Stream and Structure of Communicational Behavior. Context Analysis of a Psychotherapy Session*. Behavioral Studies Monograph #1. Philadelphia: Eastern Pennsylvania Psychiatric Institute.

Schwinger, J. (1970). The algebra of measurement, *Quantum Kinematics and Dynamics*. New York: Benjamin, pp. 1-29.

Segal, L. (1980). Focused problem resolution. In *Models of Family Therapy*, E. Tolsen & W. Reid (Eds.), New York: Columbia University Press.

Segal, L. (1986). *The Dream of Reality.* New York: W.W. Norton.

Selvini, M. (Ed.) (1988). *The Work of Mara Selvini Palazzoli*. New York: Aronson.

Selvini Palazzoli, M., Anolli, L., Di Blasio, P., Giossi, L., Pisano, I., Ricci, C., Sacchi, M., & Ugazio, V. (1986). *The Hidden Games of Organizations*. New York: Pantheon Books.

Selvini Palazzoli, M., Boscolo, L., Cecchin, G., Prata, G., (1978). *Paradox and Counterparadox*. New York: Aronson.

Selvini Palazzoli, M., Boscolo, L., Cecchin, G., Prata, G. (1980). Hypothesizing, circularity & neutrality. *Family Process*. 19, pp. 3-12.

Selvini Palazzoli, M., Cirillo, S., Selvini, M., Sorrentino, A., (1989). *Family Games: General Models of Psychotic Processes in the Family.* New York: W.W. Norton.

Selvini Palazzoli, M. et al. (1976). *Il Mago Smagato*. Milan, Italy: Feltrinelli.

Shepard, R. (1981). Psychophysical complementarity. In *Perceptual Organization,* M. Kubovy & J. R. Pomerantz (Eds.). Hillsdale, NJ: Erlbaum.

Shepard, R. (1983). Ecological constraints on internal representation: Resonant kinematics of perceiving, imagining, thinking, and dreaming. *Psychological Review*, 91 (1984): pp. 417-447.

Sluzki, C., & Ransom, D. (1976). *Double Bind: The Foundation of the Communicational Approach to the Family.* New York: Grune & Stratton.

Smith, B. (1956). *A Quarter for Growing Up*. Austin, TX: Hogg Foundation.

Smith, B. (1959). *A Family Grows*. Austin, TX: The Hogg Foundation.

Smith, D., & Williamson, L. K. (1977). *Interpersonal Communication: Roles, Rules, Strategies, and Games*. Dubuque: W.C. Brown.

Taylor, C. (1985). *Human Agency and Language*. Cambridge: Cambridge University Press.

Teismann, M. (1979). Jealousy: Systematic problem-solving therapy with couples, *Family Process*.

Thom, R. (1975). *Structural stability and morphogenesis*. Reading, MA: Benjamin.

Varela, F. (1976). Not one, not two. *Coevolution Quarterly*, 10, pp. 62-67.

Vigotsky, L. (1934). Thought in schizophrenia. *Archives of Neurology & Psychiatry*, 31: pp. 1063-1077.

Watzlawick, P. (1964). *An Anthology of Human Communication*. Palo Alto, CA: Science & Behavior Books.

Watzlawick, P. (1978). *The Language of Change: Elements of a Therapeutic Communication*. New York: Basic.

Watzlawick, P. (1979). *How Real Is Real?* Vintage Books.

Watzlawick, P. (1980). *Il linguaggio del cambiamento*, Milano, Italy: Feltrinelli.

Watzlawick, P. (1983). Hypnotherapy without trance. 2nd Congress of Ericksonian Approaches to Psychotherapy, Phoenix, AZ.

Watzlawick, P. (1984). *The Invented Reality.* New York: W.W. Norton.

Watzlawick, P. (1985a). If you desire to see, learn how to act. Address at "The Evolution of Psychotherapy" conference, Phoenix, AZ.

Watzlawick, P. (1985b). Hypnotherapeutic principles in family therapy. International Congress "Familizar Realities." Heidelberg, Germany.

Watzlawick, P., Beavin, J., Jackson, D. (1967). *Pragmatics of Human Communication*. New York: W.W. Norton.

Watzlawick, P., Weakland, J., Fisch, R. (1974). *Change: Principles of Problem Formation and Problem Resolution*. New York: W.W. Norton.

Watzlawick, P. & Weakland, J. (1977). *The Interactional View.* Studies at the Mental Research Institute, 1965-1977. New York: W.W. Norton.

Weakland, J. (1972). We became family therapists. In *The Book of Family Therapy*, A. Ferber, M. Mendelson, A. Napier (Eds.). New York: Science House, pp. 132-133.

Weakland, J. (1974). "The double-bind theory" by self-reflexive hindsight. *Family Process*, 13, pp. 269-277.

Weakland, J. (1977a). Piano player. Unpublished video tape, Mental Research Institute.

Weakland, J. (1977b). "Family Somatics"–A neglected edge. *Family Process,* 16, pp. 263-272.

Weakland, J., Fisch, R., Watzlawick, P., Bodin, A. (1974). Brief therapy: Focused problem resolution. *Family Process*, 13, p. 141.

Weakland, J. & Jackson, D. (1958). Patient and therapists observations on the circumstances of a schizophrenic episode. *AMA Archives of Neurology & Psychiatry*, 79, pp. 554-574.

Weakland, J. & Riskin, J. (1989). The Satir interview–Some points in question. *Milton H. Erickson Foundation Newsletter*, 9, pp. 1-5.

Weiner, N. (1948). *Cybernetics of Control & Communication in the Animal and the Machine*. New York: Wiley.

Wilmot, W. (1979). *Dyadic Communication*. Reading, MA: Addison.

Wong-Gi, I., Wilner, R., & Breit, M. (1983). Jealousy: Interventions in couples therapy. *Family Process*, 22 (2), pp. 211-220.

Wynne, L. C., Singer, A. (1963). Thought disorders and the family relations of schizophrenics. *Archives of General Psychiatry*, 9, pp. 191-206; 12, pp. 187-220, 201-212.

Zuk, G. (1981). Homage to Don D. Jackson. *International Journal of Family Therapy*, 3 (1), pp. 3-4.

Index

For Product Safety Concerns and Information please contact our EU representative GPSR@taylorandfrancis.com Taylor & Francis Verlag GmbH, Kaufingerstraße 24, 80331 München, Germany

Batch number: 10726009

Printed by Printforce, the Netherlands